Story of God Bible Commentary
Series Endorsements

"Getting a story is about more than merely enjoying it. It means hearing it, understanding it, and above all, being impacted by it. This commentary series hopes that its readers not only hear and understand the story, but are impacted by it to live in as Christian a way as possible. The editors and contributors set that table very well and open up the biblical story in ways that move us to act with sensitivity and understanding. That makes hearing the story as these authors tell it well worth the time. Well done."

Darrell L. Bock
Dallas Theological Seminary

"The Story of God Bible Commentary series invites readers to probe how the message of the text relates to our situations today. Engagingly readable, it not only explores the biblical text but offers a range of applications and interesting illustrations."

Craig S. Keener
Asbury Theological Seminary

"I love the Story of God Bible Commentary series. It makes the text sing, and helps us hear the story afresh."

John Ortberg
Senior Pastor of Menlo Park Presbyterian Church

"In this promising new series of commentaries, believing biblical scholars bring not only their expertise but their own commitment to Jesus and insights into today's culture to the Scriptures. The result is a commentary series that is anchored in the text but lives and breathes in the world of today's church with its variegated pattern of socioeconomic, ethnic, and national diversity. Pastors, Bible study leaders, and Christians of all types who are looking for a substantive and practical guide through the Scriptures will find these volumes helpful."

Frank Thielman
Beeson Divinity School

"The Story of God Bible Commentary series is unique in its approach to exploring the Bible. Its easy-to-use format and practical guidance brings God's grand story to modern-day life so anyone can understand how it applies today."

Andy Stanley
North Point Ministries

"I'm a storyteller. Through writing and speaking I talk and teach about understanding the Story of God throughout Scripture and about letting God reveal more of His story as I live it out. Thus I am thrilled to have a commentary series based on the Story of God—a commentary that helps me to Listen to the Story, that Explains the Story, and then encourages me to probe how to Live the Story. A perfect tool for helping every follower of Jesus to walk in the story that God is writing for them."

Judy Douglass
Director of Women's Resources, Cru

"The Bible is the story of God and his dealings with humanity from creation to new creation. The Bible is made up more of stories than of any other literary genre. Even the psalms, proverbs, prophecies, letters, and the Apocalypse make complete sense only when set in the context of the grand narrative of the entire Bible. This commentary series breaks new ground by taking all these observations seriously. It asks commentators to listen to the text, to explain the text, and to live the text. Some of the material in these sections overlaps with introduction, detailed textual analysis and application, respectively, but only some. The most riveting and valuable part of the commentaries are the stories that can appear in any of these sections, from any part of the globe and any part of church history, illustrating the text in any of these areas. Ideal for preaching and teaching."

Craig L. Blomberg
Denver Seminary

"Pastors and lay people will welcome this new series, which seeks to make the message of the Scriptures clear and to guide readers in appropriating biblical texts for life today."

Daniel I. Block
Wheaton College and Graduate School

"An extremely valuable, and long overdue series that includes comment on the cultural context of the text, careful exegesis, and guidance on reading the whole Bible as a unity that testifies to Christ as our Savior and Lord."

Graeme Goldsworthy
author of *According to Plan*

1 PETER

The Story of God Bible Commentary

1 PETER

Dennis R. Edwards

Tremper Longman III & Scot McKnight
General Editors

ZONDERVAN

1 Peter
Copyright © 2017 by Dennis R. Edwards

This title is also available as a Zondervan ebook.

Requests for information should be addressed to:
Zondervan, 3900 *Sparks Dr. SE, Grand Rapids, Michigan 49546*

ISBN 978-0-310-32730-1

Cover design: Ron Huizinga
Cover image: iStockphoto®
Interior composition: Kait Lamphere

Printed in the United States of Ameria

17 18 19 20 21 22 23 24 25 26 27 /DHV/ 20 19 18 17 16 15 14 13 12 11 10 9 8 7 6 5 4 3 2 1

To Susan Steele Edwards,

whose inner beauty is of great worth in God's sight

(1 Peter 3:4)

Old Testament series

New Testament series

Contents

Acknowledgments

Since my college days I wrestled internally over what I felt was a call of God on my life. I told every spiritual leader I knew about my feelings. Eventually, my pastor at the time, Rev. John Chestnut, encouraged me to attend Trinity Evangelical Divinity School in Deerfield, Illinois. I thank Pastor Chestnut for caring about what God was doing in my life and—despite our geographic and cultural distance—for continuing to be a pastor to me over the last thirty-plus years.

When I arrived at seminary I had no idea what to expect and knew nothing about the faculty. I found myself in summer Greek Exegesis, taught by Dr. Scot McKnight, and then later studying the Gospels under him. He was funny, engaging, practical, and thorough. He has continually encouraged me in my desire to rightly divide the word of truth (2 Tim 2:15 KJV). His passion for the church as well as academic excellence motivates me to be similarly minded.

Dr. Lynn Cohick and I met at an academic symposium years ago and she, as one of the editors of this volume, has been a thoughtful and keen observer, offering sound advice to me. I respect her scholarship and her pastoral spirit. I am also grateful for Katya Covrett, executive editor at Zondervan Academic, who treated me like one of the team even though I spend more time in the pastorate than in academia.

God has allowed me to serve as a church planter twice in my life, and also twice as pastor of established churches. I must acknowledge the wonderful people who have been part of New Community Evangelical Free Church (Brooklyn, New York), Washington Community Fellowship (Washington, DC), Peace Fellowship (Washington, DC), and The Sanctuary Covenant Church (Minneapolis, Minnesota). As I worked through this commentary, so many memories from years of pastoral service flooded my mind.

As a husband and father I strive to champion the work of my wife and children. But I have received so much more than I have given! I am blessed beyond measure. My wife Susan, my son Jonathan (along with his wife, Erica, and my grandson Mays), my son Jason, along with my daughters Joanna and Jessica, have continually cheered me on. They are remarkable people who strive to do what is good in this world (1 Pet 3:11).

The Story of God Bible Commentary Series

The Word of God may not change, but culture does. Think of what we have seen in the last twenty years: we now communicate predominantly through the internet and email; we read our news on iPads and computers; we can talk on the phone to our friends while we are driving, while we are playing golf, while we are taking long walks; and we can get in touch with others from the middle of nowhere. We carry in our hands small devices that connect us to the world and to a myriad of sources of information. Churches have changed; the "Nones" are rising in numbers and volume, and atheists are bold to assert their views in public forums. The days of home Bible studies are waning; there is a marked rise in activist missional groups in churches, and pastors are more and more preaching topical sermons, some of which are not directly connected to the Bible. Divorce rates are not going down, marriages are more stressed, rearing children is more demanding, and civil unions and same-sex marriages are knocking at the door of the church.

Progress can be found in many directions. While church attendance numbers are waning in Europe and North America, churches are growing in the South and the East. More and more women are finding a voice in churches; the plea of the former generation of leaders that Christians be concerned not just with evangelism but with justice is being answered today in new and vigorous ways. Resources for studying the Bible are more available today than ever before, and preachers and pastors are meeting the challenge of speaking a sure Word of God into shifting cultures.

Readers of the Bible change, too. These cultural shifts, our own personal developments, the progress in intellectual questions, as well as growth in biblical studies and theology and discoveries of new texts and new paradigms for understanding the contexts of the Bible—each of these elements works on an interpreter so that the person who reads the Bible today asks different questions from different angles.

Culture shifts, but the Word of God remains. That is why we as editors of The Story of God Bible Commentary series, a commentary based on the New International Version 2011 (NIV 2011), are excited to participate in this new series of commentaries on the Bible. This series is designed to address this generation with the same Word of God. We are asking the authors to explain what the Bible says to the sorts of readers who pick up commentaries so they can understand not only what Scripture says but what it means for today. The Bible does not change, but relating it to our culture changes constantly and in differing ways in different contexts.

When we, the New Testament editors, sat down in prayer and discussion to choose authors for this series, we realized we had found fertile ground. Our list of potential authors staggered in length and quality. We wanted the authors to be exceptional scholars, faithful Christians, committed evangelicals, and theologically diverse, and we wanted this series to represent the changing face of both American and world evangelicalism: ethnic and gender diversity. I believe this series has a wider diversity of authors than any commentary series in evangelical history.

The title of this series, emphasizing as it does the "Story" of the Bible, reveals the intent of the series. We want to explain each passage of the Bible in light of the Bible's grand Story. The Bible's grand Story, of course, connects this series to the classic expression *regula fidei*, the "rule of faith," which was the Bible's story coming to fulfillment in Jesus as the Messiah, Lord, and Savior of all. In brief, we see the narrative built around the following biblical themes: creation and fall, covenant and redemption, law and prophets, and especially God's charge to humans as his image-bearers to rule under God. The theme of God as King and God's kingdom guides us to see the importance of Israel's kings as they come to fulfillment in Jesus, Lord and King over all, and the direction of history toward the new heavens and new earth, where God will be all in all. With these guiding themes, each passage is examined from three angles.

Listen to the Story. We believe that if the Bible is God speaking, then the most important posture of the Christian before the Bible is to listen. So our first section cites the text of Scripture and lists a selection of important biblical and sometimes noncanonical parallels; then each author introduces that passage. The introductions to the passages sometimes open up discussion to the theme of the passage while other times they tie this passage to its context in the specific book. But since the focus of this series is the Story of God in the Bible, the introduction leads the reader into reading this text in light of the Bible's Story.

Explain the Story. The authors follow up listening to the text by explaining each passage in light of the Bible's grand Story. This is not an academic series, so the footnotes are limited to the kinds of texts typical Bible readers and preachers readily will have on hand. Authors are given the freedom to explain the text as they read it, though you should not be surprised to find occasional listings of other options for reading the text. Authors explore biblical backgrounds, historical context, cultural codes, and theological interpretations. Authors engage in word studies and interpret unique phrases and clauses as they attempt to build a sound and living reading of the text in light of the Story of God in the Bible.

Authors will not shy away from problems in the texts. Whether one is examining the meaning of "perfect" in Matthew 5:48, the problems with Christology in the hymn of Philippians 2:6–11, the challenge of understanding Paul in light of the swirling debates about the old, new, and post-new perspectives, the endless debates about eschatology, or the vagaries of atonement theories, the authors will dive in, discuss evidence, and do their best to sort out a reasonable and living reading of those issues for the church today.

Live the Story. Reading the Bible is not just about discovering what it meant back then; the intent of The Story of God Bible Commentary series is to probe how this text might be lived out today as that story continues to march on in the life of the church. At times our authors will tell stories about what this looks like; at other times they may offer some suggestions for living it out; but always you will discover the struggle involved as we seek to live out the Bible's grand Story in our world.

We are not offering suggestions for "application" so much as digging deeper; we are concerned in this section with seeking out how this text, in light of the Story of God in the Bible, compels us to live in our world so that our own story lines up with the Bible's Story.

Scot McKnight, general editor New Testament
Lynn Cohick, Joel Willitts, and Michael Bird, editors

Abbreviations

AB	Anchor Bible
ABD	*Anchor Bible Dictionary*. Edited by D. N. Freedman. 6 vols. New York: Doubleday, 1992.
ACCS	Ancient Christian Commentary on Scripture
AnBib	Analecta Biblica
ANF	Roberts, A., and J. Donaldson, eds. *Ante-Nicene Fathers*. 10 vols. Christian Literature Publishing Co., 1885–87; reprint, Peabody, MA: Hendrickson, 1994.
BDAG	Bauer, W., F. W. Danker, W. F. Arndt, and F. W. Gingrich. *A Greek-English Lexicon of the New Testament and Other Early Christian Literature*. 3rd ed. Chicago: University of Chicago Press, 2000.
BECNT	Baker Exegetical Commentary on the New Testament
BHGNT	Baylor Handbook on the Greek New Testament
BNTC	Black's New Testament Commentaries
BTB	*Biblical Theology Bulletin*
BTCB	Brazos Theological Commentary on the Bible
Did.	Didache
DLNT	*Dictionary of the Later New Testament and Its Developments*. Edited by Ralph P. Martin and Peter H. Davids. Downers Grove, IL: InterVarsity Press, 1997.
DNTB	*Dictionary of New Testament Background*. Edited by C. A. Evans and S. E. Porter. Downers Grove, IL: InterVarsity Press, 2000.
DPL	*Dictionary of Paul and His Letters*. Edited by G. F. Hawthorne and R. P. Martin. Downers Grove, IL: InterVarsity Press, 1993.
ExAud	*Ex Auditu*
Hist. eccl.	Eusebius, *Ecclesiastical History*
Holmes	Holmes, Michael W. *The Apostolic Fathers: Greek Texts and English Translations*. Updated ed. Grand Rapids: Baker Academic, 1999.

JBL	*Journal of Biblical Literature*
LNTS	The Library of New Testament Studies
LXX	The Septuagint, the Greek Old Testament
KJV	King James Version
MT	Masoretic Text
NDBT	*New Dictionary of Biblical Theology.* Edited by B. Rosner, T. D. Alexander, G. Goldsworthy, and D. A. Carson. Downers Grove, IL: InterVarsity Press, 2000.
NICNT	New International Commentary on the New Testament
NIV	New International Version
NovTSup	Novum Testamentum Supplements
NRSV	New Revised Standard Version
NTL	New Testament Library
NTS	*New Testament Studies*
SBLDS	Society of Biblical Literature Dissertation Series
SBLMS	Society of Biblical Literature Monograph Series
SGBC	Story of God Bible Commentary
SHBC	Smyth and Helwys Bible Commentary
SNTSMS	Society for New Testament Studies Monograph Series
THNTC	Two Horizons New Testament Commentary
TNTC	Tyndale New Testament Commentaries
WBC	Word Biblical Commentary
ZECNT	Zondervan Exegetical Commentary on the New Testament

Introduction

Most people in our culture have heard of the apostle Peter, at the very least because of those jokes about him guarding the gates of heaven. And of course, Bible students know that Jesus assigned Peter a prominent place among the twelve apostles.[1] Yet, "in view of the prominence of the Apostle Peter both in the Gospels and in later Christian tradition, it is surprising that almost from the beginning the two epistles attributed to him in the NT have occupied a rather modest place in the canon and in the historical reconstruction of Christian beginnings."[2] Indeed, John Hall Elliott, who has written extensively on 1 Peter, has memorably described the letter as an "exegetical step-child."[3]

Despite relative disinterest at particular periods in Christian history in 1 Peter, which is an encyclical letter addressed to churches in five provinces of Asia Minor, it has consistently proven to be a source of encouragement as well as challenge to faithful readers. For example, Elliott points out that the early Christian authors Clement of Rome (first-century AD) and Polycarp of Smyrna (second-century AD) "were inspired by [1 Peter's] words of consolation, exhortation, and hope."[4] Many years later, Martin Luther, who felt free to disparage the letter of James,[5] raved about 1 Peter: "This epistle of Peter is one of the grandest of the New Testament, and it is the true, pure gospel."[6] In our own generation, Karen Jobes asserts that "Peter's principles remain significant for the church today, living in times when social values and structures are changing at a rapid pace. The epistle is especially relevant in the Majority

---

1. Recently, Robert H. Gundry has advanced the controversial thesis that the Gospel of Matthew depicts the apostle Peter as an example of apostasy and failed discipleship (*Peter: False Disciple and Apostate According to Saint Matthew* [Grand Rapids: Eerdmans, 2015]). Gundry's conclusion, while intriguing, represents a minority viewpoint. He notes that his study "deals neither with the historical Peter nor with the received Peter" but focuses on Matthew's portrait of him (2). While Gundry's analysis may fill out the picture of a complex and frail human being, it does not diminish Peter's legacy.

2. J. Ramsey Michaels, *1 Peter*, WBC 49 (Waco: Word, 1988), xxxi.

3. John H. Elliott, *1 Peter: A New Translation with Introduction and Commentary*, AB 37B (New York: Doubleday, 2000), 3.

4. Ibid., 4.

5. Luther famously wrote, "Therefore, St. James' epistle is really an epistle of straw, compared to these others [John, 1 John, Romans, Galatians, Ephesians, 1 Peter], for it has nothing of the nature of the gospel about it" (J. Pelikan and H. T. Lehmann, ed., *Luther's Works*, 55 vols. [Fortress/Concordia, 1957], 35:362). Although Luther's chief concern was the apparent contradiction James 2 presents to Pauline thought, particularly Romans 4–5, he was also disturbed by the absence of teaching about the passion and resurrection of Jesus and about the Holy Spirit (*Luther's Works*, 35:396).

6. Martin Luther, *Commentary on Peter and Jude*, ed. John N. Lenker (Grand Rapids: Kregel, 1990), 10.

World, where Christianity is no longer a missionary religion but is becoming indigenous in cultures that were not formed by the Judeo-Christian tradition. First Peter's emphasis on Christian engagement with society makes it a relevant and thought-provoking book for all times and places."[7]

Having served as a pastor for over twenty-five years, I can echo Jobes's observation about 1 Peter's relevance. I have found its themes especially applicable for Christians who have dwelled on the margins of society. Such marginal status may become increasingly normative for believers. First Peter will assist us by affirming our Christian identity, guiding us in our relationships within and without the Christian community, with Jesus as our model, and reminding us that salvation is future, something to which we zealously look forward. Despite the present challenges of living among people hostile to Christian faith, we have a "living hope" (1 Pet 1:3).

The Letter's Author, Date, and Provenance

The first word of 1 Peter is the author's name, *Petros*, and he identifies himself as an apostle of Jesus Christ. There is little question that the letter purports to be from the person we know as Simon, who was called "Rock" by the Lord Jesus (Matt 16:17–18).[8] Contemporary scholarship, however, has called into question Peter's authorship, suggesting that an unknown Christian wrote in Peter's name in the late first- or the early second-century AD.[9] Some scholars even hypothesize the existence of a "Petrine circle," out of which came 1 and 2 Peter.[10] There are a range of issues that cast a shadow of doubt over Petrine authorship, but the main arguments are three: (1) the Greek of 1 Peter appears to be too sophisticated for an uneducated Galilean fisherman to have written (see Acts 4:13), and it seems doubtful that Peter would have used the Greek OT (i.e., the Septuagint), as 1 Peter does; (2) 1 Peter seems to depend upon so-called deutero-Pauline writings, i.e., those letters where Paul's authorship is questioned and are taken to have been written in the late first- or the early second-century AD; (3) the situation of Peter's readers seems to reflect a time later in the church's development when persecution was more widespread.[11]

---

7. Karen H. Jobes, *1 Peter*, BECNT (Grand Rapids: Baker Academic, 2005), 4.

8. See my discussion of 1:1–2.

9. For information on pseudonymous authorship or pseudepigraphal writings within the NT, compare Raymond E. Brown, *An Introduction to the New Testament* (New York: Doubleday, 1997), 585–89, with D. A. Carson, "Pseudonymity and Pseudepigraphy," *DNTB* 857–64.

10. David G. Horrell, *Becoming Christian: Essays on 1 Peter and the Making of Christian Identity*, LNTS 394 (London: Bloomsbury T&T Clark, 2013), 7–44.

11. Virtually all commentaries discuss the question of Peter's authorship, with varying degrees of detail. Jobes, *1 Peter*, 5–18, is exceptionally thorough in her treatment of the issue.

The major commentaries on 1 Peter lack consensus concerning these doubts of Peter's authorship. For example, Jobes notes that regarding (1), "the quality of the Greek is a somewhat subjective judgment."[12] Jobes concludes that "the author of 1 Peter may well have been a Semitic speaker for whom Greek was a second language."[13] Other scholars suggest that Peter used a secretary (called an amanuensis), who was more proficient in Greek. Regarding (2), Peter's dependence upon Pauline or deutero-Pauline writings, there is no clear evidence that Peter depended upon Pauline literature; they may simply have both shared common Christian tradition. Paul J. Achtemeier, after an extensive comparison of the two authors, concludes, "The notion of the dependence of 1 Peter on Pauline theology, to say nothing of literary dependence on the Pauline corpus, seems often to have been exaggerated."[14] As for (3), related to the historical situation, state-sanctioned persecutions occurred under emperors Nero (AD 54–68), Domitian (AD 81–96), and Trajan (AD 98–117). However, most scholars acknowledge that Peter's readers are not facing official, empire-wide persecution, but rather local, unorganized, and sporadic oppression. Consequently, the references to suffering in the letter give no firm indication of its date, and do not contribute definitively to the debate over Petrine authorship.

Some scholars have noted features of the letter that suggest that the apostle Peter is the actual author. For example, Larry R. Helyer discusses passages that evoke moments in Peter's life, such as Jesus's washing of the disciples' feet and how that might be reflected in 1 Peter 5:5–6.[15] After weighing the arguments, one need not reject Petrine authorship of 1 Peter.

If Peter is genuinely the author of 1 Peter, then the most likely date of composition is sometime before AD 64, the date of his supposed martyrdom under Emperor Nero.[16] Related to the question of date is the tradition that Peter spent time in Rome, the city where he likely penned the letter (as well as 2 Peter, although there are also objections to Petrine authorship of that writing).

At the close of the letter, Peter sends greetings from "Babylon" (5:13). Noted church reformer John Calvin took "Babylon" to be the literal city in Mesopotamia: "Since Peter had Mark as his companion when he wrote this Epistle, it

---

12. Jobes, *1 Peter*, 7.

13. Ibid.

14. Paul J. Achtemeier, *1 Peter: A Commentary on First Peter*, Hermeneia (Minneapolis: Fortress, 1996), 19.

15. Larry R. Helyer, *The Life and Witness of Peter* (Downers Grove, IL: IVP Academic, 2012), 108. Helyer's book is an excellent treatment of the life of Peter, including extrabiblical traditions surrounding him and writings associated with him.

16. Helyer, *Life and Witness*, 112, suggests a time as early as the AD 50s, while Wayne A. Grudem, *The First Epistle of Peter: An Introduction and Commentary*, TNTC (Leicester: Inter-Varsity Press, 1988), 38, narrows the timeframe to "between AD 62 and 64."

is very probable that he was at Babylon; and this was in accordance with his vocation, for we know that he was appointed an apostle especially to the Jews. He therefore visited chiefly those parts of the world where there was the greatest number of that nation."[17] Nevertheless, Calvin appears to have been attracted to this opinion because of ecclesiastical politics; he, like other leaders of the Protestant Reformation, wanted to invalidate claims associating Peter with the papacy in Rome.[18] Against Calvin's reasoning is the fact that the ancient city of Babylon had few inhabitants in the middle of the first-century AD and consisted of little more than ruins.[19] Contemporary scholars are in general agreement that "Babylon" is a cipher for Rome (see my analysis of 5:12–14).

"By the time Eusebius writes his magnum opus … Peter's post-NT career is summarized as follows: 'Peter appears to have preached through Pontus, Galatia, Bithynia, Cappadocia and Asia, to the Jews that were scattered abroad; who also, finally coming to Rome, was crucified with his head downward, having requested of himself to suffer in this way.'"[20] It seems best to conclude that Peter wrote 1 Peter from Rome to Christians in Asia Minor who were being ostracized because of their faith.

The Letter's Recipients

Eusebius supposes that it was Peter who had evangelized the Christians of the five regions of Asia Minor noted in 1:1: Pontus, Galatia, Cappadocia, Asia, and Bithynia. The order of the provinces is sometimes thought to reveal the route of a courier after having disembarked at a port along the Black Sea.[21] These five provinces contained people from a range of backgrounds, living in rural areas (Galatia and Cappadocia) as well as large cities (e.g., Smyrna). As noted above, while the Christians were probably not under a state-sanctioned mass persecution, they were subjected to local social tensions, suspicions, and alienation. Even if Peter was not the one who evangelized those regions, he was aware of the Christians' difficulties.

---

17. John Calvin, *Hebrews and 1 and 2 Peter*, Calvin's New Testament Commentaries Series 12 (Grand Rapids: Eerdmans, 1994), 323.

18. Calvin, *Hebrews and 1 and 2 Peter*, 322–23, admits, "Many of the old commentators thought that Rome is here [in 1 Pet 5:13] symbolically denoted…. But this old comment has no colour of truth, nor do I see why it was approved by [church historian] Eusebius and others, except that they were already led astray by the error that Peter had been at Rome."

19. Grudem, *First Peter*, 34.

20. Helyer, *Life and Witness*, 277, after considering various early writings associating Peter with Rome, and citing Eusebius, *Hist. eccl.* 3.1.

21. Richard Bolling Vinson, Richard Francis Wilson, and Watson E. Mills, *1 and 2 Peter, Jude*, SHBC (Macon: Smyth and Helwys, 2010), 38, however, speculate as to where a courier from Rome might begin. They then suggest the "places are simply listed in the order that the author thought of them."

In 1:18 Peter writes of "the empty way of life handed down to you from your ancestors," and in 2:10 asserts that "once you were not a people." Some scholars take those words, along with other hints, to mean that the readers of 1 Peter were Gentiles. However, as we see throughout this commentary, Peter makes references to the OT that seem targeted to people of Jewish background. For example, 1:19 mentions a lamb "without blemish or defect," alluding to the Jewish sacrificial system, and 1:1 and 2:9 touch upon the concept of election, of being chosen people. Yet Peter's frequent references to Israel's story with God may just be his way of communicating that Gentiles have been drawn into that same story. As J. Ramsey Michaels notes with regard to Gentile converts, "The Jewish past became their past."[22] It seems best to conclude that although the Christians to whom Peter writes were predominately Gentile in background, they were a mixed community, composed of Gentile and some Jewish believers in Jesus.[23]

The readers' designation as "exiles" that are "scattered" adds to the confusion. As I discuss in the section on 1:1–2, scholars struggle with how literally to understand the terms *parepidēmos* ("exiles") and *diaspora* ("scattered"). *Parepidēmos* is rare in the NT (Heb 11:13; 1 Pet 1:1; 2:11); it has a metaphorical sense in Hebrews 11:13, referring to those whose real home is heaven but who sojourn on the earth. Meanwhile, *diaspora* is sometimes thought to be a technical term indicating Jews living outside of Palestine, perhaps as the victims of expulsion.

It may be that some of Peter's readers were literally aliens in Asia Minor, possibly due to forced colonization.[24] But this cannot be the whole story: Peter also uses the terms *parepidēmos* and *diaspora* rhetorically to emphasize how his readers, like immigrants throughout time, are socially disconnected from the dominant culture. In 1 Peter, the Christian believers are alienated from a hostile society whose values are at odds with the teachings of Jesus.

First Peter and the Story of God

While working through the Greek text of 1 Peter, I was struck by two things: Peter's dependence upon the OT and the unusually high volume of words that occur nowhere else in the NT.[25] One need not draw any major theological

---

22. Michaels, *1 Peter*, l.
23. E.g., Grudem, *First Peter*, 39; Elliott, *1 Peter*, 95–96.
24. Jobes, *1 Peter*, 28–41.
25. One-time occurrences of words are called *hapax legomena*. First Peter's sixty-two hapaxes (along with 2 Peter's fifty-four), constitute a comparatively large percentage of the 686 within the entire NT. See Kenneth O. Gangel, "2 Peter," in *The Bible Knowledge Commentary: An Exposition of the Scriptures*, ed. John F. Walvoord and Roy B. Zuck (Wheaton: Victor, 1983), 2:860.

conclusions from the rarity of some of Peter's words, but his use of the
OT is theologically important: Peter uses the OT to connect his readers to
the story of God in which God draws people into a community.[26] As Scot
McKnight puts it, "The story of the Bible is creation, fall, *and then covenant community*—page after page of community—*as the context* in which
our wonderful *redemption* takes place."[27] The story of God, from creation,
through the call of Abraham, through the rescue of Israelites out of Egypt,
through King David, through the ministry of the OT prophets, and ultimately through the person of Jesus Christ, is a story of divine love. God's love
unfolds through Scripture, showing his intentions to construct a community
of people devoted to him.

A powerful scriptural example is found in the prophet Hosea, a man God
used to illustrate selfless, reconciling love. Hosea's wife was Gomer, a woman
of questionable character (Hos 1:2). The prophet was later cuckolded: his wife
took up with another man (Hos 3:1). Gomer's behavior served to illustrate
Israel's infidelity with God, while Hosea's tenacious devotion illustrated God's
love (Hos 14:4–5). Early in the prophet's story, there is a glimpse of God's
grace stemming from the naming of Hosea and Gomer's children. One child
is named Lo-Ruhamah, which means, "not loved," illustrating God's disap-
pointment in Israel. A subsequent child is named Lo-Ammi, which means,
"not my people," indicating how far God's people had wandered from him.
However, in Hosea 1:10 God promises a divine reversal: "Yet the Israelites
will be like the sand on the seashore, which cannot be measured or counted.
In the place where it was said to them, 'You are not my people,' they will be
called 'children of the living God.'" And in that same oracle God commands,
"Say of your brothers, 'My people,' and of your sisters, 'My loved one'" (Hos
2:1). Peter connects his readers to the story of God that unfolds in Hosea by
applying the prophet's words directly: "Once you were not a people, but now
you are the people of God; once you had not received mercy, but now you
have received mercy" (1 Pet 2:10).

There are many places where Peter places his readers within the story of
God, starting with his use of the term "elect" (1:1), an allusion to God's election of Israel. Achtemeier observes that, "1 Peter relies on the writings of the
people of Israel for language to describe the new people of God.... In a way
virtually unique among Christian canonical writings, 1 Peter has appropriated
the language of Israel for the church in such a way that Israel as a totality has

---

26. Elliott, *1 Peter*, 12–17, and Peter H. Davids, *The First Epistle of Peter*, NICNT (Grand
Rapids: Eerdmans, 1990), 23–24, offer detailed lists of Peter's use of the OT.

27. Scot McKnight, *The Blue Parakeet: Rethinking How You Read the Bible* (Grand Rapids:
Zondervan, 2008), 73 (emphasis original).

become for this letter the controlling metaphor in terms of which its theology is expressed."[28] Peter demonstrates that the Christian community is to be a united people of God, not merely a group of individuals who happen to possess similar beliefs. As the one people of God, they stand in solidarity with all sisters and brothers, even when oppressed by naysayers and devilish detractors. The united people of God must not compromise, not even on the chance that such compromise might alleviate their harsh conditions.

The Letter's Major Themes
(Suffering, Holiness, Salvation)

As I write this section, our nation is reeling from a horrible attack. A young white man, who was attending a Bible Study and prayer gathering at a predominately African-American church in South Carolina, killed nine church members, including the senior pastor, Rev. Clementa Pickney.[29] The young shooter allegedly was motivated by hatred and a desire to terrorize African Americans. The victims were thus targeted because of their race but also because that church was known for its commitment to their neighbors. I view the Emanuel African Methodist Episcopal Church in Charleston as eerily connected to the world of Peter's readers in that the believers of Asia Minor were not under the threat of government-sanctioned brutality but were subjected to random and localized displays of contempt.

Suffering is one of the major themes of 1 Peter. The letter itself does not focus on violent attack (but see 2:19–20) but rather on alienation, shame, slander, and other abuses. Peter likens these bad experiences to being burned in a fire (1:6–7; 4:12). Elliott concludes that neighbors attacked the Christians through "a barrage of verbal abuse designed to demean, discredit, and shame the believers as social and moral deviants endangering the common good."[30] By publicly shaming them, they were trying to pressure the believers to conform to the values and behaviors of the larger society. Peter's words serve as encouragement to keep his readers from becoming demoralized and possibly even giving up on their faith.

Holiness is another theme that Peter stresses, using Greek terms that are related to the adjective *hagios* ("holy" or "sanctified"), such as in 1:14–16 and 2:9. In particular, he develops how Christian conduct might serve as a

---

28. Achtemeier, *1 Peter*, 69.
29. The shooting occurred on the evening of June 17, 2015 at Emanuel African Methodist Episcopal Church in Charleston, South Carolina.
30. John H. Elliott, "Disgraced yet Graced. The Gospel according to 1 Peter in the Key of Honor and Shame," *BTB* 24 (1995): 173.

witness to unbelievers (e.g., 2:15; 3:13). He starts off by citing Leviticus 19:2, "Be holy, because I am holy" (1 Pet 1:16) and thus sets the tone for his later admonitions.

Salvation is another important topic for Peter and is related to other theological concepts such as Christology and eschatology (the study of the end times). First Peter opens with teaching on "salvation," with three of the four occurrences of the word appearing in the first chapter (1:5, 9, 10) as part of the introduction to the entire letter (the other occurrence is 2:2). Salvation begins with new birth (1:3) but finds its culmination in the future (1:9). Jesus is the one who makes salvation possible through his death and resurrection (1:3; 3:21), and it is upon his return that salvation will be made complete (1:7, 13; 4:7; 5:4, 10).

Even as we list the individual themes that emerge from reading 1 Peter, I hasten to note that foundational to everything—even Peter's use of the OT—is the person and ministry of Jesus Christ. These themes of suffering, holiness, and salvation derive their energy from the life of Jesus. Through numerous references to him (including those found in traditional formulas, such as in 3:18–19), Peter uses the life, suffering, death, and resurrection of Jesus as the basis for Christian belief and behavior; the Lord continually serves as a model for the community (e.g., 2:21–24).

An Outline of 1 Peter

The following outline demonstrates that 1 Peter, like most of the letters of the NT, fits the typical pattern of Greco-Roman letters:

The Opening Greeting (1:1–2). These verses contain a formulaic opening: "A to B, greetings," where the sender "A" greets the recipient(s) "B," often with some sort of remembrance or wish for the recipient's good health.

The Introduction (1:3–12). This section is where central themes are put forward. Generally, the introduction of a Greco-Roman letter might contain a blessing or a prayer of thanksgiving to God or the gods; in non-Christian letters, writers sometimes gave thanks to pagan deities. Peter opens this section offering praise to God. The major themes of suffering, holiness, and salvation are touched on in this introduction. Verses 6–9 mention suffering and trials. Holiness, or upright behavior, is linked to Peter's comments about new birth (v. 3), genuine faith (v. 7), and the community's love for Jesus, which flows from that faith (v. 8). Salvation is prominent throughout the introduction (e.g., vv. 3–5, 9–10).

The Body of the Letter (1:13–5:11). This is where the main message is found.
1:13–2:10 is the body opening, where the exhortations begin.

2:11–4:11 is the heart of the letter, where Peter discloses practical
instructions regarding how believers should live the holy lives
encouraged in the previous section. Peter begins this section
with "dear friends" (2:11), the same words that begin the next
section (4:12).

4:12–5:11 is the body closing, a section that recapitulates earlier
points and offers final motivational comments and reminders.

The Conclusion (5:12–14). This is the section that usually contains final
greetings and sometimes a final praise, or doxology. Peter has already
offered a closing doxology at 5:11.

1 Peter 1:1-2

 LISTEN to the Story

> [1]Peter, an apostle of Jesus Christ,
> To God's elect, exiles scattered throughout the provinces of Pontus,
> Galatia, Cappadocia, Asia and Bithynia, [2]who have been chosen according
> to the foreknowledge of God the Father, through the sanctifying work of
> the Spirit, to be obedient to Jesus Christ and sprinkled with his blood:
> Grace and peace be yours in abundance.

Listening to the Text in the Story: Genesis 23:4; Exod 24:3–8; Psalm 39:12;
Isaiah 53:1–12.

"I would not encourage any person to come here that could live middling well at home as they might meet with many dificulties [*sic*] by coming here. But any Boy or Girl that has to labour for their living this is The Country for them."[1] Those sentences allude to the reality of how tough life can be for immigrants to the USA. In this case it was a man from Ireland in 1852, but there are legions of stories—and letters—of people who arrived to a distant land to discover that opportunities often came at a hefty price. Immigrants often endure alienation because they stand out from the host culture, struggling with a new language and slowly becoming familiar with local customs and rituals. Immigrants may become victims of xenophobia on the part of new neighbors who resist change in their communities and fail to offer a sympathetic ear. Immigrants are often aliens in the starkest sense of that term in that they do not fit into the established patterns of the host culture.

The recipients of Peter's first letter experienced a similar reality. They were different from their non-Christian neighbors—some perhaps because of immigrant status, but all because of their allegiance to Jesus Christ as opposed

---

1. "Michael Hogan, Albany, NY, to aunt Catherine Nolan, County Carlow, Ireland, March 17, 1852," *Letters to and from Irish Immigrants to America, 1830s–1880s,* http://risdyeswecan.blogspot.com/2010/02/letters-to-and-from-irish-immigrants-to.html.

to anything or anyone else, up to and including the emperor. People on the margins have little power and influence in society. Yet they may still make a profound impact on the world when they are able to persevere and live according to the ways of the Lord Jesus. Even though such believers are called upon to suffer, they may still "live such good lives among the pagans" that, even if accused of wrongdoing, they will cause those unbelievers to witness genuine goodness and "glorify God on the day he visits us" (2:12). Christians today, even in the USA, could benefit from Peter's words to people on the margins. We do well to hear that suffering for our faith in Jesus not only puts us in solidarity with our Lord but also serves to refine us, making us more effective witnesses in the world.

EXPLAIN the Story

As noted in the introduction, 1 Peter is a typical Greco-Roman letter and thus similar to the Pauline letters. Peter's introduction, however, is not a simple one. Peter here demonstrates his familiarity with OT ideas, especially evident in the images he uses to address and describe his readers.

The Writer of the Letter (1:1a)

For most readers of the NT, Peter needs little introduction.[2] We know him as the outspoken and even brash disciple of Jesus who, along with James and John, was part of the Lord's inner circle. Although his given name was Simon, Jesus called him "rock" (*Petros*). He is famous for his bold declaration of Jesus's identity (Matt 16:16), for being called into the leadership of God's people (Matt 16:17–19), but then also for rebuking Jesus directly afterwards (Matt 16:22). Peter is notorious for having three times denied knowing Jesus on the night the Lord was betrayed (Matt 26:75). However, the Lord reaffirmed Peter's call to serve God's people with another incident involving three responses: he invited Peter to declare his love three times and followed up each response with a command that Peter care for the Lord's sheep (John 21:15–17).

Acts 2:14–40 demonstrates Peter's leadership as he preaches on the Day of Pentecost, when the Holy Spirit was poured out upon some 120 disciples of Jesus who were gathered in prayer after the Lord's ascension.

The first several chapters of the book of Acts depict Peter as a leader of the church in Jerusalem. For example, after his powerful Pentecost sermon,

---

2. Please see the section on authorship in the introduction. At the end of the letter Peter mentions Silas and Mark. Since they are not named here as coauthors of the letter, I'll discuss them at 5:12–14.

Peter performs wonders in Jerusalem (Acts 3:1–10), continues to preach (Acts 3:11–26), faces persecution (e.g., Acts 4:1–22; 5:17–42; 12:1–19), and exercises discipline within the budding Christian community (Acts 5:1–11). Furthermore, after a vision in Joppa he meets with a Gentile named Cornelius (Acts 10:1–48) and then returns to Jerusalem to convey the importance of mission to the Gentiles (Acts 11:1–18). However, Peter disappears after Acts 15:7 (although see v. 14) as the ministry of Saul of Tarsus takes center stage.

Church history and legend offer answers to some questions concerning the ongoing ministry and fate of the apostles. One such source, *The Acts of Peter*, claims that Peter encountered the risen Lord Jesus on a road outside of Rome. In this meeting Peter asks the Lord, "Where are you going?" (in Latin: *Quo vadis?*). Jesus indicates that he is going to Rome to be crucified again, a reference to the martyrdom of his followers there. Peter then finds the courage to return to Rome. Upon his return Peter is arrested and crucified—opting to hang upside down on the cross because he deemed himself unworthy to die in the same manner as his Lord. This is why, in some ancient art, Peter is depicted along with an upside-down cross. Peter's martyrdom (as well as the apostle Paul's) is thought to have occurred under Emperor Nero.[3] First Peter 5:13 may support the tradition that Peter ended his days in Rome, since it mentions that he is in "Babylon," which is likely a reference to Rome.

Peter, like Paul, refers to himself as an apostle, which means that his authority proceeds directly from the Lord Jesus. Indeed, in a vision that also involves another set of three interactions with Jesus, the Lord invites Peter into mission to the Gentiles. Acts 10:1–11:18 recounts Peter's evangelistic encounter with Cornelius and his household, followed by Peter's response to the criticism by Jewish believers who had been made aware of his table fellowship with Gentiles. Jesus called Peter as apostle to minister to both Jews and Gentiles, as he does with this letter, in which he depends heavily upon the Jewish Scriptures.

The Recipients of the Letter (1:1b–2)

In the introduction I spell out some details concerning the geographic location of the letter's addressees. They resided among a diverse population with various expressions of polytheism, within five regions of Asia Minor (modern-day Turkey) that covered a large geographic area, some 129,000 square miles. The Christians would have come from both Jewish and Gentile backgrounds.

Alongside those geographic references, Peter speaks of the social status of his readers with a series of three Greek words: *eklektos* ("chosen" or "elect"),

---

3. For an overall picture of Peter's story, including extrabiblical tradition, see Helyer, *Life and Witness*, 272–81.

parepidēmos ("exile" or "sojourner"), and *diaspora* ("scattered," or "dispersed"). All three words conjure up images of the OT people of God. The OT refers to Israel as "chosen" or "elect" on numerous occasions (e.g., Deut 7:6–8; Isa 41:8–9), and Christians came to be similarly identified (e.g., Rom 8:33; Col 3:12; 2 Tim 2:10). God is the one who elects (as the NIV makes explicit with the addition of "God's" in v. 1). Election in this context refers to God's invitation, or calling, to be part of a people who will live distinctly from the rest of the world (see 1 Pet 2:9). That way of life is characterized by holiness, where believers adopt the character of the one who does the choosing (see 1:13–21).

God's chosen people are at the same time strangers. *Parepidēmos* is a rare term in biblical literature (in the LXX: Gen 23:4; Ps 38:13; in the NT: Heb 11:13; 1 Pet 1:1; 2:11) and points to one living in a foreign land (willingly or by force). Perhaps because of their rarity, there is some scholarly debate regarding *parepidēmos* and the next term, *diaspora*. The issue is whether these words are used literally, or metaphorically, or perhaps both ways at once. In a purely metaphorical understanding, Peter's readers would be said to be members of a heavenly home, and of necessity they must withdraw from their temporal earthly home. Peter does not make a sharp contrast between heavenly and earthly homes (as Phil 3:20 does), but earlier commentators adopted such a view of this text. However, through the work of more recent scholarship, closer attention has been given to the socio-political reality of Peter's readers.[4] Since Peter mentions real geographic regions, a literal sense of *diaspora* is not out of the question.

Even so, a strictly literal understanding of *diaspora* would make it a technical term referring to the forced expulsion of Jews, a sad event that has happened at various times throughout history (see Acts 18:2). Consequently, with a solely literal, nonmetaphorical view of *parepidēmos* and *diaspora*, we would perceive Peter's readers to be largely Jewish Christians displaced from Palestine and its environs.[5] This is problematic since there is some evidence that Peter's audience consisted predominately of Gentile Christians.[6] Paul Achtemeier thus voices the opinion of many commentators when he writes that "the whole tenor of 1 Peter … argues for this [*diaspora*] to be metaphorical, and hence to refer to all Christians."[7]

There is perhaps a third way, if one affirms the socio-rhetorical realities as well as the metaphorical language on Peter's part. Thus, Joel B. Green

---

4. John H. Elliott, *A Home for the Homeless: A Sociological Exegesis of 1 Peter, Its Situation and Strategy* (Philadelphia: Fortress, 1981).

5. Elliott, *1 Peter*, 313.

6. Joel B. Green, *1 Peter*, THNTC (Grand Rapids: Eerdmans, 2007), 15.

7. Achtemeier, *1 Peter*, 82.

claims that "the dichotomy, metaphorical versus nonmetaphorical, is itself wrongheaded."[8] Karen Jobes, in discussing the Roman policy of urbanization through colonization, points out that Emperor Claudius (AD 41–54) established Roman cities—"colonies" of people transplanted from Rome—in all five of the regions named here in 1 Peter 1:1.[9] She hypothesizes that "if the theory of Roman colonization is correct, Peter uses the sociohistorical situation of his readers to explain their sociospiritual situation."[10]

Peter's closing, 5:12–14, reinforces this same status of his readers. In 5:13 the word *syneklektē* ("co-elect" or the NIV's "chosen together") echoes *eklektos*; the mention of Babylon (5:13) is meant to evoke images of exile and dispersion. Consequently, the entire letter is framed with the concept that believers are an alienated community and simultaneously members of God's chosen people. What has become clear to readers throughout the centuries is that the author focuses on believers who are alienated from the surrounding secular society, mainly because of their faith. Thus, believers face abuse in a variety of forms but are called to demonstrate their faith among, as the apostle Paul says, "a warped and crooked generation" (Phil 2:15).

The Trinity at Work (1:2)

Verse 2 highlights God the Father, the Holy Spirit, and Jesus Christ. God has had a plan since before creation to build a community of people devoted to him ("to be obedient") through the ministry of Jesus Christ (1:20). God the Father's foreknowledge set the plan of election in motion. Foreknowledge is not simply "knowledge," or even knowledge before an event; rather, it means that whatever happens does so in accord with God's purpose.[11] Such words serve as encouragement on at least two accounts. The first is that God, as Father, is not uncaring about his people's situation. The second reason for encouragement is that because of his foreknowledge, God is not caught off guard or taken by surprise at the suffering of his people; in fact, it happens within his overall plan of salvation. Just as his own son, Jesus Christ, suffered before being exalted, so will Peter's readers face persecution while yet enjoying the hope for future salvation and vindication (1:3–12).

The Holy Spirit carries out God's plan of election by setting apart God's people (the technical word is "sanctify," *hagiazō*). Peter will elaborate upon the Spirit's work of sanctification throughout the letter (e.g., 1:15–16, 22;

---

8. Green, *1 Peter*, 16.
9. Jobes, *1 Peter*, 29.
10. Ibid., 38.
11. *Prognōsis* ("foreknowledge") is rare in the NT; see also Acts 2:23, where the word comes from Peter's lips. Peter will later use the cognate verb (*proginōskō*) in 1:20, see also Rom 8:29 and 11:2.

2:5, 9).[12] Divine foreknowledge and sanctification are the two elements that prepare the reader for subsequent discussion, starting immediately with an analysis of their salvation (1:3–12) and an admonition concerning holiness (1:13–21). The theme of obedience also shows up throughout the letter, especially in the main part of the body, 2:11–4:11; it is linked to the Lord Jesus Christ, the member of the Trinity mentioned at the outset of Peter's greeting.

The purpose of election, which happens according to the foreknowledge of God and is carried out by the Holy Spirit's sanctifying work, is literally, "obedience and sprinkling of the blood of Jesus Christ."[13] Obedience and sprinkling of blood should be taken together as one single idea that has its background in the Mosaic covenant as described in Exodus 24:3–8:

> When Moses went and told the people all the LORD's words and laws, they responded with one voice, "Everything the LORD has said we will do." Moses then wrote down everything the LORD had said. He got up early the next morning and built an altar at the foot of the mountain and set up twelve stone pillars representing the twelve tribes of Israel. Then he sent young Israelite men, and they offered burnt offerings and sacrificed young bulls as fellowship offerings to the LORD. Moses took half of the blood and put it in bowls, and the other half he splashed against the altar. Then he took the Book of the Covenant and read it to the people. They responded, "We will do everything the LORD has said; we will obey." Moses then took the blood, sprinkled it on the people and said, "This is the blood of the covenant that the LORD has made with you in accordance with all these words."

In the ceremony described in Exodus, the newly formed nation makes several pledges of obedience, i.e., to "do everything the LORD has said." Accompanying those confessions of the people are rituals involving the blood of sacrificed animals, which is splashed not only upon the altar but also sprinkled upon the people. The sprinkling of blood is the means by which the people are cleansed and the covenant sealed. For Peter, Jesus is the sacrifice that was anticipated in Exodus 24. Peter may well have Exodus in mind here, as he does in 2:9, where he relies upon Exodus 19:5–6.

God's purpose in election is to form a consecrated people who are obedient to him as Jesus Christ himself is, having been cleansed through the blood

---

12. See my treatment of 1:13–21 as well as subsequent discussions concerning holiness.

13. There is confusion surrounding the syntax of the Greek phrase related to obedience and sprinkling of blood. We hold that the word *eis* ("toward"), which begins the phrase, indicates purpose (see my explanation of 1:3–5).

of Jesus and set apart by the Holy Spirit. Whatever life throws at us, it cannot slow down God's plan, not even when we suffer because of our faith in Jesus.

To these tenacious believers, then, Peter wishes abundant grace and peace, i.e., God's favor along with the well-being, or wholeness (*shalom*), that he gives. He will end his letter with a similar wish for peace (5:14).

LIVE the Story

Earlier I mentioned how immigrants—even in our time—might feel the alienation that stems from a lack of familiarity with a new setting as well as from xenophobia on the part of the host culture. History is full of the stories of people who have been made to feel disconnected. Such was the case with Peter's first readers. Peter writes to people on the margins. Therefore, we have an opportunity to learn from words addressed not to people in the upper echelons of society but to those pushed to the side. I wonder if we Christians in America are open to receiving words addressed to people who are on the bottom and not the top. My experiences from years of involvement in Christian service suggest that we typically only want to hear messages addressed to and delivered by powerful and influential people. Or we are willing to hear from *former* aliens and strangers, but only after those people have been removed from such status—presumably by their own hard work and self-determination. However, Peter's readers were not on the path of upward mobility. They were objects of shame but were instructed to live faithfully, following the way of Jesus, as evidence of God's work in their lives and as witnesses to their accusers.

As an African American, I am continually amazed at the endurance of my forebears, many of whom became Christians despite the evils of slavery and American Christianity's mixed sentiments concerning that institution. Additionally, I am motivated and encouraged when I recall that our Lord Jesus was a voice from the margins and that such a place can be one of honor and not disdain.

An Example from among African-American Aliens

In the classic work *The Souls of Black Folk*, W. E. B. Du Bois struggles with how African Americans have been made to feel like strangers in their own land. From the outset Du Bois gives voice to the archetypal young man who cries, "Why did God make me an outcast and stranger in mine own house?"[14] Theologian Arthur Sutherland suggests that in *The Souls of Black Folk* Du Bois

---

14. W. E. B. Du Bois, *The Souls of Black Folk* (New York: Dover, 1994 [orig. 1903]), 2.

"relies upon a cluster of ideas in describing black folk as strangers; he uses out-casts, exiles, vagabonds, the helpless, and the pitiable."[15]

Yet, despite the alienation that we African Americans have long experi-enced, the world has been profoundly impacted by our tenacious faith. There are innumerable heroes from the margins who will be forever nameless. One person whose name is well-known is Rosa Parks. Most Americans are familiar with her as the woman from Alabama who refused to give up her seat and move to the rear of a public bus, sparking the Montgomery Bus Boycott, which lasted 381 days and helped to propel Dr. Martin Luther King Jr. to national notoriety.

Rosa Parks is a classic example of a Christian believer on the margins. She was a lifelong member of the African Methodist Episcopal Church and her faith in Jesus was always an integral part of her life. Biographer Douglas Brin-kley writes concerning Ms. Parks's devotion that "the teachings of Jesus Christ had convinced her … as they had Martin Luther King, Jr., that a heart filled with love could conquer anything, even bigotry. 'I remember finding such comfort and peace while reading the Bible,' Parks averred. 'Its teaching became a way of life and helped me in dealing with my day-to-day problems.'"[16]

Ms. Parks's legacy has been profound, but not because she was especially charismatic or held a place of prominence in the country. On the contrary, she was not widely known and respected until well after her simple act of defiance. Yet, upon her death at 92 years old in 2005, she was honored with numerous memorial services and her body was given the high honor of lying in state at the U. S. Capitol rotunda. She serves as an example of someone from the margins of society who faced discrimination and alienation, much the way Peter's readers did, but whose faith allowed her to make a lasting impact on those who observed her.

Jesus Christ: Stranger and Alien

Throughout his letter Peter offers Jesus as an example of one who endured suf-fering (e.g., 2:21–24). But it seems that Christians in America do not get that the Bible portrays Jesus as someone with little social status. On more than one occasion, people who follow Prosperity Teaching (or the Prosperity Gospel) have told me that Jesus must have been wealthy because he had a treasurer (see John 13:29). It is helpful, especially in light of such ludicrous speculations, to recall our Lord's marginal status in the world.

---

15. Arthur Sutherland, *I Was a Stranger: A Christian Theology of Hospitality* (Nashville: Abing-don, 2006), 13.

16. Douglas Brinkley, *"Rosa Parks," New York Times,* http://www.nytimes.com/books/first/b/brinkley-parks.html.

First, Jesus refers to himself as *homeless*: "Foxes have dens and birds have nests, but the Son of Man has no place to lay his head" (Matt 8:20//Luke 9:58). Scot McKnight imagines how life may have been for this homeless Jesus: "The Jesus we follow seems to have had nothing. He lived in a dry, hot, and dusty world. What food he ate he received by fishing, by farming, or by donations. The summers were long and filled with famine-causing heat; the houses in places like Capernaum were made of black basalt and were sturdy but hardly cool enough to make life comfortable. To cool off people waded in the Sea of Galilee. He lived on little; he lived from the generosity of others; he undoubtedly knew some hunger and thirst."[17] Instead of seeing a savior flush with cash and living "high on the hog," we should see a man of low status, with few material goods, yet clearly in close fellowship with the Father and the Holy Spirit.

Second, Jesus is described as *rejected*. In the prologue to the Gospel of John, the writer prepares the reader for much of what will appear in the rest of the book, including the rejection of Jesus: "He was in the world, and though the world was made through him, the world did not recognize him. He came to that which was his own, but his own did not receive him" (John 1:10–11). Later in the Gospel, on at least two occasions, he was faced with the prospect of being put to death by stoning (8:59; 10:31–33). To be sure, there are glimpses of the apparent popularity of Jesus in the crowds who witnessed his ministry of teaching and healing, but we must remember that he was ultimately rejected. For example, after the famous bread-of-life discourse of John 6, rather than gaining more followers, Jesus lost many of those he already had: "From this time many of his disciples turned back and no longer followed him" (John 6:66). Often our images of the best and most effective ministers are those who are able to attract a crowd; Jesus, on the other hand, shows us how to thin out a crowd! By common measures, Jesus does not fit our image of a successful leader.

Finally, I would like to let the prophet Isaiah speak. In a passage that we understand to be about Jesus (see how it is described in Acts 8:26–40) and that is often read around Easter, we see a marginalized savior, one who was made to feel like a stranger in this world, much like Peter's audience. Please allow me to encourage you to meditate on the words and images of Isaiah 53:1–12:

> Who has believed our message
> and to whom has the arm of the LORD been revealed?
> He grew up before him like a tender shoot,

---

17. Scot McKnight, *The Sermon on the Mount*, SGBC (Grand Rapids: Zondervan, 2013), 204.

and like a root out of dry ground.
He had no beauty or majesty to attract us to him,
    nothing in his appearance that we should desire him.
He was despised and rejected by mankind,
    a man of suffering, and familiar with pain.
Like one from whom people hide their faces
    he was despised, and we held him in low esteem.
Surely he took up our pain
    and bore our suffering,
yet we considered him punished by God,
    stricken by him, and afflicted.
But he was pierced for our transgressions,
    he was crushed for our iniquities;
the punishment that brought us peace was on him,
    and by his wounds we are healed.
We all, like sheep, have gone astray,
    each of us has turned to our own way;
and the LORD has laid on him
    the iniquity of us all.
He was oppressed and afflicted,
    yet he did not open his mouth;
he was led like a lamb to the slaughter,
    and as a sheep before its shearers is silent,
    so he did not open his mouth.
By oppression and judgment he was taken away.
    Yet who of his generation protested?
For he was cut off from the land of the living;
    for the transgression of my people he was punished.
He was assigned a grave with the wicked,
    and with the rich in his death,
though he had done no violence,
    nor was any deceit in his mouth.
Yet it was the LORD's will to crush him and cause him to suffer,
    and though the LORD makes his life an offering for sin,
he will see his offspring and prolong his days,
    and the will of the LORD will prosper in his hand.
After he has suffered,
    he will see the light of life and be satisfied;
by his knowledge my righteous servant will justify many,
    and he will bear their iniquities.

Therefore I will give him a portion among the great,
 and he will divide the spoils with the strong,
because he poured out his life unto death,
 and was numbered with the transgressors.
For he bore the sin of many,
 and made intercession for the transgressors.

CHAPTER 2

1 Peter 1:3-12

 LISTEN to the Story

³Praise be to the God and Father of our Lord Jesus Christ! In his great mercy he has given us new birth into a living hope through the resurrection of Jesus Christ from the dead, ⁴and into an inheritance that can never perish, spoil or fade. This inheritance is kept in heaven for you, ⁵who through faith are shielded by God's power until the coming of the salvation that is ready to be revealed in the last time. ⁶In all this you greatly rejoice, though now for a little while you may have had to suffer grief in all kinds of trials. ⁷These have come so that the proven genuineness of your faith—of greater worth than gold, which perishes even though refined by fire—may result in praise, glory and honor when Jesus Christ is revealed. ⁸Though you have not seen him, you love him; and even though you do not see him now, you believe in him and are filled with an inexpressible and glorious joy, ⁹for you are receiving the end result of your faith, the salvation of your souls. ¹⁰Concerning this salvation, the prophets, who spoke of the grace that was to come to you, searched intently and with the greatest care, ¹¹trying to find out the time and circumstances to which the Spirit of Christ in them was pointing when he predicted the sufferings of the Messiah and the glories that would follow. ¹²It was revealed to them that they were not serving themselves but you, when they spoke of the things that have now been told you by those who have preached the gospel to you by the Holy Spirit sent from heaven. Even angels long to look into these things.

Listening to the Text in the Story: Exodus 20:6; 34:6, 10; Psalms 31:10; 32:5; Hosea 2:20; John 3:3–7; Ephesians 1:3–14.

The life of faith in Jesus is one of dynamic tension where believers are simultaneously pulled in two directions. On the one hand, followers of Jesus are pulled *upward*: we are heirs to promises of a secure future (e.g., Eph 1:3–14); we are God's children and special possession (1 Pet 2:9–10). We are called to live with an upward focus (Col 3:1–4) and to find encouragement as we consider Jesus and all that he has done for us (Heb 12:1–3). On the other hand, we believers are dragged *downward*, toward life's corruption. Satan has influence in this world (Eph 2:2); there is also the personal struggle to resist sin (e.g., Col 3:5–9) and the old patterns of life (1 Pet 1:14). To compound matters, living as witnesses of Jesus may cause us to suffer on account of our faith since we attract the ire of those who oppose him and his message.

This first letter of Peter addresses those very tensions. His readers faced pressure from a pagan society and needed to be encouraged to remain steadfast in following the Lord Jesus, who also suffered while on the earth. In Peter's opening, 1:3–12, he acknowledges the reality of suffering and likens it to the refining fire. Peter does not ignore the existence of pain but treats it as a relatively small matter when compared to the benefits of new birth through faith in Jesus. Consequently, even though the Christian life is one of tension, in the end it is a life of joy in the midst of suffering. Joy invites believers to transcend circumstances since joy is founded upon the promises of God.

EXPLAIN the Story

In typical Greco-Roman letters the author would offer a prayer or thanksgiving after the opening address (1:1–2), which in turn served to introduce the body of the letter.[1] Peter's thanksgiving (1:3–12) takes the form of a doxology, a prayer of praise in which he touches on themes that will appear later; his doxology is a fitting introduction to the entire letter.[2] Specifically, Peter relates the affliction of his readers and their hope of glory (1:6–7) to the sufferings and glories of the Messiah (1:10–12). His instruction regarding holy living (1:13–22), his admonition concerning purity through God's word (1:22–2:3), and his exhortation for his readers to live out their special identity as God's people (2:4–10) are ways he picks up on the themes of hope, new birth, salvation, and the *parousia* introduced in 1:3–12.

The middle of the letter likewise expands on these opening themes as Peter addresses the concrete situation of his audience: in 2:11–4:11, he associates the suffering of Christ with that of his readers. And in the conclusion of the

---

1. See my outline in the introduction. For more on Greco-Roman letters, see Brown, *Introduction to the New Testament*, 410–16; P. T. O'Brien, "Letters, Letter Forms," *DPL* 550–53.

2. I make some use here of a detailed and helpful discussion of how 1:3–12 introduces the entire letter by David W. Kendall, "The Literary and Theological Function of 1 Peter 1:3–12," in *Perspectives on First Peter*, National Association of Baptist Professors of Religion Special Studies 9 (Macon, GA: Mercer University Press, 1986), 103–20.

letter, 4:12–5:11, he reiterates themes from the body of the letter and again draws a close relationship with the introduction. There is a recurrence of three key words: (1) "trial" or "ordeal" (*peirosmos*) (1:6; 4:12); (2) "sufferings" (1:11; 4:13; 5:1, 9); (3) "a little while" (1:6; 5:10). These words, along with an emphasis on ultimate salvation as well as the sovereignty of God, demonstrate that the introduction and conclusion focus on matters associated with the end times, or eschatology. Careful consideration of Peter's introduction, therefore, prepares us to receive the message of the entire letter.

Praise to God for New Birth (1:3–5)

Peter introduces his letter with a doxology, which is a formulaic praise to God. The English word "eulogy" derives from the Greek, meaning "praise be," *eulogētos*. That expression is a common element in prayers of praise found in Scripture. Luke 1:68 is the beginning of Zechariah's prayer known as the *Benedictus*, which is the Latin equivalent for "eulogy." The word is used in Pauline doxologies and in his discussions concerning the nature of God (Rom 1:25; 9:5; 2 Cor 1:3; 11:31; Eph 1:3). Peter's prayer of praise, however, does not derive from Luke or Paul but from common Jewish practice, as shown in numerous instances in the Septuagint (LXX), the Greek Old Testament (e.g., Gen 14:20; 24:27; Exod 18:10; Ruth 4:14). It is said that good theology gives rise to doxology, and Peter's words of praise are rooted in his understanding of salvation, which has been made possible through Jesus Christ.

It is by God's mercy that Peter and his readers have been transformed. Mercy is pity or kindness to those in need. God's mercy (NIV: "love") is celebrated prominently in the OT, particularly in his relationship with his people (e.g., Exod 20:6; 34:7; Pss 32:10; 33:5, 22; Hos 2:19). In fact, in 2:10 Peter alludes to Hosea 1–2, where the prophet's own marriage serves to illustrate God's mercy. Additionally, Peter exclaims that God's mercy is abundant, or great, indicating that God is not stingy or reluctant to show love, as some human parents might be. Peter's words correspond to the celebration of God's transforming work in Ephesians 2:4–5, "But because of his great love for us, God, who is rich in mercy, made us alive with Christ even when we were dead in transgressions—it is by grace you have been saved." The transformation of which Peter speaks is described as new birth.

Although Peter's specific vocabulary is unique to this letter, the concept of new birth is not. In the NT the verb *anagennaō* as such appears only here and in 1:23, but the notion of new birth is present in the teachings of Jesus, notably in John 3:3–7, where the Lord holds an evening conversation with a Pharisee named Nicodemus:

Jesus replied, "Very truly I tell you, no one can see the kingdom of God
unless they are born again." "How can someone be born when they are
old?" Nicodemus asked. "Surely they cannot enter a second time into their
mother's womb to be born!" Jesus answered, "Very truly I tell you, no one
can enter the kingdom of God unless they are born of water and the Spirit.
Flesh gives birth to flesh, but the Spirit gives birth to spirit. You should
not be surprised at my saying, 'You must be born again.'"

Many biblical scholars see Ezekiel 36:25–27 as a backdrop for the words
of Jesus to Nicodemus.[3] Ezekiel prophesies, "I will sprinkle clean water on
you, and you will be clean; I will cleanse you from all your impurities and
from all your idols. I will give you a new heart and put a new spirit in you;
I will remove from you your heart of stone and give you a heart of flesh.
And I will put my Spirit in you and move you to follow my decrees and
be careful to keep my laws." Ezekiel brings together "water" and "spirit"
to signify not only spiritual cleansing but also transformation by the Holy
Spirit. Jesus too mentions cleansing and transformation through water and
Spirit in his discussion of the new birth. Peter concurs with Ezekiel and Jesus
regarding cleansing, transformation, and new birth. The sanctifying work of
the Holy Spirit (v. 2), the sprinkling of the blood of Jesus (v. 2), holy living
(1:13–21), the regenerating power of Scripture (1:23), and the waters of
baptism (3:21) are some of the themes by which Peter opens up for us the
concept of new birth.

New birth suggests new parentage (see 1:14). God is not only the creator
(4:19)—who, after all, might remain aloof from his creation—but is also the
Father, a title denoting familiarity, and possibly even intimacy. The concept
of new birth corresponds to the divine initiative, i.e., "foreknowledge," noted
in v. 2. Christian believers become part of a new family through the mercy of
God and the ministry of Jesus. The benefits of being in this new family include
the hope for a bright future, even if its members are now undergoing trials.

With three prepositional phrases, each introduced with the Greek *eis*,
which may often indicate purpose, Peter points to the goals of new birth in
vv. 3–5:

1. Into (*eis*) a living hope
2. Into (*eis*) an inheritance
3. Until (*eis*) … salvation[4]

---

3. Martin Williams, *The Doctrine of Salvation in the First Letter of Peter*, SNTSMS 149 (Cambridge: Cambridge University Press, 2011), 133.

4. The preposition *eis* is not here translated to indicate purpose in the NIV. The NRSV, however, does translate it in this way ("for a salvation").

First, the new birth leads to hope. As I will note in my discussion of 1:13–21, hope is not an abstract sense of optimism but a confident expectation of a good outcome based upon the work of God. Jesus is the foundation of Christian hope. Because Jesus has been raised from the dead and is alive, Christian hope can be described as a "living" hope. Such hope is in contrast to pagan religions, which are dead exercises in futility (see Eph 2:12).

Second, the new birth leads to an inheritance. To receive an inheritance means that someone is part of a family. Karen Jobes theorizes that Peter's readers, alienated because of their faith, may have lost their natural inheritance and family rights.[5] If so, such disinheritance would have contributed to the shame and hopelessness that Peter's readers struggled against.

In the OT, the land of Canaan was seen as Israel's inheritance (e.g., Num 34:2). Peter does not elaborate on the contents of the Christian's inheritance but rather describes it in terms of salvation. The inheritance is future and eternal. It is also secure, as noted by three similar adjectives, each possessing the Greek letter *alpha* ("a" in transliteration) as a prefix indicating negation: *aphtharton* (imperishable; see 1:23), *amianton* (unspoilable; see Heb 7:26), and *amaranton* (unfading; cf. 5:4). Michaels explains that "each of these words in its own way drives home the point that the inheritance of which Peter speaks is an eternal one (cf. Heb 9:15). In general, *aphtharton* refers to freedom from death and decay, *amianton* to freedom from uncleanness or moral impurity, and *amaranton* to freedom from the natural ravages of time."[6]

This inheritance is like the treasure Jesus preaches about in the Sermon on the Mount (Matt 6:19–21), one that is "stored up" in heaven; for his part, Peter describes the inheritance as "kept in heaven for you." Just as the inheritance is kept safe in heaven, the Christian believers are guarded while on earth until the time they can fully enjoy it. It is God's own power that watches over his people, a power which they experience through faith. Of the five times Peter mentions faith in this letter, three are in this opening paragraph (vv. 5, 7, 9; see 1:21; 5:9). Faith is foundational to Peter's entire message. Jobes notes the irony regarding the faith of Peter's readers: "Paradoxically, it is their faith in Christ that has put them in jeopardy with respect to their society, but it is that very faith in Christ that identifies them as legitimate heirs, whom God powerfully protects."[7]

Third, the new birth leads to salvation, the climax of the Christian experience: "Salvation describes the ultimate rescue of Christians from their current

5. Jobes, *1 Peter*, 85.
6. Michaels, *1 Peter*, 21 (I transliterated the Greek words).
7. Jobes, *1 Peter*, 87.

oppression."[8] Salvation is a broad term that may be used to describe deliverances of various sorts, including military threats, sickness, physical danger, and sin. Peter views salvation comprehensively, envisioning deliverance of God's people from oppression on earth as well as from God's final judgment (see 4:17).[9] Throughout the NT salvation is described as having present benefits (e.g., Eph 2:8; 1 Pet 3:21) but also a final and ultimate fulfillment (1 Pet 1:9). Here in v. 5 Peter anticipates the future coming of Christ, called the *parousia* in other places in the NT (e.g., Matt 24:37; 1 Cor 15:23; 1 Thess 2:19). The *parousia* is a time when God will bring an end to the world as we know it (4:7), executing judgment upon his enemies (4:5, 17–18) while vindicating his people.

The *parousia* arrives "in the last time," or *eschatos*, the Greek word behind our term "eschatology," the study of the end of time from Scripture. The Lord himself, along with the fullness of salvation, are to be revealed at the last time (1:13). Peter does not indicate when that time will be, but he notes that salvation is "ready to be revealed." As Peter Davids puts it, "The curtain is about to go up. Only the final signal is awaited."[10]

Rejoicing through Present Trials (1:6–9)

The Christian life embraces paradoxes. For example, Jesus says that those who lose their lives will find them (Matt 10:39) and those who wish to be great must be servants (Matt 20:26). In v. 6 Peter offers another seeming contradiction: the Christian might experience both joy and grief at one and the same time. The goals of new birth (living hope, inheritance, and salvation) are the "all this" that allow for great rejoicing despite the present trials.[11] At this point Peter does not give any details about what trials confront his readers; they may take a variety of forms.[12] Later he will refer to slander (2:12), harsh treatment (2:18–20), and verbal abuse (4:4, 14). Whatever the present trials may be, they are a source of grief and distress.

"Suffer grief" translates an expression that indicates that there is considerable emotional pain (e.g., Matt 17:23; 2 Cor 2:2, 4, 5). At least three gospel facts might mitigate the anguish Peter's readers face: (1) the final ends of the

---

8. Achtemeier, *1 Peter*, 97.

9. I discuss salvation again, in some detail, in my treatment of 1:22–2:3.

10. Davids, *First Peter*, 54.

11. As it stands in the Greek, the expression "you greatly rejoice" (so the NIV) could be taken as a command or as a statement. Even though Paul commands rejoicing in Phil 4:4 (with different vocabulary), it does not appear that Peter gives a command here but instead commends his readers that they are now rejoicing.

12. "All kinds" is the same word that is translated "various" in 4:10, which explains that God's grace is manifested to the believers through a variety of spiritual gifts.

new birth, particularly salvation (which Peter will elaborate upon in vv. 9–12), (2) the knowledge that their suffering is temporary (v. 6), and (3) the assurance that suffering is not pointless but has a divine purpose (v. 7).

Peter says that the present trials last only for a little while, something he reiterates in 5:10. He does not try to minimize the severity of his readers' struggles or suggest that those afflictions are unimportant. Yet in the larger scope of God's plans, any time spent in suffering is a short time in comparison with the limitless inheritance that awaits believers.

Suffering is not accidental but purposeful and therefore necessary ("had to" in 1:6). It is the duty of Peter and other servants of God to point this out, even if it is not a formula for becoming a popular preacher. The NT teaches that suffering is part of Christian experience, especially in light of the end of days. For example, Jesus warns that suffering "must take place" (e.g., Mark 13:7; cf. Rev 1:1; 4:1); Paul exhorted believers that "we must go through many hardships" (Acts 14:22), and he also wrote to the Philippians that God grants suffering just as he grants faith (Phil 1:29). Peter later admonishes his readers not to be surprised at their "fiery ordeal" (4:12).

The purpose of suffering (v. 7) is to bring about praise, glory, and honor at the *parousia*. Peter is ambiguous regarding who gives and receives this praise, glory, and honor. Perhaps they are offered to God by the believers; perhaps they are showered upon the believers by God. We need not choose between these options since both are valid: God will vindicate his people (v. 9), commend them (2:19–20), confer blessings upon them (3:9–12), reward the faithful with "the crown of glory" (5:4), and exalt his people at the proper time (5:6). Yet, simultaneously, God is the one who receives praise and glory in all things (4:11).

Suffering that has a purpose, that is, suffering that results in praise, glory, and honor, is a sort of testing that demonstrates the genuineness of Christian faith. Peter employs the image of refining, as he will again in 4:12, to describe how faith is proven to be genuine (see Prov 27:21). In the refining process, metal ore is heated to the point where impurities can be separated and the pure metal retrieved. This metaphor is already useful as it stands, but Peter pushes it further: even purified gold, the most precious metal known to his readers, is still perishable (see 1:18). Faith in the meantime, which is also tested through "fire," will reveal itself to be more precious than gold, even purified gold. In v. 7 Peter returns to the topic of the *parousia*, and he will bring it up again before the end of the chapter (1:13). Yet in verses 8–9 Peter highlights a present aspect of Christian life, while we await the promises of the future. Everyday life is characterized by faith in a Lord who is invisible to his followers. Peter himself loved Jesus because he once lived and worked with him (5:1; John 21:15–19). The readers of this letter could not make such a claim; they had never seen Jesus and certainly could not see him at the present time (v. 8). Yet Peter appreciates that these true believers are able to love Jesus and believe in him despite not being able to see him; in much the way Paul acknowledges that "we live by faith, not by sight" (2 Cor 5:7). Consequently, they are blessed to experience joy beyond words ("inexpressible," *aneklalētos*, is another of Peter's rare words, occurring only here in the NT).

According to John 20:24, the apostle Thomas, known as Doubting Thomas, was not present when the Lord first appeared to the other disciples. Thomas later said, "Unless I see the nail marks in his hands and put my finger where the nails were, and put my hand into his side, I will not believe" (John 20:25). John 20:29 is the Lord's response to Thomas's amazement at seeing the risen Jesus: "Because you have seen me, you have believed; blessed are those who have not seen and yet have believed." Peter's words here make us think of that blessing Jesus gave Thomas. Believers who were not privileged to see the resurrected Jesus before his ascension are nevertheless blessed; and that blessing includes great joy even while in the throes of oppression.

Joy is one characteristic of the life of faith on earth, and the reward for such faith, according to v. 9, is ultimate salvation. Full deliverance is described as the rescue of your "souls," which refers to the whole person, including the body. "Soul" has a similar sense in 3:20, when Peter refers to the salvation of eight souls (NIV: "people").[13] God's protection is experienced by faith (v. 4), faith is proven through the refining fire of trials (v. 7), and faith leads to God's final deliverance for his people.

Witnesses to the Wonder of Salvation (1:10–12)

Right after pointing to the goal, or "end result" of salvation, Peter reflects on the past, when people had to view salvation as even more remotely future. The Greek syntax of vv. 10–12 is difficult, but the sense is clear: it is a comparison of what the OT prophets knew of salvation and what Peter's readers were already experiencing. The ancient prophets were given insights and prophesied concerning future salvation, described as "grace that was to come" (v. 10). It was "the Spirit of Christ" who revealed the sufferings of the Messiah (Christ), and also his subsequent glorification. Peter stresses the preexistence of Christ by using an unusual expression ("Spirit of Christ" is atypical in the NT) to denote how OT prophets received their revelations. Similarly, the Holy Spirit energizes evangelists in Peter's day who preach the good news (v. 12). Although the prophets searched intently and investigated, they did

---

13. Peter uses the word "soul" six times in his letter (1:9, 22; 2:11, 25; 3:20; 4:19). For a detailed discussion of Peter's understanding of "soul," see Reinhard Feldmeier, *The First Letter of Peter: A Commentary on the Greek Text*, trans. Peter H. Davids (Waco, TX: Baylor University Press, 2008), 87–92.

not know details concerning the time or circumstances surrounding the suffering and glorification of Christ. (Something similar could be said about our own vantage point: we do not know the time or the full circumstances associated with the *parousia*, Christ's second coming.) Furthermore, the prophets were shown that their insights did not serve them but were for subsequent generations. Peter spotlights the privileged status of his readers, as they are the ones served by the ancient prophets. These believers received through Spirit-energized preaching what the prophets had been saying many years earlier.

Peter does not specify any particular OT text or name of any specific prophet. It is similar to Jesus on the road to Emmaus with two disciples, who "beginning with Moses and all the Prophets ... explained to them what was said in all the Scriptures concerning himself" (Luke 24:27). The whole OT prophetic witness argues for the Messiah's suffering and glorification, which led to salvation. What believers have received is so magnificent that even angels— who are close to God—desire to get a better look into the sufferings and glorification of the Messiah, which are part of God's redemptive plan for humanity.

LIVE the Story

Dynamic Tension: A Paradox of the Christian Faith

The Christian life is one of paradoxes. Some paradoxes come from the Lord Jesus Christ's description of what it means to experience genuine existence as people of the kingdom of God. For example:

- Whoever finds their life will lose it, and whoever loses their life for my sake will find it (Matt 10:39).
- For whoever wants to save their life will lose it, but whoever loses their life for me will find it (Matt 16:25).
- Instead, whoever wants to become great among you must be your servant (Mark 10:43).

Similarly, it is also paradoxical that humility is a path toward significance:

- For those who exalt themselves will be humbled, and those who humble themselves will be exalted (Matt 23:12).
- Humble yourselves before the Lord, and he will lift you up (Jas 4:10).
- Humble yourselves, therefore, under God's mighty hand, that he may lift you up in due time (1 Pet 5:6).

Also, the contrast between godly and worldly wisdom may appear paradoxical: God chose the foolish things of the world to shame the wise; God chose the weak things of the world to shame the strong (1 Cor 1:27).

The dynamic tension that Christians experience trying to live a life of joyful expectation of final salvation while facing suffering is also paradoxical. John Calvin, in his commentary on 1 Peter 1:6, describes it in this way:

> It seems somewhat inconsistent when he [Peter] says that the faithful, who exult with joy, are at the same time sorrowful, for these are contrary feelings, but the faithful know by experience that these things can exist together much better than can be expressed in words. However, to explain the matter in a few words, it may be put thus: the faithful are not logs of wood, nor have they so divested themselves of human feelings as to be unaffected by sorrow, unafraid of danger, unhurt by poverty, and untouched by hard and unbearable persecutions. Hence they experience sorrow because of evils, but it is so mitigated by faith they never cease at the same time to rejoice. Thus sorrow does not prevent their joy, but rather gives place to it."[14]

Similarly, Martin Luther notes the tension behind 1 Peter 1:6: "Here the apostle sets forth how the Christians fare in the world. Before God in heaven they are the beloved children of the eternal, heavenly inheritance—assured of their salvation, as has been said. But upon earth they are not only sorrowful, cast down, and forsaken, but they must also suffer many temptations from the devil and from the wicked world."[15]

Calvin surmises that words cannot fully capture the reality of the believer's tension; meanwhile, Luther, upon further reflection, relies upon poetry, citing Psalm 116:10 ("I trusted in the LORD when I said, 'I am greatly afflicted'"). Poetry and hymnody serve us well as tools to express our feelings when experiencing what may be paradoxical: living faithfully and expectantly according to the promises of God while simultaneously facing the trials and temptations of life in the present.

Israel's Songbook and the Paradox of Faithful Living

The Psalms are a good starting point for meditating upon the paradoxical nature of the life of faith by means of artistic expression. Tremper Longman III points out that "as we read the Psalms, we are entering into the sanctuary, the place where God meets men and women in a special way. We will see that the conversation between God and his people is direct, intense, intimate, and above all, honest. Thus, the Psalms are a kind of literary sanctuary in the Scripture. The place where God meets his people in a special way, where his people may address him with their praise and lament."[16]

---

14. Calvin, *Hebrews and 1 and 2 Peter*, 234.
15. Luther, *Peter and Jude*, 43.
16. Tremper Longman III, *How to Read the Psalms* (Downers Grove, IL: InterVarsity Press, 1988), 11–12.

Let's think of one psalm in particular, Psalm 130. Eugene H. Peterson's translation, *The Message*, captures the raw emotion of the psalmist:

Help, GOD—the bottom has fallen out of my life!
     Master, hear my cry for help!
Listen hard! Open your ears!
     Listen to my cries for mercy.
If you, GOD, kept records on wrongdoings,
     who would stand a chance?
As it turns out, forgiveness is your habit,
     and that's why you're worshiped.
I pray to GOD—my life a prayer—
     and wait for what he'll say and do.
My life's on the line before God, my Lord,
     waiting and watching till morning,
     waiting and watching till morning.
O Israel, wait and watch for GOD—
     with GOD's arrival comes love,
     with GOD's arrival comes generous redemption.
No doubt about it—he'll redeem Israel,
     buy back Israel from captivity to sin.

In his commentary on that psalm, Peterson observes that "a Christian is a person who decides to face and live through suffering. If we do not make that decision, we are endangered on every side. A man or woman of faith who fails to acknowledge and deal with suffering becomes, at last, either a cynic or a melancholic or a suicide."[17]

Prayer and meditation on the Psalms can help us to gain perspective on the challenge of 1 Peter 1:3–12 as we try to live joyfully in light of the hope of ultimate salvation, while simultaneously experiencing the tests and trials associated with our life in a broken world.

One legacy of the Psalms is the rich tradition of musical expressions that expresses the feelings of people trying to make sense of their experience of suffering while holding onto faith in God. There are many examples, but I offer the uniquely American voices found in the Negro Spirituals.

Negro Spirituals: The Music of Dynamic Tension

Slaves who were brought from Africa to what would become the United States of America were thrust into an environment heavily influenced by

---

17. Eugene H. Peterson, *A Long Obedience in the Same Direction: Discipleship in an Instant Society* (Downers Grove, IL: InterVarsity Press, 1980), 133.

Christianity. This is not to say that all slave owners were devout Christians, but abolitionist Christians were initially in the minority. Consequently, slaves would come to interpret their plight through the lens of the biblical narratives. People who were born into slavery came to connect their story to the biblical story. Such connection is analogous to how Peter incorporates his Gentile readers into Israel's story with God. The Story of God Biblical Commentary series recognizes that Christian believers are invited to join our personal narratives with the biblical story of God and his people, in the same way that many slaves did.

Arthur Sutherland asserts that "the spirituals emerged not just because of slavery, but because the slaves were working people surrounded by the preaching and teaching of the gospel.... The creators of the spirituals knew the biblical narratives, and they knew the importance of ancestors in African religion. Daniel, Moses, and Jacob became not just figures caught in the pages of the past but living and active participants, even protectors, in the present who could be appealed to for survival."[18] Songs grew out of the dynamic tension of living with faith in the God who promises deliverance while simultaneously experiencing the slave master's whip. Sutherland further observes that although the spirituals were fundamentally work songs that provided some measure of relief from backbreaking labor, they also served to help build a measure of community. The spirituals helped the slaves to affirm that they were not defined by their work; their identity was rooted in a spiritual reality that transcended their circumstances.

There are many Negro Spirituals that illustrate the dynamic tension American slaves felt; here is but one example:

> I want Jesus to walk with me
> I want Jesus to walk with me
> All along my pilgrim journey
> I want Jesus to walk with me.
> In my trials, Lord, walk with me
> In my trials, Lord, walk with me
> When the shades of life are falling
> Lord, I want Jesus to walk with me.
> In my sorrow, Lord, walk with me
> In my sorrows, Lord, walk with me
> When my heart is aching,
> Lord, I want Jesus to walk with me.
> In my troubles, Lord, walk with me

---

18. Sutherland, *I Was a Stranger*, 5.

In my troubles, Lord, walk with me
When my life becomes a burden,
Lord, I want Jesus to walk with me.

Negro Spirituals are not the only musical forms that communicate expectations of God's deliverance while undergoing suffering—and that with joy. My point is that we ought not underestimate the power of song, poetry, and other artistic expressions to communicate the reality that Peter describes in 1 Peter 1:3–9. That is why we should celebrate those among us with the creative gifts of the Holy Spirit to articulate the promises of the new birth, even when we must suffer for a time. Through the help of such artistic people we can experience "inexpressible and glorious joy" along our journey.

CHAPTER 3

1 Peter 1:13-21

 LISTEN to the Story

> [13]Therefore, with minds that are alert and fully sober, set your hope on the grace to be brought to you when Jesus Christ is revealed at his coming. [14]As obedient children, do not conform to the evil desires you had when you lived in ignorance. [15]But just as he who called you is holy, so be holy in all you do; [16]for it is written: "Be holy, because I am holy."
>
> [17]Since you call on a Father who judges each person's work impartially, live out your time as foreigners here in reverent fear. [18]For you know that it was not with perishable things such as silver or gold that you were redeemed from the empty way of life handed down to you from your ancestors, [19]but with the precious blood of Christ, a lamb without blemish or defect. [20]He was chosen before the creation of the world, but was revealed in these last times for your sake. [21]Through him you believe in God, who raised him from the dead and glorified him, and so your faith and hope are in God.
>
> *Listening to the Text in the Story:* Exodus 3:1–6; Leviticus 11:44–45; 19:1–37; Matthew 5:48.

Every follower of Jesus knows how difficult it is to live a consistently upright life, despite the fact that Peter calls his readers to follow God's command in Leviticus: "be holy for I am holy." Holiness describes the essence of God's nature, one that is very different from human nature. "Throughout Scripture, holiness is pre-eminently a characteristic of God himself. The terminology is used to signify that God is wholly other, distinct and separate from everything that he has made, and different from the gods of human imagination."[1]

Recall, for example, the story of Moses being summoned by a bush that burned yet was not consumed. The voice said, "Do not come any closer. Take off your sandals, for the place where you are standing is holy ground"

---

1. David G. Peterson, "Holiness," *NDBT* 544.

(Exod 3:5). God introduced himself and "at this, Moses hid his face, because he was afraid to look at God" (Exod 3:6). The holiness of God demands our reverential fear.

However, the holiness of God simultaneously serves as motivation for the ethical behavior of God's people. The holiness of God's people is found only in their relationship with him, and consequently God's people are invited to live in such a way that showcases that relationship. The Torah provided instruction on how Israel was to live holy lives. Later, God sent prophets to exhort his people to live as holy, distinct from the pagan nations around them; hence the recurring calls to "return to God" (e.g., Isa 31:6; Jer 3:12, 14; Hos 6:1; Joel 2:13).

In a manner reminiscent of the OT prophets, Peter calls on God's people to live holy lives as they await their future salvation. The resurrection of Jesus assures the resurrection of his followers while the impeccable life of Jesus provides the model for his followers' behavior. Just as Jesus was the perfect sacrificial lamb, his followers are to pursue holiness in their everyday lives. So their future is promising (1:3–12), even if the present is replete with suffering.

EXPLAIN the Story

Because of their confidence in the physical return of Jesus Christ, believers have the motivation to live upright lives while they wait. These beleaguered Christians are not to focus on their opposition or their particular trials; rather, they are to focus on living lives of complete devotion to Jesus Christ. In order to *behave* in a godly fashion, believers must first be *thinking* in a godly fashion; right behavior follows right thinking. The "therefore" of v. 13 signals a transition from Peter's declaration of God's blessings to a string of imperatives, which focus on some practical dimensions of the Christian's hope.

Peter's central concern for his readers at this point in his letter is that they have a lifestyle characterized by holiness. Holy living is the appropriate response of believers who have received a new birth (1:3), a living hope (1:3), joy (1:8), and salvation (1:9). The standard for the believer's holiness is God's holiness—a defining characteristic of God. It is the bodily return of Jesus Christ that musters hope, which in turn provides motivation for a life of holiness. As people who live in visible contrast to the broader society, believers have an intimate relationship with God: he is Father to his people. This relationship is possible because of the redeeming work of Christ, whose sacrificial death, resurrection, and glorification engender faith and hope in God.

The call to holiness may be seen as literally the center of Peter's discussion, as it is possible to discern a symmetrical (i.e., chiastic) pattern to his admonition:

A. The believer's hope (v. 13)
B. The revelation of Jesus Christ (v. 13)
C. A reminder of prior sinful living (v. 14)
D. A call to holiness based upon God's character (vv. 15–17)
C. A reminder of prior sinful living (vv. 18–19)
B. The revelation of Jesus Christ (v. 20)
A. The believer's hope (v. 21)

Peter develops his argument *logically*, appealing to an understanding of the ministry of Jesus on earth as well as an understanding of human sin and the holiness of God. His argument is also *temporal* (vv. 13–21).[2] With relatively few words, Peter manages to reflect upon years of salvation history—the history of the work of God to rescue sinful humanity through the death and resurrection of Jesus. Peter starts out by looking to the future (i.e., the return of Christ). His plea for holy living then returns us to the present time (i.e., the current status of the redeemed as foreigners in the world). But it is Peter's references to the past that are most wide-ranging. He deals with the recent past when commenting on the former lives of the believers (vv. 14, 18). He then takes his readers further back in time by using the OT ritual of animal sacrifice to describe the death of Jesus (v. 19) and then goes even further back—to before creation—when describing God's unique call of Jesus (v. 20). By looking accurately and honestly at the past as well as putting hope in the future, believers are able to live holy in the present.

The Believer's Hope (1:13 and 1:21)

The section begins and ends with hope (v. 13 and v. 21). The opening exhortation of v. 13 is for the communities of believers to have hope that is anchored in the *parousia*, the second coming of Christ.[3] "Hope" in the NT is not an

---

2. Green, *1 Peter*, 36–47, notes the importance of time in these verses and structures this section using a "temporal map."

3. Peter uses the word *apocalypsis* (which BDAG defines as "revelation," "disclosure") rather than *parousia* ("presence," "coming," "advent"). The former word may be used to refer to the ministry of Christ during his first advent (e.g., "Now to him who is able to establish you in accordance with my gospel, the message I proclaim about Jesus Christ, in keeping with the revelation of the mystery hidden for long ages past" [Rom 16:25]). However, it may also describe the Second Coming (e.g., "Therefore you do not lack any spiritual gift as you eagerly wait for our Lord Jesus Christ to be revealed" [1 Cor 1:7]), as it does here in 1 Peter.

abstract feeling of optimism but a confident expectation of a good outcome based upon the work of God. At this point it may be helpful to take a look at a few of the NT passages that treat the topic of hope in order to appreciate the role it has in Christian faith as well as its relationship to the return of Christ. Recall the words of the apostle Paul to the church at Rome:

> Therefore, since we have been justified through faith, we have peace with God through our Lord Jesus Christ, through whom we have gained access by faith into this grace in which we now stand. And we boast in the hope of the glory of God. Not only so, but we also glory in our sufferings, because we know that suffering produces perseverance; perseverance, character; and character, hope. And hope does not put us to shame, because God's love has been poured out into our hearts through the Holy Spirit, who has been given to us. (Rom 5:1–5)

Later on in Romans, Paul characterizes God as the "God of hope": "May the God of hope fill you with all joy and peace as you trust in him, so that you may overflow with hope by the power of the Holy Spirit" (15:13). God's work in the believer's life gives hope, and God's plan to have the Lord Jesus Christ return to earth is also a source of hope.

Titus 2:13 gives an encouragement similar to what we find here in 1 Peter. The appearance of Christ at the second coming is a "blessed hope" that provides motivation for the moral living described in Titus 2:12, 14.

> For the grace of God has appeared that offers salvation to all people. It teaches us to say "No" to ungodliness and worldly passions, and to live self-controlled, upright and godly lives in this present age, while we wait for the blessed hope—the appearing of the glory of our great God and Savior, Jesus Christ, who gave himself for us to redeem us from all wickedness and to purify for himself a people that are his very own, eager to do what is good. (Titus 2:11–14)

That is, God works through Jesus to form a people who are his own special possession (see a parallel in 1 Pet 2:9). The ministry of Jesus purifies God's people. Jesus will return one day, but in the meantime his followers are to live with hopeful expectation. While waiting for Jesus to return, God's people learn—by God's grace—to reject sinfulness and to live upright lives. The writers of the NT frequently offer the return of Christ, or the consummation of the present age, as motivation for upright behavior (other examples include Rom 13:11–14 and 1 John 2:2–3). Peter himself will come back to this very idea in 4:7.[4]

---

4. See the later discussion regarding 4:7, where Peter says, "The end of all things is near. Therefore be alert and of sober mind so that you may pray." Once again the end of the age is in view and

Hope is what can sustain Christians in the here and now while they await their inheritance at the end of time. Hope is confidence rooted in something concrete, and for Peter the substance of the believers' hope is the "grace to be brought to you."[5] Certainly these believers had already come to know God's grace (see 1:10), but the coming of Jesus Christ will bring a fuller, climactic experience. Although Christians may speak of being "saved" in the present, ultimate salvation is yet to happen.[6]

For Peter this is not a new hope, per se, but a renewed vigor to keep on hoping. After all, these readers have already had hope since they first became believers (1:21), a "living hope" (1:3) that must now be nurtured through deliberate action. That deliberate action is described with rich imagery. The phrase, "with minds that are alert" translates an expression that literally reads "girding the loins of your mind." Girding one's loins carries the idea of removing any impediment, such as a long garment, so that a man might undertake strenuous activity, such as combat. In the same way, mental preparedness is part of what it means to have hope.

It also helps the mind to stay sharp by staying completely sober. As Paul Achtemeier observes, "Drunken people in long garments are not very good at hard labor."[7] "Sober" includes being free from the intoxication of alcohol and other drugs, but it also refers to spiritual alertness.[8] In addition to the three times the word is used in 1 Peter (1:13; 4:7; 5:8), the verb indicating sobriety (*nēphō*) occurs only three other times in the NT, all in Pauline literature, and has the same ethical implications:[9]

So then, let us not be like others, who are asleep, but let us be awake and sober. (1 Thess 5:6)

But since we belong to the day, let us be sober, putting on faith and love as a breastplate, and the hope of salvation as a helmet. (1 Thess 5:8)

---

there is also an appeal to sobriety of mind, the same appeal that Peter makes here at 1:13 and finally at 5:8 ("Be alert and of sober mind. Your enemy the devil prowls around like a roaring lion looking for someone to devour").

5. Several commentators note how an early Christian prayer links divine grace with the return of Christ and the end of the present age ("May grace come, and may this world pass away," Did. 10:6, Lightfoot).

6. For example, "Since we have now been justified by his blood, how much more shall we be saved from God's wrath through him! For if, while we were God's enemies, we were reconciled to him through the death of his Son, how much more, having been reconciled, shall we be saved through his life!" (Rom 5:9–10). Note our earlier discussion of 1 Pet 1:3–12.

7. Achtemeier, *1 Peter*, 118.

8. "This exhortation to soberness (as the parallel exhortation to vigilance) finds its home in the New Testament mainly in eschatological contexts" (Feldmeier, *First Peter*, 100).

9. The adjective *nēphalios* ("temperate, sober, self-controlled, level-headed") is found in 1 Timothy and Titus describing upright overseers (or "elders"), female deacons, and older men and women.

But you, keep your head in all situations, endure hardship, do the work of an evangelist, discharge all the duties of your ministry. (2 Tim 4:5)

For Peter's readers, pagan life was a life full of "debauchery, lust, drunkenness, orgies, carousing and detestable idolatry" (4:3). The Christian has to constantly struggle not to be pulled into these activities, and for believers facing persecution that pressure can seem unbearable. In order to act correctly, one must think correctly. Being sober means having a spiritual alertness that allows one to focus on keeping faith in God rather than succumbing to the pressures and temptations of human nature. Hope is possible, even for beleaguered Christians, when they remember the grace of God shown in the resurrection, glorification, and return of the Lord Jesus Christ. As John Calvin noted, since the "fruition" of grace "will not be until Christ appears from heaven, for in Him is hid the salvation of the godly, there is need in the meantime of hope, since the grace of Christ is offered to us in vain, if we do not patiently wait until the coming of Christ."[10]

The Revelation of Jesus Christ (1:13 and 1:20)

Peter refers to Christ being "revealed" in 1:13 and also 1:20. In 1:13 the revelation of Jesus Christ is the second coming; the revelation of Jesus that Peter has in mind in 1:20 is the Lord's ministry on earth—especially his sacrificial death.[11] Both appearances unfold some aspect of God's plan for humanity. The second coming will be the ultimate revelation of God's grace and glory as history reaches a climax. On the last day all will be overwhelmed by God's presence, bringing delight for Christ's followers (with a joy even more pronounced than their present joy—1:8), and ultimate justice upon Christ's enemies.

According to the Gospels, Christ came to show God's grace and glory toward sinful, needy humanity. As John 1:14 has it, "The Word became flesh and made his dwelling among us. We have seen his glory, the glory of the one and only Son, who came from the Father, full of grace and truth." The oft-quoted John 3:16 puts it this way: "For God so loved the world that he gave his one and only Son, that whoever believes in him shall not perish but have eternal life," teaching that the sacrificial death of Christ is a revelation of God's love. For Peter, reflecting on both of Christ's comings will have a great impact on believers even at the present time.

In 1:20 Peter returns to the idea of God's foreknowledge (see v. 2), making clear that God orchestrated events for the salvation of his church a long time

---

10. Calvin, *Hebrews and 1 and 2 Peter*, 244.
11. See the discussion of Christ's atonement in the next subsection, my discussion of 1:14 and 1:18–19.

ago—before the creation of the world. The selection of the Son was part of a "pretemporal divine plan" in which God was pleased to allow his unique Son to die on behalf of his creation.[12] The NT is replete with references to the pre-existence of Christ, and several passages make explicit God's pretemporal design. For example, the description of God found in 2 Timothy 1:9–10 makes a similar point to that found here in 1 Peter 1:20:

> He has saved us and called us to a holy life—not because of anything we have done but because of his own purpose and grace. This grace was given us in Christ Jesus before the beginning of time, but it has now been revealed through the appearing of our Savior, Christ Jesus, who has destroyed death and has brought life and immortality to light through the gospel.

As noted earlier, the physical return of Jesus Christ is to be the foundation of hope for these weary saints. Indeed, in 1:7 the apostle associates the return of Christ with a promise of reward: the reward will be that the faith of these Christians will be proven genuine so that there will be praise, glory, and honor at the revelation of Christ.[13] A similar idea appears near the end of the letter (4:13) when he urges believers to rejoice even in the middle of suffering because the revelation of Jesus Christ will bring great joy.

"Revelation" or "appearing" shows up in several passages:[14]

> who through faith are shielded by God's power until the coming of the salvation that is ready to be revealed in the last time. (1:5)

> It was revealed to them that they were not serving themselves but you, when they spoke of the things that have now been told you by those who have preached the gospel to you by the Holy Spirit sent from heaven. Even angels long to look into these things. (1:12)

> To the elders among you, I appeal as a fellow elder and a witness of Christ's sufferings who also will share in the glory to be revealed. (5:1)

> And when the Chief Shepherd appears, you will receive the crown of glory that will never fade away. (5:4)

This truth is especially encouraging for believers who are ostracized, persecuted, and oppressed. These faithful followers of Jesus can be confident of

---

12. See Feldmeier, *First Peter*, 119.

13. Just as in v. 13, Peter uses the word *apocalypsis* ("revelation") in 1:7 to refer to the return of Christ, rather than the term *parousia* ("coming").

14. In most cases Peter uses the noun *apocalypsis*, or some form of the verb *apocalyptō* ("reveal, disclose"). However, in 1:20 and 5:4 he uses forms of the verb *phaneroō* ("cause to become visible").

a bright future because the blood of the Lord Jesus Christ has redeemed their present lives.

A Reminder of Prior Sinful Living (1:14 and 1:18–19)

Redemption through the blood of Jesus Christ not only secures a marvelous future for believers but also a changed lifestyle in the present (1:3), one of obedience and humility. I say "humility," because Peter encourages his adult readers to submit to the Father as "obedient children." Rather than following their earthly forebearers whose way of life was empty, believers are to be holy, like their heavenly Father. Peter's words are radical, especially when one considers how Gentiles, as well as Jews, placed great value on tradition and the ways of one's ancestors. But conversion to Jesus means that they are no longer bound to those old customs and rituals; that lifestyle was one of sin and ruin.

Peter describes the pre-Christian state of his readers as one of "ignorance." This is similar to what Peter says (Acts 3:17) as he preaches about the crucifixion of Jesus and describes the unconverted state of Jewish leaders ("Now, fellow Israelites, I know that you acted in ignorance, as did your leaders"). The apostle Paul likewise refers to unbelieving Gentiles as ignorant (Acts 17:30, in his speech at the Areopagus in Athens; see also Eph 4:18: "They are darkened in their understanding and separated from the life of God because of the ignorance that is in them due to the hardening of their hearts"). To become a follower of Jesus means to be changed from the inside out, and from ignorance to enlightenment.

The actual process of conversion is mystical, and not easily understood.[15] Richard V. Peace uses the apostle Paul's conversion as a paradigm, since it "is considered normative" in the minds of many.[16] Peace writes that what "drives conversion" is fresh insight, which involves people calling into question assumptions they had made about themselves.[17] Insight is enlightenment, and conversion to Christian faith involves an enlightened understanding of God, as well as a new self-understanding.

In contrast to the old ways of ignorance, the apostle pushes his readers toward a state of readiness (1:13). What Christians know should have an

---

15. Richard V. Peace, *Conversion in the New Testament: Paul and the Twelve* (Grand Rapids: Eerdmans, 1999), 1, asserts that, "The church has not always been clear about conversion. In fact, there is a wide difference of opinion as to what constitutes conversion." Scot McKnight has also explored the topic of conversion on several occasions, notably in *Turning to Jesus: The Sociology of Conversion in the Gospels* (Louisville: Westminster John Knox, 2002), and together with Hauna Ondrey, *Finding Faith, Losing Faith: Stories of Conversion and Apostasy* (Waco: Baylor University Press, 2008). McKnight's studies combine biblical analysis with contemporary stories of converts (including converts *away from* the faith, to apostasy).

16. Peace, *Conversion*, 11.

17. Ibid., 52.

impact on what they do. Christians are not to govern their lives according to previous patterns; they are no longer to conform to evil desires.[18] Peter does not here elaborate on the nature of the evil desires that these believers once had, but he will do so later in 2:1; 4:2–4. The latter passage contains a list of sins associated with "reckless, wild living," "debauchery, lust, drunkenness, orgies, carousing and detestable idolatry."

These human desires are inherited according to 1:18. Peter does not say exactly how evil passions are transferred from one generation to another, nor does he speak of Adam's fall or "original sin." The main emphasis here seems to be the role of family influence: his audience is made up of "children" of a new birth who must obey their true Father and no longer mimic the ways of their biological ancestors (1:3, 23).

That way of life handed down from the ancestors is empty, futile, even useless. The rest of Peter's letter, by contrast, speaks of a good life that is fruitful and useful (e.g., 3:8–12). This new, holy life is made possible by the sacrificial death of Christ that redeems sinful humanity: "Peter does not *merely* present Christ's redemptive suffering as a *motivation* for holy living, but as the very *basis* for it."[19]

Redemption is one of those powerful terms which the NT uses to describe the work Jesus Christ has done to rescue sinful humanity.[20] You may have heard redemption described as Christ "buying us back," as one might do when recovering a precious item that had been left at the pawnshop. This is useful but should not be pressed too far: the pawnbroker in this analogy might seem to be Satan, but of course when it comes to our souls, Satan has received no payment![21] Another analogy is that redemption is like a ransom paid to kidnappers for the release of hostages. And of course, Jesus does redeem us from the bondage of sin's control.[22] But once again, unbelievers are bound by sin

---

18. The verb translated, "do not be conformed" comes from *syschēmatizō*. The only other NT occurrence of this word is in Rom 12:2 ("Do not conform to the pattern of this world, but be transformed by the renewing of your mind. Then you will be able to test and approve what God's will is—his good, pleasing and perfect will").

19. Williams, *Doctrine of Salvation*, 82 (emphasis original).

20. There are other images and metaphors used in the NT with "salvation" being the most common (e.g., "justification," "adoption," and "reconciliation"). See Michael F. Bird, *Evangelical Theology: A Biblical and Systematic Introduction* (Grand Rapids: Zondervan, 2013), 548–79, and Leon Morris, *The Atonement: Its Meaning and Significance* (Downers Grove, IL: InterVarsity Press, 1983).

21. See Morris, *Atonement*. Morris avers that the early church fathers did indeed see Satan as the one to whom ransom was to be paid. This was based on those fathers' view that since sinners belonged to Satan, God would need to broker a deal with Satan to gain release of those sinners. The deal would include God offering his Son in exchange for sinners' souls. However, Morris notes that such theories involving Satan "do no more than amuse us these days …" (129).

22. Such as seen in Rom 6:6 ("For we know that our old self was crucified with him so that the body ruled by sin might be done away with, that we should no longer be slaves to sin") and Gal 5:1 ("It is for freedom that Christ has set us free. Stand firm, then, and do not let yourselves be burdened again by a yoke of slavery").

itself, not by Satan. And in fact, the Scriptures indicate that Satan plays no positive part—and gets no credit—in the story of human redemption, and we do not want to imagine that Satan deserves payment or has bargaining rights equal to God's. Yes, it is true that redemption (*lytrōsis*) typically involves the payment of the ransom (*lytron*): "For even the Son of Man did not come to be served, but to serve, and to give his life as a ransom for many" (Mark 10:45 // Matt 20:28). However, the biblical passages emphasize God's action of deliverance, not the receipt (nor recipient) of payments. Leon Morris wrote, "In the New Testament there is never any hint of a recipient of the ransom. In other words, we must understand redemption as a useful metaphor which enables us to see some aspects of Christ's great saving work with clarity but which is not an exact description of the whole process of salvation."[23]

An even better explanation of redemption comes from the manumission of slaves in ancient times, since in the NT redemption usually refers to the release of a person from slavery or even the liberation of a nation from foreign domination.[24] Because slavery was omnipresent throughout the Roman Empire, Peter's readers probably thought about redemption from slavery when they heard the word "redeem." That family of words in both the Greek Old Testament and the New Testament carry the sense of "releasing" and "setting free" (i.e., "liberation"), as well as the idea of "ransom."[25] These words are used as part of a theology of liberation, a holistic notion of redemption that includes the deliverance of one's soul from sin, as well as the deliverance of one's entire being from the domination of evil structures, such as Egypt and Babylon. For example, after Moses, Israel's liberator, receives his commission, God instructs him to "say to the Israelites: I am the LORD, and I will bring you out from under the yoke of the Egyptians. I will free you from being slaves to them, and I will redeem (LXX: *lytrōsomai*) you with an outstretched arm and with mighty acts of judgment" (Exod 6:6). When Israel sang of their liberation from Egypt, they used the same terms, e.g., "With your mighty arm you redeemed (LXX: *elytrōsō*) your people, the descendants of Jacob and Joseph" (Ps 77:15 = 76:16 LXX). The prophet Isaiah, centuries after the exodus, uses the language of redemption to announce good news of salvation, particularly as it relates to the return from exile and the restoration of Jerusalem. One example is found in this oracle: "But now, this is what the

---

23. Morris, *Atonement*, 129.

24. Compare the concepts as they are found, for example, in Rom 3:24 and Eph 1:7 with Luke 2:38 and 24:21; the former verses describe a more personal freedom from the bondage of slavery and the latter verses refer to the nation of Israel's political independence.

25. The words include the verb *lytroō* ("to redeem," or "to set free") and the nouns *lytrōsis* ("ransoming," "releasing," "redemption"), *apolytrōsis* ("release," "redemption," "deliverance"), and (*anti-*) *lytron*, "ransom."

LORD says—he who created you, Jacob, he who formed you, Israel: Do not fear, for I have redeemed (LXX: *elytrōsamēn*) you; I have summoned you by name; you are mine" (Isa 43:1). Darrin W. Snyder Belousek traces the notion of redemption from Moses through the prophets and concludes that "seen against its canonical backdrop, the purpose of the cross of Christ is fulfillment of God's promise of redemption—begun with exodus from slavery, continued through covenant, renewed in return and restoration from exile, consummated through cross [*sic*]."[26] Furthermore, the holistic aspect of redemption may be seen in Paul's words to the Romans that brings together human freedom from sin with the liberation of all of creation: "For the creation waits in eager expectation for the children of God to be revealed. For the creation was subjected to frustration, not by its own choice, but by the will of the one who subjected it, in hope that the creation itself will be liberated from its bondage to decay and brought into the freedom and glory of the children of God" (Rom 8:19–21).

God ransoms the sinner with Christ's blood, not with silver or gold. Reinhard Feldmeier suggests that "the contrast between precious metal and blood marks rather a contrast between two ways of life and their opposite theological valuation. For gold and silver are the means of the violent procurement of life at the cost of others: its procurement already costs life; whoever gathers it, exploits others."[27] Feldmeier goes on to point out that "ancient mines were for the most part notorious as places of the agonizing death of those who were condemned to work in them." Peter may be using irony here: silver and gold could take one's life blood, but it is through blood—that of Christ—that believers are rescued from spiritual slavery and given real life.

The blood of Christ draws the reader's attention to the OT Law and its numerous sacrifices and offerings. Sacrifices occurred at specified times and for a variety of reasons, but perhaps the most notable occasion was the Day of Atonement (*Yom Kippur*). Leviticus 16 explains its rituals in detail. This was the annual event when the high priest of Israel offered a solemn sacrifice for the sins of the nation. The priest's responsibilities included the slaughter of a bull and a goat—with various applications of blood—in addition to a burnt offering of a ram. Peter, along with other NT writers, affirms that the blood of Jesus also functioned as sacrifice, but with such efficacy that no more sacrifices need be made. "The death of Jesus is to be seen as a sacrifice which accomplishes in reality what the old sacrifices pointed to but could not do."[28]

---

26. Darrin W. Snyder Belousek, *Atonement, Justice, and Peace: The Message of the Cross and the Mission of the Church* (Grand Rapids: Eerdmans, 2012), 133–34.

27. Feldmeier, *First Peter*, 118n61.

28. Morris, *Atonement*, 63.

The sacrifice of Jesus is a once-for-all event; the writer of Hebrews echoes Peter's point and sums it up well:

> So Christ was sacrificed once to take away the sins of many; and he will appear a second time, not to bear sin, but to bring salvation to those who are waiting for him. (Heb 9:28)

The animals for Israel's sacrifices were to be free of any defect or blemish, and this is how Peter describes the "lamb" who is the Lord Jesus. The image of a lamb points to yet another powerful OT ritual, that of Passover. According to Exodus 12, the lamb is the central feature of that *Seder* meal. Peter is in harmony with the Gospel of John, which is the only Gospel that refers to Jesus as the "Lamb of God." John the Baptist uses the expression to greet and introduce the Lord Jesus (1:29, 36), thus anticipating his sacrificial death. The meticulous OT rituals that involved the sacrificial death of animals were a constant sober reminder of how serious sin is; its consequences always involve death. These sacrifices were designed to help God's people appreciate his holiness and to understand that they are to be holy, just as God is holy.[29]

A Call to Holiness Based upon God's Character (1:15–17)

Since the holiness of God is such an expansive topic, worthy of entire volumes, we can only begin to touch upon it here.[30] Scot McKnight challenges the popular notion that "holiness" means "separation," or "distinction." He says, "Holiness cannot be reduced to separation or difference. At a deeper level, holiness means 'devoted.'"[31] God's devotion is to God (each person of the Trinity fully devoted to each other). It is this complete and holy devotion that leads to a separation or distinction from that which is common or profane. God does not *possess* holiness; he *is* holy. Consequently, God acts in ways consistent with his character; his deeds are holy because he is holy. James Bryan Smith in his thoughtful book *The Good and Beautiful God* writes, "The essence of God is holiness. Holiness is a divine attribute. God is pure. There is no sin, evil or darkness in God."[32] Rather than defining holiness by listing all

---

29. In the book of Leviticus God several times repeats the command, in so many words, "be holy for I am holy" (11:44, 45; 19:2; 20:7, 26). The Lord Jesus makes a similar appeal in the Sermon on the Mount: "Be perfect, therefore, as your heavenly Father is perfect" (Matt 5:48).

30. The reader might wish to consider the following: R. C. Sproul, *The Holiness of God*, rev. ed. (Carol Stream, IL: Tyndale House, 2000); A. W. Tozer, *The Knowledge of the Holy: The Attributes of God: Their Meaning in the Christian Life* (San Francisco: Harper Collins, 1992); J. I. Packer, *Knowing God* (Downers Grove, IL: InterVarsity Press, 1979).

31. Scot McKnight, *A Fellowship of Differents: Showing the World God's Design for Life Together* (Grand Rapids: Zondervan, 2014), 117.

32. James Bryan Smith, *The Good and Beautiful God: Falling in Love with the God Jesus Knows* (Downers Grove, IL: InterVarsity Press, 2009), 122.

that God does (an impossible enterprise), it is better to step back and consider the big picture: God does what is consistent with his nature.[33]

Conversely, we humans do what is consistent with our own nature: we sin. Therefore, in order for human beings to be holy, we need a new nature. Just as God's holiness is more than the sum of his actions, holiness for human beings does not consist merely of a list of "dos and don'ts." It is about being distinct from the broader society, but as a result of having a new nature. That new nature is one of love, goodness, and obedience to God.

That new nature comes from God, as Peter has already explained: "In his great mercy he has given us new birth into a living hope through the resurrection of Jesus Christ from the dead" (1:3b). The other letter that bears Peter's name also emphasizes the new nature:

His divine power has given us everything we need for a godly life through our knowledge of him who called us by his own glory and goodness. Through these he has given us his very great and precious promises, so that through them you may participate in the divine nature, having escaped the corruption in the world caused by evil desires. (2 Pet 1:3–4)

In these verses from 2 Peter, holy living is possible through participation "in the divine nature," including a transformation of the ordinary, sinful nature.

The believers to whom Peter writes are being "sanctified" and have experienced a "new birth." Sanctification means being set apart for a divine purpose. The NT writers recognize that even though believers have already received the Spirit of God and may already be "saints" or "sanctified," the reality is that we still struggle to do the right thing. Consequently, the Bible is full of commands and reminders for all disciples to be more like Jesus; i.e., to practice self-denial and follow his word and life. Believers throughout time are urged to act like what they are declared to be—children of God![34]

On a practical level, holiness means conforming to the ways of God rather than the ways of the prevailing culture. The culture of the first century was decadent. For example, consider the list of vices found at 1 Peter 4:3: "debauchery, lust, drunkenness, orgies, carousing and detestable idolatry." There are similar lists of vices found throughout the NT, notably in the apostle Paul's letters (e.g., Gal 5:19–21a and Col 3:5).

---

33. "Holiness is an essential part of God's nature. God cannot *not* be holy in the same way that God cannot *not* be love" (Smith, *The Good and Beautiful God*, 122–23, emphasis original).

34. N. T. Wright in *After You Believe: Why Christian Character Matters* (New York: Harper Collins, 2010), 93, reflects on the concept of sanctification as found in Pauline literature; he writes that holiness "or sanctification" is "the learning in the present of the habits which anticipate the ultimate future." The same could be said of the teaching here in 1 Peter.

As "foreigners," Peter's readers find themselves "living among hostile natives who are ignorant of their origins, their families, their history, and who are suspicious of their commitments and conduct."[35] Christians are treated as unwelcomed immigrants because their very testimony puts them out of sync with the prevailing culture. The Christians strive to live lives of holiness in nonconformity to evil actions and attitudes along with conformity to the life of Jesus. The benefits of such holy living include the hope of divine inheritance (1:4). Also, those committed to holiness experience divine protection, even through trials (1:5); they revel in unfathomable joy (1:8), receive God's commendation (2:20), enjoy God's favor (5:5), rely on God's care (5:7), and count on God's strength (5:10). Holiness requires separation; it also necessitates a nearness to God. In 1:15 the apostle Peter connects holiness to God's divine calling, a calling that invites people to be part of God's unique community. He continues to apply the truth of Leviticus. Leviticus 20:26 reads: "You are to be holy to me because I, the LORD, am holy, and I have set you apart from the nations to be my own." In Leviticus God's election of Israel is part of the basis for the nation's holiness.[36] So also is the case in 1 Peter: because believers are called by God to be his special people and possession (1 Pet 2:9–10), we are to behave in ways that reflect well on our heavenly parent.

But not only is God our Father, the one who hears us when we call (1:18); he is also judge of all humanity. "Paternal authority includes the right and responsibility of judging and disciplining the behavior of family members. The notion of God as judge is a biblical commonplace and recurs elsewhere in 1 Peter (2:23; 4:5, 6, 17; cf. 2:12)."[37] The fact that God is a judge who does not play favorites provides some of the motivation for holy living. We will be helped if we adopt an attitude of "reverent fear," the Greek word *phobos*, whose meaning can range from sheer terror and fright to reverence and respect. When it comes to human attitudes toward God, the NT focuses on those latter aspects. Peter urges his readers to have a sober mindset (cf. v. 13) about their relationship with God. When they approach God with awe and respect, recognizing him as holy, believers will know to keep an appropriate distance from sinful, worldly behaviors and move themselves toward holy living.

The teaching of A. W. Tozer provides a helpful perspective at this point:

> To Israel first and later to His Church God spoke, saying, "Be ye holy; for I am holy." He did not say "Be ye holy as I am holy," for that would be

---

35. Elliott, *1 Peter*, 368. See my discussion of the theme in my comments on 1 Pet 1:1 and later at 2:11.

36. See John G. Gammie, *Holiness in Israel*, Overtures to Biblical Theology (Minneapolis: Fortress, 1989), 33.

37. Elliott, *1 Peter*, 365.

to demand of us absolute holiness, something that belongs to God alone. Before the uncreated fire of God's holiness angels veil their faces. Yea, the heavens are not clean, and the stars are not pure in His sight. No honest man can say "I am holy," but neither is any honest man willing to ignore the solemn words of the inspired writher, "Follow peace with all men, and holiness, without which no man shall see the Lord."

Caught in this dilemma, what are we Christians to do? We must like Moses cover ourselves with faith and humility while we steal a look at the God whom no man can see and live. The broken and the contrite heart He will not despise. We must hide our unholiness in the wounds of Christ as Moses hid himself in the cleft of the rock while the glory of God passed by. We must take refuge from God in God. Above all we must believe that God sees us perfect in His Son while He disciplines and chastens and purges us that we may be partakers of his holiness.[38]

LIVE the Story

Sam's Story

During my years as a church planter in Brooklyn, New York, I had the pleasure of meeting Sam.[39] Sam had found our young church after responding to an evangelistic appeal by the Rev. Billy Graham at his 1991 rally in Central Park. A large man with an awkward gait and intense facial features, Sam appeared older than his fifty-five years. Indeed, his life had been scarred—literally and figuratively—by the rough streets of New York. Sam was not a well-educated man and he had retired from being a sanitation worker for the New York City Transit Authority.

Sam had been a drug addict for several years. And as if that weren't bad enough, Sam had regularly abused narcotics in front of one of his wife's several children. The impressionable youngster had later become a drug addict herself, and by the time our paths crossed she was an adult with five children of her own, all of whom were saddled with tremendous, life-controlling problems. Indeed, these children were experiencing an "empty way of life" (1 Pet 1:18) that had been handed down by their mother who herself had previously inherited a way of life handed down from her stepfather. When I met Sam he was desperately trying to break that cycle.

Because of his commitment to live for the Lord Jesus, Sam was trying to become a positive influence on the children of his stepdaughter; for this, he

---

38. Tozer, *Knowledge of the Holy*, 106–7.
39. Not his real name.

enlisted the help of several of us in our young congregation. But Sam's mission wasn't just about those children; he wanted to touch as many lives as he could in a positive way. He would tell how he felt that he owed the Lord every minute because of how much life he had wasted earlier. He was highly motivated to make up for lost time. And despite his rough exterior, he was about as gentle a man as one could imagine. He became a true inspiration to everyone in our fellowship, as we all came to know his love for his family, his dedication to the Lord, and his service to our congregation.

The Lord had given Sam a new nature; no longer was he trying to pursue a life of self-centered evil behavior but instead he was actively trying to pursue the good. He was on a path of holiness, or sanctification, as he waited for the return of the Lord Jesus. When I last was in touch with Sam, he was trying to live the message of 1 Peter 1:13–21. He had a living hope (1:3, 13, 21) because of an encounter with the living Lord Jesus, who had been revealed to him (1:20) through the preaching of the gospel message. Sam, had rejected his prior sinful life (1:14, 18) and was pursing the holiness of God. Since holiness involves separation from evil, Sam did what any recovering addict has to do: separate from old haunts, acquaintances, and drug contacts in order to remain clean. But Sam's physical separation from old patterns was the result of a separation that had already taken place in his mind.

Qualitative Holiness

I think of the commitment to holiness made in one's heart and mind as a *qualitative* dimension of holiness, while the physical act of separation—or rejection of certain activities—may be considered a *quantitative* dimension. I use the word quantitative because such actions might give the impression of being scientifically measurable, as if believers could calculate their level of holiness by what or whom they avoid. A quantitative notion of holiness focuses mainly on avoiding certain people so as not to be tainted by their actions or avoiding certain actions that might be considered sinful (even if the reasons for that label are not clear). When I was a child, for example, many in my family attended a church that used the moniker "holiness" as a shorthand description of its beliefs and practices, sometimes in place of mentioning the denomination by name. Holiness was defined by how well we kept our distance from the unsaved. We could not attend movies of any kind or any rating, nor could we attend a party thrown by unbelievers. We certainly were not to be found in a place where smoking or drinking took place, even if we did not participate. Maybe you have heard the sanctification jingle: "Don't smoke, don't chew; don't go with girls who do!" At one time the use of tobacco and alcohol, playing card games, wearing certain clothing or accessories, and even eating certain foods could be enough to consider one unholy. You probably have your own stories of how holiness is defined by Christians, whether they could back it up from the Bible or not. These are Christians who seek to define holiness quantitatively; they try to measure what actions make one holy and which do not. Sometimes the motivation behind this quantitative understanding is pure, but unfortunately it can lead to a legalistic understanding of Christianity rather than a more accurate notion of a relationship with God.

This quantitative view of holiness might seem consistent with the Leviticus passages that Peter reflects upon. Yet we know that believers have always been encouraged to let their lights shine, precisely by being present with unbelievers (as the Lord says in Matthew 5:16, "In the same way, let your light shine before others, that they may see your good deeds and glorify your Father in heaven"). Even my friend Sam continued to live in Brooklyn after his conversion, while at the same time he avoided previous practices.

Qualitatively, holiness means a change in one's heart and mind, which leads to upright behavior. The life of God's people reflects God's heart, and our actions should spring from hearts that are in sync with him. Even in the OT we see that God was much more interested in the state of his people's hearts more than their religious behaviors and rituals. For example, the well-known passages of Amos 5:22–24 and Micah 6:6–8 demonstrate that God is more passionate about justice, mercy, human compassion, and true godly devotion than he is about showy, expensive corporate worship:

> Even though you bring me burnt offerings and grain offerings,
> I will not accept them.
> Though you bring choice fellowship offerings,
> I will have no regard for them.
> Away with the noise of your songs!
> I will not listen to the music of your harps.
> But let justice roll on like a river,
> righteousness like a never-failing stream! (Amos 5:22–24)

> With what shall I come before the LORD
> and bow down before the exalted God?
> Shall I come before him with burnt offerings,
> with calves a year old?
> Will the LORD be pleased with thousands of rams,
> with ten thousand rivers of olive oil?
> Shall I offer my firstborn for my transgression,
> the fruit of my body for the sin of my soul?
> He has shown you, O mortal, what is good.

And what does the Lord require of you?
To act justly and to love mercy
and to walk humbly with your God. (Mic 6:6–8)

Isaiah 58 deals a major blow to those who seek to define holiness in merely
ritualistic terms. Pious practices are no substitute for true faith in God:

Is this the kind of fast I have chosen,
    only a day for people to humble themselves?
Is it only for bowing one's head like a reed
    and for lying in sackcloth and ashes?
Is that what you call a fast,
    a day acceptable to the Lord?
Is not this the kind of fasting I have chosen:
to loose the chains of injustice
    and untie the cords of the yoke,
to set the oppressed free
    and break every yoke?
Is it not to share your food with the hungry
    and to provide the poor wanderer with shelter—
when you see the naked, to clothe them,
    and not to turn away from your own flesh and blood? (Isa 58:5–7)

Yet one must take care to avoid going to an extreme. Christian faith isn't
a system of "anything goes"! Christians must first and foremost separate from
the world's system in terms of perspective and attitude, that is, *qualitatively*.
The result may be that certain actions and associations are avoided, but that
will be as a consequence of one's new nature, not merely because the action in
and of itself is wrong or the association in question is too sinful. For example,
in my opinion Christian believers may in good conscience go to see movies in
the theater. But the thoughtful Christian will reflect on the movie, evaluating
its message as well as the medium, and draw a conclusion about what he or
she will do. Walking into the theater does not make a person unholy, but the
wholesale buying of an unwholesome message might! For example, the movie
Fifty Shades of Grey, based on the novel by the same title, sparked widespread
discussion about sexuality and the sexual degradation of women. A *quantitative* view of holiness might keep one from viewing the movie or reading
the book, but a *qualitative* view of holiness would go further, encouraging
Christians to affirm a better view of human sexuality. This type of qualitative
separation requires thoughtful deliberation—"an alert and fully sober" mind,
as Peter says.

Life in the Spirit

Each of us, even if we didn't live as tough a life as Sam, has inherited an empty way of life from our ancestors—especially our first ancestor, Adam—and each of us needs to receive a new nature. When we place our faith in the Lord Jesus Christ as the spotless Lamb of God who takes away the sin of the world, we receive new lives through the ministry of the Holy Spirit. The Holy Spirit will help us to develop new appetites so that we can separate from sinful habits of the past and move toward a life of holiness. That separation starts in our minds as we exercise sober judgment and have a respectful attitude toward God. And since right behavior will follow right thinking, we will make conscious choices to separate from those things that would drag us down and not lift us up.

There may be some comfort in knowing that we are not the first generation of believers to struggle with living holy lives in the midst of an often decadent society. Theophylact (a medieval bishop and biblical scholar) concluded, "To be conformed to the things of this world means to be surrounded by them. Even today there are some weak-willed people who say that when they are in Rome, they have to do what the Romans do. But whether they do this knowingly or in ignorance, the message here is clear. We are to abandon this world and be conformed to the One who alone is truly holy."[40]

---

40. Gerald L. Bray, ed., *James, 1–2 Peter, 1–3 John, Jude*, ACCS New Testament 11 (Downers Grove, IL: Intervarsity Press, 2000), 77.

LISTEN to the Story

²²Now that you have purified yourselves by obeying the truth so that you have sincere love for each other, love one another deeply, from the heart. ²³For you have been born again, not of perishable seed, but of imperishable, through the living and enduring word of God. ²⁴For,

"All people are like grass,
    and all their glory is like the flowers of the field;
the grass withers and the flowers fall,
    ²⁵but the word of the Lord endures forever."

And this is the word that was preached to you.
²:¹Therefore, rid yourselves of all malice and all deceit, hypocrisy, envy, and slander of every kind. ²Like newborn babies, crave pure spiritual milk, so that by it you may grow up in your salvation, ³now that you have tasted that the Lord is good.

Listening to the Text in the Story: Psalms 34:8–14; 119:89–105; Isaiah 40:1–8; John 15:9–12.

"Don't work harder; work smarter!" That is, some tasks are completed by planning and ingenuity rather than through brute strength. The solution to some problem may come more readily when we stop trying to force it to happen and approach the challenge in an entirely different way. Perhaps when it comes to being holy, we Christians don't need to work harder but to work smarter.

"Working harder" in this context leads us back around to the false idea that holiness is measurable and quantifiable—gauged by how well one can keep the "dos and don'ts"—as opposed to how one nurtures a relationship with God. Focusing upon duties more than a relationship with God can lead to viewing Christianity as a rigid legalistic system rather than a dynamic journey. Upright behavior follows from one's intimate relationship with God, not merely from a sense of duty. We keep the Lord's commands because we love him (John 14:15; 1 John 5:3).

Yet no one can behave perfectly all the time. Therefore, when we fail to live impeccably—which is inevitable—we might end up trying to convince ourselves that we must work harder next time, as if all that is required for holiness is to roll up our sleeves, grit our teeth, and apply greater determination. Even though we are called to "work out" our salvation (Phil 2:12), holiness is not achieved through human effort. As the Philippians were also told, it is God who works in us "to will and to act in order to fulfill his good purpose" (Phil 2:13). So instead of working harder, we need to work smarter. This means that we receive the divine resources that God has given to his people and let them exert their full impact. The resource that Peter focuses upon in 1:22-2:3 is the word of God.[1] God's word is the glue that binds this section together, even though he also gives his readers some commands.[2]

EXPLAIN the Story

In 1:13-21 we noted that holiness starts with a nearness to God (a result of God's divine call) and is only possible through the sacrificial death of Jesus. Here, in 1:22-2:3, Peter emphasizes the role that the word of God plays in developing holy people. Human effort alone is ultimately futile, but the eternal word of the Lord is able to purify our souls and secure for us ultimate salvation.

Although the emphasis in this section is on the word of the Lord, Peter also urges the believers toward practical holiness. Sincere love, as well as the absence of malice, deceit, hypocrisy, envy, and slander, is especially important for holding together a Christian community that is under the pressure of persecution.

Sincere Love Based upon Obedience to God's Word (1:22)

Peter teaches that pure actions follow from pure hearts. After he commends them for loving Christ (1:8), he follows up with the command to "love one another deeply, from the heart." This love is also described as "sincere." Such love is made possible because these believers have purified their souls. Some scholars suggest that here Peter does not refer to conversion but to

---

1. Other resources are: the Holy Spirit, with his multifaceted and mysterious ways of ministering to us; godly counselors; wise teaching and preaching (which is based on God's word); and genuine worship.

2. Green, *1 Peter*, 48, explains, "this textual unit is held together by its heightened focus on the 'word [of God/the Lord]' (1:23, 25 [2x]; 2:2) around which the logic of this text turns." Also, Douglas Harink, *1 and 2 Peter*, BTCB (Grand Rapids: Brazos, 2009), 60, 64, who titles the section 1:22-25, "Conceived by the Word," and 2:1-3, "Nourished by the Word."

subsequent "sanctification," as if purification comes "by obeying the truth," making humans participate in their ongoing salvation.[3] For this reason Wayne Grudem asserts, "Christians are never in the New Testament said to be active agents in God's initial cleansing of their souls at conversion."[4]

Nevertheless, grammar and the flow of Peter's discussion suggest that he is referring to a past event, most likely that of conversion. The main verb of the sentence is the imperative, "love" (agapēsate). "Have purified" translates a participle, hēgnikotes, which suggests an event that took place in the past.[5] In addition to the grammar, the section seems to point to conversion in several ways, including the discussion of purification in v. 22. Joel Green observes, "The phrases in 1:22a, 23; 2:1, 3 refer, albeit in different ways, to the same moment: conversion. All are cast in the past and provide the basis for life befitting those born anew."[6]

Conversion is the work of God (1:3), but it also involves human obedience, at least from the onlooker's perspective.[7] John Elliott, in referring to the opening of v. 22, contends, "This initial phrase recalls 1:14–16 and describes the active role that the addressees played in the process of their conversion from Gentile pollution."[8] Taken together, v. 22 stresses the human dimension, whereas v. 23 indicates that new birth comes through God's word.

Purity is one more of the benefits granted to humanity because of the sacrificial death of Jesus (vv. 19–21): believers have redemption, faith, hope, and purity of soul. The participle, hēgnikotes (v. 22), is meant to remind readers of ritual cleansing associated with the OT sacramental system. This verb hagnizō is related to the verb hagiazō ("to sanctify") and the adjective hagios ("holy"; see vv. 15–16). It is used frequently in the Greek Old Testament (Septuagint) in contexts of ritual purification.[9] Similarly, the less frequent NT usage most often describes ritual purity (John 11:55; Acts 21:24, 26; 24:18). In the letters of James and 1 John, hagnizō is used to describe a genuine purity of heart yet with the ritual imagery providing background:

---

3. E.g., Grudem, First Peter, 92. Grudem seems to follow Martin Luther and John Calvin on this point. Luther translated 1:22 with imperatival force: "Purify your souls in your obedience to the truth ..." (Luther, Peter and Jude, 78). Calvin asserts, "Peter does not declare what they are but reminds them of what they ought to be" (Hebrews and 1 and 2 Peter, 251).

4. Grudem, First Peter, 93.

5. The participle hēgnikotes ("having purified") is in the perfect tense, indicating a past action whose impact continues through the time of the writing.

6. Green, 1 Peter, 49. See also Jobes, 1 Peter, 124, who concludes, "Peter is most likely saying that his readers are to love one another because of their previous conversion...."

7. Consider, for example, the apostle Paul's recounting of his conversion and call to ministry before King Agrippa. Paul emphasizes the Lord's divine initiative, but notes, "I was not disobedient to the vision from heaven" (Acts 26:19).

8. Elliott, 1 Peter, 382.

9. E.g., Exod 19:10; Num 6:3; 8:21; 11:18; 19:12; 31:19, 23.

Come near to God and he will come near to you. Wash your hands, you sinners, and purify your hearts, you double-minded. (Jas 4:8)

All who have this hope in him purify themselves, just as he is pure. (1 John 3:3)

Peter uses the term in the same manner as the authors of James and 1 John, applying the language of OT cleansing to the impact of the sacrificial death of Jesus (e.g., 1 Pet 1:18–19). Through their obedience to God's word the Christians have purified their souls. Such purity of soul allows God's people to draw near to him without fear of rejection.

Obedience is more than mental assent to some set of propositions but is conformity to a new standard (see 1:14). It is akin to "repentance," a common NT term that describes more than a simple changing of one's mind, but a new reorientation of one's life.[10] Peter's readers have reoriented their lives around "the truth," which is Peter's shorthand for the *kerygma*, i.e., the preached good news concerning Jesus, also known simply as "the word" (v. 25). Throughout the NT, "truth" is often a synonym for the good news.[11] The truth is the gospel message and for Peter that message is rooted in the OT on which he relies to support his argument (as we will see in v. 24).

God's word, that is, the preaching of the gospel, is powerful (v. 22). The word not only has the power to cleanse souls but also to produce love among believers. In fact, Peter says that "sincere love for each other" was a purpose of this cleansing.[12] "Sincere" is *anypokritos*, the opposite of hypocrisy, an adjective found only a few times in the NT and always modifying a Christian virtue (i.e., faith, love and wisdom).[13] "Sincere love" is not phony affection or flattery, where one pretends to show concern; and neither does love play favorites. These believers are to practice genuine *philadelphia*, brotherly and sisterly concern for each other (see the cognate adjective in 3:8).[14]

---

10. It is common to hear preachers say that *metanoia*, the Greek word for "repentance," derives from the two words *meta* ("change") and *nous* ("mind"), thus it is a "change of mind." However, words can often mean something much more (or even something very different) from what their etymology might indicate. While repentance "could imply merely an intellectual transformation, [the term] draws from the OT and Jewish concept that demanded a lifestyle change as well.... The idea is that of turning to God in every area of one's life, moral/ethical as well as mental" (Grant R. Osborne, *Matthew*, ZECNT [Grand Rapids: Zondervan, 2010], 110). This understanding of *metanoia* seems most typical in the NT.

11. Achtemeier, *1 Peter*, 136, gives many examples, including John 8:32; Rom 2:8; Jas 5:19; 2 Pet 2:2; 1 John 2:21.

12. The Greek text uses the preposition *eis*, which in this case indicates purpose; hence the NIV translation "so that."

13. Modifying "faith": 1 Tim 1:5 and 2 Tim 1:5; modifying "love": Rom 12:9; 2 Cor 6:6; 1 Pet 1:22; modifying "wisdom": Jas 3:17.

14. Many Christians are familiar with the important NT word for love, *agapē*, but in the context of Christian community, a few NT writers used *philadelphia* to describe mutual concern (e.g., in addition to our present context: Rom 12:10; 1 Thess 4:9; Heb. 13:1; 2 Pet. 1:7).

Philadelphia was not originally a Christian term, even though it aptly suits the context of church community. John H. Elliott points out that "in Greco-Roman society, the love of blood-brothers and siblings for one another was a highly celebrated virtue as a sign of a harmonious and mutually supportive household/family and a signal of its honorable character and public reputation."[15] *Philadelphia* was also the name of a first-century city in Asia Minor, where there was a church (Rev 1:11; 3:7); that city is included in the regions to where Peter's letter is addressed (1 Pet 1:1). Peter's readers, therefore, would have known that their neighbors used the term *philadelphia* for their blood relatives and would have appreciated the new dimension that Christian faith brought to the word, especially in the context of suffering, when true friendship and love may be most appreciated.

Peter commands his readers to love "deeply, from the heart." The admonition sounds redundant here because "deeply, from the heart" is precisely what sincerity entails. Peter seems to be saying, "Since you have love for each other, show it!" I find it noteworthy that Peter mentions love before prohibiting specific unethical behaviors (such as those found in 2:1). Love is the most important virtue, as Peter will say clearly in 4:8 ("Above all, love each other deeply, because love covers over a multitude of sins"). Love occurs as the first of the fruit of the Holy Spirit (Gal 5:22), and the apostle Paul also states explicitly that within the triad of Christian virtues—faith, hope and love—"the greatest of these is love" (1 Cor 13:13).

Brotherly and sisterly love involves serious effort, as the word "deeply" indicates. This translates the word *ektenōs*, which literally means "strained" (see also 1 Pet 4:8). The idea is that of stern resolve, fervency, and eagerness.[16] The two other occurrences of *ektenōs* in the NT describe extraordinarily ardent prayers, including those of the Lord Jesus before his crucifixion when his sweat was like drops of blood (Luke 22:44), and the prayers of the believers in Jerusalem (Acts 12:5) when Peter was imprisoned. Peter wants his readers to love intensely and with constancy.

The Enduring Word of God (1:23–25)

The purification of souls in v. 22 is characterized as a new birth in v. 23. Peter uses the same term that he employed earlier in v. 3 and that is also reminiscent of the new nature detailed in vv. 14–21. Peter reinforces his point that holiness is not manufactured through human effort but is the product of a

---

15. Elliott, *1 Peter*, 384.
16. The related verb, *ekteinō*, literally means "to stretch out." It is often used to describe someone extending the hand (more often than some other part of the body), as in a healing (e.g., Matt 12:13) or even in an arrest (e.g., Luke 22:53).

new nature, a spiritual rebirth.[17] The biological imagery continues as Peter explains that rebirth is possible through the "imperishable seed."[18] That seed is the "living and enduring" word of God. These two adjectives remind us of Peter's earlier words, in which "living" describes the believer's hope (1:3) and "enduring" is reminiscent of our eternal inheritance (1:4). Paramount in Peter's understanding of the word is its lasting quality; he describes the word as "enduring" in both vv. 23 and 25.

Once again, the OT provides background for Peter's argument; descriptions of the word of God as alive and enduring abound in the Hebrew Bible. Consider, for example, the magnificent Psalm 119, what I think of as "Ode to the Torah." Psalm 119:89 describes God's word as eternal, and verses 9, 11, 25, and 28 show the word as alive, having energy to guide, strengthen, and encourage. There are many other examples, but another notable one is the word of God observed as the creative force at the foundation of the world (Gen 1); the word was not only alive but able to give life as well. Indeed, the book of Deuteronomy shows that fidelity to the covenant meant obeying God's words, which would bring life (e.g., Deut 31:9–13). The understanding of God's word as living and lasting is found in the NT as well. For example, in Hebrews 4:12 God's word is alive and powerful: "For the word of God is alive and active. Sharper than any double-edged sword, it penetrates even to dividing soul and spirit, joints and marrow; it judges the thoughts and attitudes of the heart." The might of the Lord's word is dramatically displayed in Revelation 19:15: "Coming out of his mouth is a sharp sword with which to strike down the nations. 'He will rule them with an iron scepter.' He treads the winepress of the fury of the wrath of God Almighty." The sword from the mouth of the victorious Jesus is his triumphant word.[19]

God's seed has all the power necessary to create a new nature, one that is capable of love (v. 1 Pet 1:22). The supernatural "imperishable seed" is put in contrast to "perishable seed," that which is natural and subject to decay (v. 23). The imperishable/perishable contrast is used elsewhere in the NT to highlight the powerful nature of God when compared to the frailty of humanity. For example, in Romans 1:22–23 the apostle Paul describes how deluded some people had become in worshiping handcrafted idols instead of God:

---

17. In this section Peter reads much like the Gospel of John, especially chapters 1 and 3. Although the Greek vocabulary is different, there is a similar emphasis on the "word" (the preexistent yet incarnate Word in John 1) as well as on new birth (in the Nicodemus encounter in John 3). See Feldmeier, *First Peter,* 127–30.

18. God's word described as "seed" is reminiscent of the parable of the farmer (see Matt 13:3–23).

19. See Grant R. Osborne, *Revelation,* BECNT (Grand Rapids: Baker Academic, 2002), 685, and Mitchell G. Reddish, *Revelation,* SHBC (Macon: Smyth and Helwys, 2001), 368.

"Although they claimed to be wise, they became fools and exchanged the glory of the immortal God for images made to look like a mortal human being and birds and animals and reptiles."[20] Another example is 1 Corinthians 15:50–54, where Paul contrasts the nature of human bodies before and after resurrection:

I declare to you, brothers and sisters, that flesh and blood cannot inherit the kingdom of God, nor does the perishable inherit the imperishable. Listen, I tell you a mystery: We will not all sleep, but we will all be changed—in a flash, in the twinkling of an eye, at the last trumpet. For the trumpet will sound, the dead will be raised imperishable, and we will be changed. For the perishable must clothe itself with the imperishable, and the mortal with immortality. When the perishable has been clothed with the imperishable, and the mortal with immortality, then the saying that is written will come true: "Death has been swallowed up in victory."[21]

The human/divine contrast continues in 1:23–25, which consists mostly of a quotation from the Greek version of Isaiah 40:6b–8.[22] The passage reinforces Peter's teaching concerning the power of God's word versus the impotence of human effort. Humanity and its glory are pictured as practically insignificant, being compared to grass and wildflowers, respectively, that easily shrivel up and die.

"Flesh" is used here as metonymy for "human being." Such usage is typical in the NT and often includes the notion of moral weakness, sinfulness, and transience.[23] Peter does not focus on the sinfulness of humanity per se but upon its frailty. With parallel phrases indicative of Hebrew poetry, mere mortals are compared to grass and human glory to "the flowers of the field." "Glory" means any positive attributes that allow human beings to stand out and be noticed.[24] But despite the splendor that mortals might possess and display, their fate is like that of the grass and the wildflowers. Grass withers, a natural occurrence especially after being bombarded by the elements of

20. The Greek words translated in Romans as "mortal" and "immortal" are the same words found in 1 Pet 1:23.

21. Not only does Paul share some of Peter's vocabulary, *phthartos/aphthartos* ("perishable/imperishable"), but also the contrasts of *thnētos/athanasia* ("mortal/immortality") and *phthora/aphtharsia* ("corruption/incorruptibility").

22. These words occur in a poetic section of Isaiah that contains words of comfort. They follow the famous lines that are sung in Handel's *Messiah* and that are applied to the ministry of John the Baptist in the Gospels (Isa 40:1–5). There are some minor variations between the MT and the LXX; Peter, as noted above, quotes from the LXX.

23. A few examples out of many include Matt 26:41; Rom 7:5; 18, 25, along with several other places where the NIV translates *sarx* ("flesh") as "sinful nature." Sometimes the stereotyped pair "flesh and blood" is also used to denote "human being" (e.g., Matt 16:17; 1 Cor 15:50).

24. The MT of Isa 40:6 uses *khesed* ("mercy," "kindness," "love"), while the LXX uses *doxa* ("glory").

nature, such as wind (see Isa 40:7) or the hot sun (see Matt 13:6). Similarly, flowers eventually die and fall to the ground. But none of this is true of God's word; amazingly, the word of the Lord endures for all time.

In v. 25 Peter makes explicit that what he previously called "the truth," "imperishable seed," and "the word of God" (vv. 22, 23, and 25) all refer to the gospel message that had been preached to these believers. Peter uses the Greek term *rhēma* ("saying") in v. 25, which here refers to the spoken or preached word as opposed to the written word.[25] And there is a *de facto* connection between the good news and OT Scripture, meaning that the gospel is on a par with the word that "endures forever." He also links Jesus the Son with God the Father. In the Greek OT, Isaiah's oracle (40:8) uses the word "God," but Peter uses the word "Lord." "Lord" (*kyrios*) was typically used in the Greek OT to translate the divine name Yahweh, since devout Hebrew readers would substitute *Adonai* (LORD) in place of YHWH. Christian writers at times applied *kyrios* to Jesus, thereby equating him with Yahweh. Peter may be asserting the divinity of Jesus by referring to him as Lord in v. 25, as well as in 2:3 (which alludes to Ps 34:8).

Spiritual Nourishment through God's Word (2:1–3)

Because the word of God has such profound power, it should be a continual source of guidance. Peter directs his audience to crave more of God's word and to put away vices that could drive a wedge between members of the community, thereby mocking the notion of *philadelphia*.[26] Lists of vices and virtues were common in the Greco-Roman world, and several NT writers employ such lists, frequently using a form of *apotithēmi* ("to put away"), just as Peter does here.[27]

Each evil in the list is especially applicable to the context of interpersonal relationships, and most deal with sins involving words or speech, which makes a fitting contrast to Peter's overall emphasis on the word of God. "All of these forms of behavior were widespread in a society marked by factional rivalries and intense social competition and conflict.... Their proscription here is especially appropriate in a letter addressed to mixed communities involving groups of different ethnic origins or social levels."[28]

---

25. *Rhēma* can sometimes have a special prophetic or predictive significance (e.g., Luke 1:37, 38; John 8:47; Jude 17).

26. Even though the opening word of 2:1 in the Greek text is a participle (*apothemenoi*, "putting away"), it takes on the force of a command ("rid yourselves"), since the subsequent verb (*epipothēsate*, "crave") is an imperative. See Daniel B. Wallace, *Greek Grammar Beyond the Basics* (Grand Rapids: Zondervan, 1997), 640–45.

27. E.g., Eph 4:22, 25; Col 3:8; Heb 12:1; Jas 1:21.

28. Elliott, *1 Peter*, 398.

"Malice" translates a word that can refer to wickedness in general (*kakia*), but in the context of personal relationships it takes on the sense of "ill will" (compare to Eph 4:31 and Col 3:8). Peter will revisit the topic of "deceit" (*dolos*) later in the chapter (v. 22) as he quotes the OT while reflecting on the suffering of Christ and again when he uses the OT to encourage upright behavior even in the face of abuse (3:10). Deceit can involve trickery to gain a personal advantage, as when Jacob usurped the inheritance from his brother Esau (the LXX uses *dolos* in Gen 27:35). "Hypocrisy" is pretense and, as we have seen, is the opposite of how believers are to love (1:22). It seems that at least some strand of Jewish thought considered "envy" or jealousy as the motivation for Satan's work in the world. In the Apocrypha, the book of Wisdom declares:

> For God created us for incorruption,
>   and made us in the image of his own eternity,
> But through the devil's envy death entered the world,
>   and those who belong to his company experience it.
>   (Wis 2:23–24 NRSV)[29]

The unbelievers commit "slander" (i.e., malicious speech) against the believers (2:12; 3:16), but that sin should not be found among the Christians. Interestingly, Peter prohibits "slander of every kind." He may mean that evil speech can take on a variety of forms and be a weapon wielded against people or even God. For example, slander is how Miriam and Aaron criticized Moses (Num 12:8) and also the kind of grumbling against God that got the Israelites in trouble during their wilderness wanderings (Num 21:5, 7; Ps 78:19). Peter is concerned about any and all speech that defames another, be it a fellow believer, leader, or God.

With the sensitivity of a pastor, Peter does not demand his readers to put away sin without also informing them of how this is possible. Purified souls and new birth have come through the word of God; so will their growth in salvation. With 2:2 Peter returns to the image of new birth found in 1:3 and 1:23. He wants the recipients of his letter to act like infants who are hungry for the word of God. The bodies of newborns, which are growing rapidly, have a huge demand for nourishment. Indeed, babies energetically cry out as they crave their mother's milk. Similarly, Christian believers are to long for God's pure, spiritual milk. Since they know that God is good (2:3), they can trust that what he produces (i.e., the word) is good for them.

---

29. In the LXX the Greek word for envy, *phthonos*, occurs only in the Apocrypha. In addition to the passage listed above, it is found in Wis 6:23; 1 Macc 8:16; 3 Macc 6:7.

This milk is pure and spiritual. "Pure" translates *adolos*, a word that occurs nowhere else in the NT and was "a term used in business documents for sales of unadulterated foods."[30] We have just seen its opposite, *dolos*, "deceit," in the previous verse. The word of God is sincere; it is not interlaced with tricks designed to fool its readers. In the same way that mothers give their infants pure milk straight from their breasts, God gives words that are not tainted with impurities that might damage one's soul.

The Greek word *logikos* is translated here as "spiritual." The only other occurrence of *logikos* in the entire Greek Bible is in Romans 12:1 ("Therefore, I urge you, brothers and sisters, in view of God's mercy, to offer your bodies as a living sacrifice, holy and pleasing to God—this is your true and proper [*logikos*] worship"; the NRSV has the word "spiritual" in both Rom 12 and 1 Pet 2). The fundamental meaning of *logikos* is "rational" or "true," and it was a common term within Greek philosophy. In Romans 12:1 and 1 Peter 2:2, there may be an underlying idea of "genuineness" that would apply to worship in the Roman church and to the word of God here in 1 Peter.[31]

Milk is a metaphor for Christian instruction in 1 Corinthians 3:2; Hebrews 5:12, 13; here it symbolizes God's word. A mother's milk provides the nutrients for physical growth to maturity while God's word aids in spiritual growth, which is to "salvation." As is typically the case in the NT, salvation is presented as a future experience to which all true believers are headed, yet salvation is "something to which we are moving, not something for which we are merely waiting."[32] In the meantime, present life for believers is characterized by hope and joy (1:3, 8).[33]

The goal of every Christian's life here on earth is to fully mature, becoming the person God intends for each of us to be; simultaneously all believers together are growing into the mature fellowship we ought to be. Peter will elaborate on what it means to be God's intended community in the next section, 2:4–10. His message here in 2:2 is much like the lesson found in

---

30. Craig S. Keener, *The IVP Bible Background Commentary: New Testament* (Downers Grove, IL: IVP Academic, 1993), 712.

31. There is a school of thought that sees *logikos* as corresponding less to rationality and genuineness and more to *logos* ("word"), as the two terms are etymologically related. In fact, Feldmeier uses the compound "word-milk" (*First Peter*, 126), and the old KJV translates the same expression as "milk of the word." But note the rigorous challenge to such treatment by Jobes, *1 Peter*, 130–41. Jobes concludes that "*logikos* milk means not the word-milk but the milk that is true to the nature of the new eschatological reality established by the resurrection of Jesus Christ and into which Peter's readers have been reborn (1:3)."

32. J. Ramsey Michaels, "Going to Heaven with Jesus: From 1 Peter to Pilgrim's Progress," in *Patterns of Discipleship in the New Testament*, ed. Richard N. Longenecker (Grand Rapids: Eerdmans, 1996), 251.

33. See Williams, *Doctrine of Salvation*, 149–225.

Ephesians 5:25–27, where "water" is the chosen symbol of how God's word brings worshipers to a mature faith:

> Husbands, love your wives, just as Christ loved the church and gave himself up for her to make her holy, cleansing her by the washing with water through the word, and to present her to himself as a radiant church, without stain or wrinkle or any other blemish, but holy and blameless.

For his part, Peter commands these sojourners to crave God's word because they have already "tasted" the goodness or kindness of God. Verse 3 is an allusion to Psalm 34:8 ("Taste and see that the LORD is good; blessed is the one who takes refuge in him").[34] There may be a play on words here. "Good" is a translation of *chrēstos* (which is often understood as "kind"); it sounds like *christos* ("Messiah" or "Christ").[35] If such wordplay was intentional, it would serve to reinforce the early Christian understand that Christ is the LORD (i.e., YHWH of the OT).[36]

Because God has already displayed goodness, God's people can trust the word of God to also be good for them. "In short, the word of God, the good news, is efficacious in generating, cultivating, and sustaining new life."[37]

LIVE the Story

Scripture's Power to Change People

For many of my adult years I had been in Christian circles that seemed to study the Bible in order to be *right*, but not necessarily to be *good*. What I mean is that I frequently witnessed the Bible used as a weapon, but not always against Satan's darts (Eph 6:16); it was used to win arguments between people, often between Christians. Some of us had come to see the Bible primarily as a source of information, but we didn't always see the power that the words possess to change us into the kind of people that God wants us to be. When it came to right behavior, we often followed some list of church-approved behaviors that were considered holy, as I noted in my earlier discussion of 1:13–21. But thankfully, not all Christians live life in a legalistic fashion or see the word of God as only a repository of sound doctrine. There was no one

---

34. Psalm 34 is numbered as Psalm 33 in the Septuagint (LXX), the Greek Old Testament. Jobes, *1 Peter*, 137–38, proposes that, "Psalm 33 LXX in its entirety is in Peter's mind as he writes, for he later quotes it more extensively in 3:10–12 as the ground for his exhortations. Moreover, the language and thoughts throughout 1 Pet. 1–3 echo the language of Ps. 33 LXX in several places."

35. Mark Dubis, *1 Peter: A Handbook on the Greek Text*, BHGNT 5 (Waco: Baylor University Press, 2010), 45.

36. Achtemeier, *1 Peter*, 148.

37. Green, *1 Peter*, 54.

particular moment that I recall moving away from legalism; perhaps I am still in the process. However, the more I interacted with Christians of various backgrounds—in college, seminary, doctoral studies, teaching in various institutions, and traveling abroad—I discovered that some of my attitudes were more influenced by culture than the Bible. For example, the church of my childhood taught that all secular music was evil without realizing that many of the hymns we sang consisted of Christian messages set to secular melodies. Music is amoral; one may listen to a variety of musical genres and not be enmeshed in sin. The basic truth we must follow is that the Holy Spirit is God's provision to convert our souls and work in us to bring about what is good, and the Spirit uses the written word of God to help accomplish his goals.

The word of God has the power to influence our behavior, including drawing us to salvation in Jesus. The conversion of Augustinus Aurelius, perhaps better known to us as St. Augustine, is an example of that power. For years Augustine resisted the call of Christ upon his life. But in a garden in Milan he heard a voice, which he interpreted to mean that he should read the Bible:

> Suddenly I heard the voice of a boy or a girl I know not which— coming from the neighboring house, chanting over and over again, "Pick it up, read it; pick it up, read it" [in Latin, *Tolle lege, tolle lege*]. Immediately I ceased weeping and began most earnestly to think whether it was usual for children in some kind of game to sing such a song, but I could not remember ever having heard the like. So, damming the torrent of my tears, I got to my feet, for I could not but think that this was a divine command to open the Bible and read the first passage I should light upon....
>
> I snatched it up, opened it, and in silence read the paragraph on which my eyes first fell: "Not in rioting and drunkenness, not in chambering and wantonness, not in strife and envying, but put on the Lord Jesus Christ, and make no provision for the flesh to fulfill the lusts thereof." I wanted to read no further, nor did I need to. For instantly, as the sentence ended, there was infused in my heart something like the light of full certainty and all the gloom of doubt vanished away.[38]

The word of God does not produce the flashy feats of strength of a cartoon superhero. Nor is it "magical." You may have seen movies that have a supernatural component to them, such as *The Mummy* or the *Harry Potter* films. At some point in those movies the words found in a book are used as

---

38. "Augustine: Account of His Own Conversion," Internet History Sourcebook, www.fordham .edu/halsall/source/aug-conv.asp.

an incantation and when they are recited—even if the reader does not understand what he or she is saying—all sorts of things start to happen! The wind
starts swirling, natural laws are suspended or contradicted, and the people deal
with the special effects that the incantation brought about. The power of the
Bible is not like that. For our part, we don't read Scripture aloud as magical
incantations. The power in the word of God is designed to change us more
than to change circumstances. Richard Foster, writing about the spiritual discipline of study, offers this challenge: "Note that the central purpose [of the
study of Scripture] is not doctrinal purity (though that is no doubt involved)
but inner transformation. We come to the Scripture to be changed, not to
amass information."[39]

Scripture's Power to Build Up Christian Community

Purity comes through obedience to God's word, according to 1:22. And
such purification has social, not just personal, implications. The divisive
behaviors that Peter mentions in 2:1 take place among groups of human
beings. We are hard pressed to find any gathering—at work, church, school,
in the neighborhood, or even at home—where there isn't some sort of malice, deceit, hypocrisy, envy, or slander. In order for unity to be created and
preserved, these actions must diminish and love must be preeminent. It
takes superhuman power to overcome these typically human practices and
to develop the type of love described in 1:22. That power is available through
the word of God.

The urban congregation I started in Washington, DC, consists of people
from the inner city as well as a few from the surrounding metro area. Their
backgrounds are quite varied. Some have a good deal of formal education
while others have hardly any. Some people have stable, fairly lucrative jobs;
others have none. Some of us are African Americans while others are not.
But during the week we mingle together in group Bible studies. The presence
of the Holy Spirit and the Scriptures themselves are what give us the power
to come together and not pull apart. That is the same for any congregation. There is always tremendous potential for factionalism that could result
from malice, deceit, hypocrisy, envy, and slander. Unity, however, can come
through the ministry of God's word. The more we study and meditate upon
the *rhēma* of God, the harder it will be to hate fellow believers and disengage
from one another.

I recall an incident where two young women in our church (one African
American and one European American) were upset with an older African-

---

39. Richard J. Foster, *Celebration of Discipline: The Path to Spiritual Growth*, rev. ed. (San Francisco: Harper Collins, 1988), 69.

American man who had allegedly made sexist comments to them and whose behavior appeared inappropriate. The women approached me for counsel and eventually they, along with the man in question and my wife and me, sat down to get to the bottom of things. I led the time with an appeal to Scripture and to seeking God's will. After discussion and prayer, the evening ended with greater understanding of each other's perspectives, with hugs, and also with affirmations of our desire to yield to God's teaching on reconciliation. What happened that evening was truly a work of God to build a new level of trust and unity within the fellowship, and it came through dependence upon the truth of God's word.

The Importance of Studying and Obeying Scripture

We must have an appetite for the word of God in order for it to provide continual help for our spiritual growth. Peter instructs his readers to "crave" the word in the same way that a newborn desires milk. The vocabulary and imagery are reminiscent of Psalm 42:1 ("As the deer pants for streams of water, so my soul pants for you, my God"). Indeed, our ultimate desire is for the Lord, and his word points to him. Peter does not advocate what might be called "bibliolatry," where God's word is worshiped instead of God. Rather, he wants followers of Jesus to know that the word of God has power to transform and nurture us.

Years ago the National Dairy Board used the advertising slogan: "Milk. It does a body good." We could say of the word: "It can help God's people—the body of Christ—to be good." But hunger for the word really does not depend upon a marketing campaign. We cannot make people hunger for the word, but we can continually encourage them to read and meditate upon it and to take advantage of the interest they already have. For example, according to a recent survey by the Barna Group, "the younger the person, the less likely they are to read the Bible," but at the same time, "younger adults ... express a slightly above-average interest in gaining additional Bible knowledge."[40] There appears to be some hunger among younger people to know more about the Bible, and we teachers need to capitalize on that desire and show by our example that we too depend upon Scripture.

Let us never make a false dichotomy between academic approaches to Scripture and devotional, or spiritual, readings of Scripture. Dr. Patricia Fosarelli along with Dr. Michael Gorman write:

40. "New Research Explores How Different Generations View and Use the Bible," Barna, https://www.barna.com/research/new-research-explores-how-different-generations-view-and-use-the-bible/#.V_AldPArLNM.

There are two common, but misguided, sentiments in some quarters of the Christian church regarding the relationship between spirituality and the academic or intellectual life. One is the belief that intellectual pursuits do not benefit the spiritual life and may even be dangerous to it. The other is the belief that spirituality is somehow "beneath" those who are intellectually serious about Christianity and specifically about the literary and historical study of the Bible.[41]

Rigorous academic study of Scripture is part of our task as we are called upon to "correctly handle the word of truth" (2 Tim 2:15). Indeed, this very volume and all the commentaries in this series strive for both sound interpretation of Scripture as well as thoughtful spiritual reflection.

Not only do the Scriptures give us right theology; they provide power to purify our souls, power to build community through love, and power to nurture our spiritual growth and development. Consequently, we need to keep encouraging believers to learn and live God's word. This has always been part of faithful worship, even in OT times. Consider Psalm 1:1–2:

> Blessed is the one
>   who does not walk in step with the wicked
> or stand in the way that sinners take
>   or sit in the company of mockers,
> but whose delight is in the law of the LORD,
>   and who meditates on his law day and night.

And Psalm 119:9–11:

> How can a young person stay on the path of purity?
>   By living according to your word.
> I seek you with all my heart;
>   do not let me stray from your commands.
> I have hidden your word in my heart
>   that I might not sin against you.

These verses from the psalms speak of the discipline of meditation, in which we reflect on God's word until we recognize the very voice of God. Foster puts it this way: "Christian meditation, very simply, is the ability to hear God's voice and obey his word. It is that simple. I wish I could make it more complicated for those who like things difficult. It involves no hidden

---

41. Patricia D. Fosarelli and Michael J. Gorman, "The Bible and Spiritual Growth," in *Scripture: An Ecumenical Introduction to the Bible and Its Interpretation*, ed. Michael J. Gorman (Peabody: Hendrickson, 2005), 229.

mysteries, no secret mantras, no mental gymnastics, no esoteric flights into the cosmic consciousness. The truth of the matter is that the great God of the universe, the Creator of all things desires our fellowship."[42] Heroes of the faith from OT times, throughout the NT era, and all the way through history have found power to live on a holy trajectory through meditation on God's "living and enduring" word.

No one can achieve holiness through mere human effort. That is why "working harder" at holiness will have to give way to "working smarter," that is, by obeying Scripture. As one example, I recently counseled a woman who was not part of my congregation. She was plagued with guilt over some things from in her past, and it was making her literally ill. Together we read James 5:16 ("Therefore confess your sins to each other and pray for each other so that you may be healed. The prayer of a righteous person is powerful and effective"). This woman confessed her sins in my presence, and we had a time of prayer. Some time later she reported how much freer and lighter she felt. She had obeyed God's word and experienced its powerful results.

Scripture and the Holy Spirit

Although Peter does not discuss the Holy Spirit directly in 1:22–2:3, he does mention him in in other places (i.e., 1 Pet 1:2, 11, 12; 3:18, 19; 4:6, 14). At the outset (1:2) he acknowledges that sanctification is a work of the Holy Spirit; in fact, the NT is replete with references to that ministry (e.g., Rom 15:16; 1 Cor 1:2; 6:11; Phil 1:6; Heb 10:10). And God's word is one of the tools that the Holy Spirit uses in his sanctifying work, as is the case in 1 Timothy 4:4–5: "For everything God created is good, and nothing is to be rejected if it is received with thanksgiving, because it is consecrated by the word of God and prayer." That is why N. T. Wright says that the word is a "vehicle of the Spirit's authority"[43] and that the power of God works "through the combination of the power of the Spirit and the spoken or written word."[44]

---

42. Foster, *Celebration*, 17.
43. N. T. Wright, *Scripture and the Authority of God: How to Read the Bible Today*, rev. and expanded ed. (New York: HarperOne, 2011), 51.
44. Ibid., 117.

LISTEN to the Story

⁴As you come to him, the living Stone—rejected by humans but chosen by God and precious to him—⁵you also, like living stones, are being built into a spiritual house to be a holy priesthood, offering spiritual sacrifices acceptable to God through Jesus Christ. ⁶For in Scripture it says:

> "See, I lay a stone in Zion,
>   a chosen and precious cornerstone,
> and the one who trusts in him
>   will never be put to shame."

⁷Now to you who believe, this stone is precious. But to those who do not believe,

> "The stone the builders rejected
>   has become the cornerstone,"

⁸and,

> "A stone that causes people to stumble
>   and a rock that makes them fall."

They stumble because they disobey the message—which is also what they were destined for.

⁹But you are a chosen people, a royal priesthood, a holy nation, God's special possession, that you may declare the praises of him who called you out of darkness into his wonderful light. ¹⁰Once you were not a people, but now you are the people of God; once you had not received mercy, but now you have received mercy.

Listening to the Text in the Story: Exodus 19:3–8; Isaiah 43:1–28; Hosea 1:6–9; 2:23; Romans 9:30–33.

God expects his people to be holy, but they can find holiness only in *relationship* with him. This is the message of the whole Scripture—God desires to be in a relationship with human beings who would reciprocate his love. Ancient Israel, the OT people of God, was called to be in a unique relationship with him through the covenants. For example, the Sinai Covenant beginning with the Ten Commandments in Exodus 20 is of critical importance for Israel's understanding of how they are to relate to God. That covenant is predicated upon God's deliverance of his people, and his care for them, as described in the picturesque language of Exodus 19.[1] "In Exod 19:3–8, Israel is summoned to a special relationship with God, described by three phases: a special possession among all peoples, a kingdom of priests, a holy nation. Israel is to be set apart from other nations for God's service just as priests were set apart from other men."[2] These ethical obligations are based upon and follow the description of God's election of his people. Peter engages in a similar endeavor. Before he focuses upon ethical behavior (2:11–3:7), he establishes the uniqueness of his audience's relationship to God; and he does so using the language of Exodus 19 and other OT passages.

EXPLAIN the Story

In 2:4–10 Peter focuses on God's elect community and how their relationship to God is centered on Jesus Christ. The passage follows a symmetrical pattern with a discussion of Jesus at the center. The opening (vv. 4–5) and the closing (vv. 9–10) both focus on worship as well as the identity of God's people. In v. 4 the recipients of Peter's letter are invited to worship God, as they are to "come to him." The call to worship is echoed in v. 9, as the believers are to "declare the praises of him who called you out of darkness into his wonderful light." Also, in v. 5, as well as vv. 9–10, the believers are given symbolic identities, associating them with Israel, God's OT people. Jesus is at the center of the discussion, vv. 6–8, and attracts believers to him and repels those who reject him.

God's Chosen People Are like Living Stones That Constitute a Temple (2:4–5)

As we discussed earlier Peter used the OT to declare that the Lord is good. And based on the goodness of God, Peter now urges his audience to draw near to the Lord Jesus in worship (vv. 4–5). The worship that is described is

---

1. Bernhard W. Anderson and Katheryn Pfisterer Darr, *Understanding the Old Testament*, 4th ed. (Upper Saddle River, NJ: Prentice-Hall, 1998), note "the rhythmic style and balanced unity" of Exod 19:3b–6.

2. William Sanford Lasor, David Allan Hubbard, and Frederic William Bush, *Old Testament Survey: The Message, Form, and Background of the Old Testament*, 2nd ed. (Grand Rapids: Eerdmans, 1996), 73.

reminiscent of OT rituals in which the high priest was to enter the sanctuary—where the very presence of God was said to dwell—in order to make sacrifices for himself and the people.[3] The phrase, "as you come to him," translates an expression that is sometimes used in extrabiblical literature and in the NT to describe a worshiper approaching a deity.[4] The LXX also uses the word, in a passage that underlies Peter's statement here: "Moses said to Aaron, 'Come to the altar and sacrifice your sin offering and your burnt offering and make atonement for yourself and the people; sacrifice the offering that is for the people and make atonement for them, as the LORD has commanded.' So Aaron came to the altar and slaughtered the calf as a sin offering for himself" (Lev 9:7–8).[5]

Peter's audience is now the priesthood, and believers are to see themselves in the place of Aaron and his descendants. However, there are important differences: they are now to approach Jesus himself instead of an altar. Also, they are to offer "spiritual sacrifices" rather than slaughtered animals; and their temple is not made by human hands, such as the tabernacle or the temples in Jerusalem built under King Solomon or King Herod. Together, Peter's readers themselves constitute the temple.

Jesus, the living stone, is to be the object of worship, even though many will reject him. Peter depicts the Lord as a stone that is used to construct a building (since Peter will elaborate upon this image of Jesus as a stone in vv. 6–8, we will consider it in more detail at that point). Even though some human beings have rejected him, God has chosen him and he is "precious."[6] These two ideas go together for Peter: God's election and God's affection. Jesus is referred to as "chosen" in the same way that Peter's audience was addressed at the start of this letter (1:1) as well as later in this section (2:9). As Elliott asserts, "The election of both Jesus and believers identifies them as demarcated and dignified, elite and exalted in God's sight."[7] Yet it is important for these readers to understand that being chosen by God and being precious to him does not exempt them from suffering. The Lord Jesus is the example for them: he was chosen (1:20) and precious to God, but rejected by many and killed as a sacrificial lamb (1:19).

---

3. E.g., Lev 16:2.

4. The verb is *proserchomai* (see BDAG). The NRSV translates this participle (*proserchomenoi*) as a command, "come to him," based on the fact that it understands the verb in v. 5 *(oikodomeisthe)* to be an imperative ("let yourselves be built into"). The passage is, in essence, an invitation but concludes with a warm, nurturing tone. So while it is possible to translate them as commands, this might have the effect of giving a sterner sound than necessary.

5. A form of *proserchomai* translates "come to" in Lev 9:7 LXX and "came to" in 9:8 LXX.

6. "Precious" translates *entimos*, which is not common in the NT (only 5x), but occurs in several places in the LXX including, of course, the Isa 28:16 passage quoted by Peter here in v. 6.

7. Elliott, *1 Peter*, 411.

These worshipers are also like Jesus in being "living stones." This oxymoronic phrase evokes the image of a human temple. Jesus is the chief stone upon which Peter's listeners are built, and they are being constructed to form a temple, a "spiritual house." Peter's picture of a human temple is consistent with teaching throughout the NT where the community of God's people is seen as the replacement for the temple in Jerusalem, the locus of the Holy Spirit's presence. For example: "Don't you know that you yourselves are God's temple and that God's Spirit dwells in your midst? If anyone destroys God's temple, God will destroy that person; for God's temple is sacred, and you together are that temple" (1 Cor 3:16–17). Also, "In him the whole building is joined together and rises to become a holy temple in the Lord. And in him you too are being built together to become a dwelling in which God lives by his Spirit" (Eph 2:21–22).

Peter goes on to suggest that his audience is not only the temple but also the priesthood that performs the ministry in the temple. Just as the priests in the OT were to be holy in order to offer sacrifices (see Lev 16), the NT people of God are to be holy, separated for God's service (see our discussion of 1:13–21). The service described here is that of offering "spiritual sacrifices."

These sacrifices are qualitatively different than those found in the OT sacrificial system. Just as the house in v. 5 is "spiritual" and not material, being made of living stones and not limestone, so the sacrifices are immaterial and consist in having a heart purified by the Holy Spirit through the word of God (1:22–23). Thus the sacrifices are actions and attitudes performed by those cleansed people. Spiritual sacrifices might include those activities that Peter will address later on: the good conduct of Christian wives and husbands (3:1–7), the upright behavior of believers even in the face of abuse (3:9–16), and the discipline of controlling one's lusts (4:2–4).

Other NT teaching may give further insight into these spiritual sacrifices. The writer of Hebrews who, like Peter, uses the OT to sustain his argument, critiques the OT sacrificial system and encourages a sacrifice of praise (which Peter also mentions in 2:9), as well as other sacrificial acts of service: "Through Jesus, therefore, let us continually offer to God a sacrifice of praise—the fruit of lips that openly profess his name. And do not forget to do good and to share with others, for with such sacrifices God is pleased" (Heb 13:15–16).

The ultimate spiritual sacrifice is that of one's entire person, as the apostle Paul admonishes in Romans 12:1: "Therefore, I urge you, brothers and sisters, in view of God's mercy, to offer your bodies as a living sacrifice, holy and pleasing to God—this is your true and proper worship," a teaching that may be akin to Peter's focus at the end of this section (vv. 9–10). Elliott concludes that for Peter "the sacrifices motivated by the Spirit are best seen as encompassing the praise of God (2:9; 4:11d; 5:11) and a holy, righteous, and honorable way of life lived to the glory of God."[8]

Jesus is the Cornerstone of the Temple, Precious to Some but Rejected by Others (2:6–8)

The apostle now shifts away from the community and back to Jesus, the "stone." Peter uses three OT passages to show how Jesus can at the same time be adored by some and scorned by others. Those who find Jesus to be precious and worthy of their trust will "never be put to shame," while those who reject him will stumble and fall. Honor and shame were important values in the ancient Mediterranean world. Even though Peter's audience was subjected to shame by the broader society, God will give the believers honor, and will shame their accusers.[9]

In 2:6 Peter alludes to Isaiah 28:16 (but does not quote the LXX verbatim) and reminds us that the prophet had foretold the coming "cornerstone." Once again Peter's imagery resonates with Ephesians, where Paul shows how Jews and Gentiles were reconciled to form one community: "Consequently, you are no longer foreigners and strangers, but fellow citizens with God's people and also members of his household, built on the foundation of the apostles and prophets, with Christ Jesus himself as the chief cornerstone" (Eph 2:19–20). The Greek word for "cornerstone" (*akrogōniaios*) is used in the NT only in Ephesians 2:20 and 1 Peter 2:6, and in both it refers figuratively to Jesus. The other important term, literally translated "head of the corner" (*kephalēn gōnias*, 1 Pet 2:7; NIV: "cornerstone"), is used several times, always in citations of Psalm 118:22 (117:22 LXX) and always referring to Jesus.[10]

Those who do not believe in Jesus are like the builders who reject as worthless the stone that, ironically, turns out to be the most important. The quotation of Isaiah 8:14, found in v. 8, is meant to show that rejecting Jesus results in serious consequences.[11] The stone these unbelievers denied turns out to be the one over which they will trip. And those who stumble have only themselves to blame; they have disobeyed the word, i.e., the message of Jesus.

The "which" in the last line of v. 8 is ambiguous because its grammatical antecedent is unclear. Commentators have to answer the question: "*What has been appointed or destined by God?*" Some say that it is the *stumbling*

---

8. Ibid., 422–23.
9. See Barth L. Campbell, *Honor, Shame, and the Rhetoric of 1 Peter*, SBLDS 160 (Atlanta: Scholars Press, 1998); Green, *1 Peter*, 56; Elliott, *1 Peter*, 427.
10. The other occurrences are: Matt 21:42 // Mark 12:10 // Luke 20:17; also Acts 4:11. In this latter passage Luke notes that the quotation is uttered by none other than the apostle Peter.
11. Paul also quotes Isa 8:14 in Rom 9:33.

that has been appointed, while others say it is the *unbelief* itself. At stake is whether God has predetermined who will disobey, which is an element in one's view of divine predestination. For example, Elliott, holding the former view, asserts that Peter makes "no reference to divine predestination of nonbelievers to condemnation (and of believers to salvation). That which is 'set' or established by God is the stumbling … rather than the disobedience itself."[12] Grudem takes the other perspective, concluding, "The force of the text is to say that those who are rejecting Christ and disobeying God's word were also *destined* by God to such action."[13] For his part, Kelly is uncertain: "no more than other NT writers does [Peter] provide a clue to the solution of the baffling problems which this tension raises."[14] Given the ambiguity of the last phrase of v. 8, one should not be dogmatic about concluding from the text of 1 Peter whether God has predestined certain people to be unbelievers or alternately if God has predestined only the result of unbelief, described here as "stumbling." One pastoral insight for us is that Peter goes on to urge current unbelievers to convert, implying that they can stop rejecting Christ and come to believe (e.g., 2:12).

God's Chosen People Are Given Titles along with a Mandate to Worship (2:9–10)

Peter has indicted the obstinate ones who refuse to believe in the word of Jesus; he now praises the faithful community, using language from several places in the OT. First, he cites Exodus 19:4–6:

> "You yourselves have seen what I did to Egypt, and how I carried you on eagles' wings and brought you to myself. Now if you obey me fully and keep my covenant, then out of all nations you will be my treasured possession. Although the whole earth is mine, you will be for me a kingdom of priests and a holy nation." These are the words you are to speak to the Israelites.

This passage, with its rehearsal of God's goodness to Israel, then forms the basis for the Sinai Covenant, featuring the Ten Commandments. In Malachi 3:17 (LXX) the people of God are called his "treasured possession" (*peripoiēsis*), the same term Peter uses here. And the powerful words found in v. 10 are a clear allusion to Hosea's prophecy, which describes God's love for

---

12. Elliott, *1 Peter*, 433–34.
13. Grudem, *First Peter*, 114. Grudem then goes on to give an extended note on "election and reprobation in Scripture," dealing with topics such as universal salvation, who is to blame for the punishment of unbelievers, and how the concept of predestination is meant to be a comfort.
14. J. N. D. Kelly, *The Epistles of Peter and of Jude*, BNTC 17 (Grand Rapids: Baker, 2001), 94.

his wayward people. In Hosea 1:6–9 the prophet is told to name his children Lo-Ruhamah ("not loved" or "not pitied") and Lo-Ammi ("not my people") because of Israel's disobedience. But it is God's intention to woo his people back. In fact, Hosea 2:23 says:

> I will plant her for myself in the land;
>   I will show my love to the one I called "Not my loved one."
> I will say to those called "Not my people," "You are my people";
>   and they will say, "You are my God."

Peter appropriates the language describing the OT people of God and applies it to his audience. Like Israel of the OT, these believers are God's "chosen people," his elect ones. And as God's beloved and chosen people, they have been called to worship; they are to declare God's praises because he has called them from their former way of life characterized by darkness (see 1:14) to a new life in the light, even as they live in a hostile environment.

LIVE the Story

The Priesthood of Believers
The phrase "the priesthood of every believer," which is based on 1 Peter 2:9, is common in some Protestant circles. The idea arose from the Reformation when Martin Luther and others came to believe that Roman Catholic clergy were abusing their spiritual authority. The doctrine of the priesthood of every believer is typically taken to mean that each individual believer has the same rights and authority as ordained clergy. Martin Luther championed this perspective. In commenting on this verse, he writes, "For we must again state this word *priest* should become as common as the word *Christian*. For to be a priest belongs not to an office that is external."[15] Jobes observes that "since Luther's time, this interpretation of 1 Peter 2:5, 9 has at times been used to bring the Christian laity into sharp tension with the ordained clergy. Moreover, it is often taken to mean the individual believer has a spiritual authority equal to that of the ordained priest or minister."[16]

Certainly some ordained clergy have abused their spiritual authority, but authority is not Peter's concern in this section. Rather, he focuses on the role of the entire community, collectively, as people who are set apart for God's service and who are separate from the rest of the population with regard to moral purity.

15. Luther, *Peter and Jude*, 104 (emphasis original).
16. Jobes, *1 Peter*, 160.

Christians and Status

Despite claims that the church in America is under persecution, it is hard to find evidence that Christians are marginalized in this country. I am old enough to have witnessed the increase in Christian influence—particularly in the political arena—during the last quarter of the twentieth century. *Newsweek* magazine famously dubbed 1976, the year that President Jimmy Carter was elected, the "Year of the Evangelical." Organizations such as the Moral Majority and the Family Research Council gathered steam, while the airways were full of ministry personalities gathering personal wealth through television programs. Americans became familiar with the terms "megachurch" and "seeker-friendly" as some churches gained high profiles. Conversations about church growth were common inside as well as outside the seminaries. As a young man following my own call to ministry during this time, I well remember the many conversations about clever ways to increase church attendance. Soong-Chan Rah observed that "as popular expressions of church growth began to dominate American evangelicalism, the megachurch obsession came to the forefront. The models of ministry in the American church became the megachurch pastors, such as Rick Warren, Bill Hybels, T. D. Jakes, and Joel Osteen. With the megachurch model becoming the model of evangelical church success, an overwhelming pragmatism began to shape ministry. Literature and resources on church growth became much more practical in nature."[17]

This pragmatic approach often led to churches doing as much as they could to make themselves attractive to the broader society. Everything including musical performances, theatrical lighting, regular dramatic performances, and other creative uses of artistic expression, as well as the removal of traditional symbols such as crosses, was used to communicate that the contemporary church was nothing like the stereotyped church of the past—steeped in tradition, with music from Europe and the American frontier, and projecting mostly a somber tone (like Rev. Lovejoy of *The Simpsons* television program). In light of all the efforts to make church in America appealing, we might ask: "Is the church really rejected by Americans?" in the way that Jesus, the living stone, is rejected by humans?

In Peter's time the Christians did not fit well into their cultural context. Elliott argues that Peter's readers lived "on the margins of political and social life."[18] And these Christians stood little chance of ever becoming popular or attractive as the church "represented a place of belonging for the displaced

---

17. Soong-Chan Rah, *The Next Evangelicalism: Releasing the Church from Western Cultural Captivity* (Downers Grove, IL: InterVarsity Press, 2009), 96.
18. Elliott, *Home for the Homeless*, 83.

and the disenfranchised. It was an alternate and self-sufficient society where people could cultivate in common the values and ideals which were at variance with those of the society at large. As a sect, Christianity appealed to persons already in tension with the world."[19] From my pastoral experience, it often feels as if the church pursues those people who are most comfortable with the world's systems and does not often appeal to those who are living in tension with the world. Meanwhile, Peter's audience aroused suspicion from their unbelieving neighbors, which led to slander and scorn, as we'll see later in 1 Peter 2.

In a world where honor and shame were of tremendous significance, the Christian community found no honor among their unbelieving contemporaries and were indeed subjected to shame and ridicule. The Christians needed to understand that their status in the eyes of God mattered more than their status in the eyes of humans, hence the language of election that Peter uses. Elliott's analysis of the concept of election in 1 Peter is helpful:

> In 1 Peter specifically the stress on the divine election of Christians serves several related purposes. First, it serves to reassure these strangers and aliens in Asia Minor society of the honor and prestige which is theirs through membership in the Christian community. United, through faith, with Jesus Christ, the 'elect' of God, they have a share in the eliteness and exaltation (2:4–10; 3:21–22). God has chosen them (1:1–2) and will continue to exalt those who are humble (5:5–7).... Participation in this elect community of God is solely through faith in Jesus Christ. Status here is gained not through blood ties nor by meeting social prerequisites; it is available to all classes and races of mankind as a divine gift.[20]

Obviously the cultural context of Peter's community and that of the contemporary Western church is different, but perhaps we can find ways to remind ourselves that our status is a divine one, granted by God, and not found through attempts to appease unbelievers. The old King James Version translated the phrase "God's special possession" (in v. 9) as "peculiar people." To contemporary ears, the word "peculiar" may trigger synonyms such as "bizarre," "eccentric," and "odd." And that may be how unbelievers view the Christian community. Certainly that was the case in Peter's time. But perhaps even today we could use that old KJV word, "peculiar," and think of other synonyms to apply to ourselves, such as "curious," "exceptional," "extraordinary," "remarkable," or "mysterious." These words suggest that God's people are an intriguing group that, notwithstanding its proximity to and dealings

---

19. Ibid., 77–78.
20. Ibid., 127.

with the broader society, lives in such a good way that they invite the interest of onlookers (see 1 Pet 2:11–12).

Rejecting Jesus

Peter quotes Isaiah 28:16 and applies it to Jesus: "See, I lay a stone in Zion, a chosen and precious cornerstone, and the one who trusts in him will never be put to shame." Those who believe in the living stone (2:4) will have honor in God's eyes, no matter the status they may hold in the eyes of the world. But for the unbelievers, the stone is a barrier; in 2:8 Peter draws from a different place in Isaiah (8:14). Jesus is the reason that some people face destruction. "Stumbling" and "falling" are euphemisms for the sad spiritual state of those who reject Jesus. There is no neutral position when it comes to him: either people will follow him and be built upon the Lord as the cornerstone, or else they will fall over him and come to ruin. As Calvin said many years ago, "there is no middle way between these two; we must either build on Him, or be dashed against Him."[21]

Such a message of "no middle way" is a difficult one to accept today—and sometimes a difficult one to preach. Jobes is on target regarding these verses: "Moreover, rejection of Christ is not an amoral decision; it is itself an instance of sin. This is a message that our religiously pluralistic society today finds just as offensive as did first-century polytheistic society."[22] The notion that all of life hinges on how one responds to Jesus is offensive to many today, and we preachers run the risk of either downplaying the message or coming off as self-righteous, judgmental holy-rollers.

Peter's point is that Jesus is the touchstone, the unique point of reference. Salvation comes through belief in him through the gospel message; destruction comes upon those who disobey, or reject, the message of Jesus, which is tantamount to rejecting him. That is why we Christians must ensure that people are faced with the message of Jesus and not the particular opinions, viewpoints, or cultural habits of church people. A few decades back, my wife and I, along with our newborn first child, visited a church in a community to which we had recently moved. We knew nothing of the church other than its name and the denominational tag that went with it (we didn't know at that time that the denominational label had many different versions!). We sat in an adult Sunday school class where the teacher railed against one of the political candidates in the upcoming presidential election. We stayed around for the worship service and that same teacher was the preacher for the morning. He continued his rant against that same candidate and I didn't get a clear

---

21. Calvin, *Hebrews and 1 and 2 Peter*, 264.
22. Jobes, *1 Peter*, 154.

message from the Scriptures that day, even though I was made quite certain of the preacher's political views. I have come to believe that such things happen in all sorts of churches—both on the left as well as the right of the political spectrum. It may be possible that people are not always encountering the living stone and his message in our churches but instead are running into a subculture of American Christianity.

We may also have met those people who claim to love Jesus but are not attracted to any local church community; they remind us of the bumper sticker, "Lord, deliver me from your followers." Those people appear to be turned off by the lives of church people that are often characterized by non- (but not necessarily "anti-") biblical practices, such as using specialized vocabulary, insistence upon certain political views, and forming an insular subculture based on race, class, or some other human-generated category. People who reject the message of some churches may actually be rejecting the image projected by those churches.

Our goal is to allow our peculiarity (see the section directly above) to point to Jesus and not be a distraction. We preachers need to admit that sometimes our congregations do things and say things out of habit and cultural preference, not because of a mandate from our Lord. Church members need to learn that their lifestyles may be formed as much—and sometimes more—by American values rather than by biblical ones. When we acknowledge that that might be the case, we may help the onlookers know that we understand that the message of Christ stands on its own even though we may live it out in particular ways within our cultural context. We want people to make a decision about the person of Christ and not be confused by the idiosyncrasies of certain Christians.

Missional Identity

Michael W. Goheen discusses the missional aspect of Peter's words in 2:9–10. He says, "In this text Peter draws on three Old Testament passages to describe the unique status and missional vocation of the church."[23] (The three passages are Exod 19:3–6; Hos 2:23; Isa 43:20–21.) Furthermore:

> The terms 'royal priesthood' and 'holy nation' are taken from early in Israel's history, from the address of God to Israel at Sinai (Exod 19:3–6). These are the words God spoke to Israel right after the exodus and its liberation from Egypt, defining its role in redemptive history; these words are foundational and constitutive for Israel's' identity and very

---

23. Michael W. Goheen, *A Light to the Nations: The Missional Church and the Biblical Story* (Grand Rapids: Baker Academic, 2011), 160.

being as the people of God. Peter tells the church that now that same missional role belongs to *them*: *they* are a 'royal priesthood and a 'holy nation'.... What is especially noteworthy about Peter's words is their missional thrust. Exodus 19:3–6 had been absolutely crucial in defining Israel's missional identity. Now the church takes up that vocation to be a holy people and a priestly kingdom in the midst of and for the sake of the nations.[24]

In Exodus 19 "Israel's response to God is conceived in terms of personal commitment to God, but this is not simply a vertical relationship. Israel's commitment will immediately entail service to the neighbor, indeed the entire creation."[25] "Israel, led and taught by God, will become a light to the nations!"[26] Peter intended his use of the Exodus passage to have a missional thrust. At least one reason that God's people are chosen and beloved is so that we can be a witness to the world.

Our status as chosen and beloved people of God results in praise to God. Praise can be a form of witness. Several OT passages, particularly in the Psalms, communicate the power of praise for those outside the community of the faithful. Psalm 18:49 says, "Therefore I will praise you, LORD, among the nations; I will sing the praises of your name." The "nations" are Gentiles, those who were not part of God's covenant people. A similar exclamation is offered in Psalm 57:9: "I will praise you, Lord, among the nations; I will sing of you among the peoples." And a final example may be found in the command of Psalm 105:1: "Give praise to the LORD, proclaim his name; make known among the nations what he has done." The apostle Paul uses the OT to make a similar point when he cites Psalm 18:49:

> And, moreover, that the Gentiles might glorify God for his mercy. As it is written:
> "Therefore I will praise you among the Gentiles;
>   I will sing the praises of your name." (Rom 15:9)

As on the day of Pentecost, in Acts 2:5–12, when many people heard the followers of Jesus miraculously praising God in recognizable languages, the people of God continue to witness through praise. Practically speaking, this means that even our corporate worship, which includes giving God praise in song, testimony, and other spoken words, can have a missional function.

---

24. Ibid., 160 (emphasis original).
25. Bruce C. Birch, et al., *A Theological Introduction to the Old Testament*, 2nd ed. (Nashville: Abingdon, 2005), 128.
26. Abel Ndjerareou, "Exodus," in *Africa Bible Commentary*, ed. Tokunboh Adeyemo (Nairobi: Word Alive, 2006), 109.

The missional emphasis in Peter's teaching is based upon the status of the Christian community, a status described with OT images that emphasizes praise and holy living. Even though Peter has already issued a call to holiness (1:13–21), he will return to the topic with some specific situations in mind, as we'll see in the following section, 2:11–17.

CHAPTER 6

1 Peter 2:11–17

 ## LISTEN to the Story

[11]Dear friends, I urge you, as foreigners and exiles, to abstain from sinful desires, which wage war against your soul. [12]Live such good lives among the pagans that, though they accuse you of doing wrong, they may see your good deeds and glorify God on the day he visits us.

[13]Submit yourselves for the Lord's sake to every human authority: whether to the emperor, as the supreme authority, [14]or to governors, who are sent by him to punish those who do wrong and to commend those who do right. [15]For it is God's will that by doing good you should silence the ignorant talk of foolish people. [16]Live as free people, but do not use your freedom as a cover-up for evil; live as God's slaves. [17]Show proper respect to everyone, love the family of believers, fear God, honor the emperor.

Listening to the Text in the Story: Genesis 39:1–6; Daniel 1:1–20; 2:46–49.

Since the beginning of time, God has been forming a people to be in intimate relationship with him. The stories of Abraham, Sarah, the other Patriarchs and Matriarchs—indeed the entire saga of ancient Israel found in the OT—witness to God's desire to be in close, loving fellowship with human beings. The testimony of the New Testament is that God has removed the barrier that prevents such fellowship through the life, death, and resurrection of his Son, Jesus Christ.

As we read this passage in Peter, we should remember OT heroes of the faith who managed to honor God as well as secular authorities. In "Listening to the Text in the Story," I have listed the stories of Joseph and Daniel, two of the most prominent of those heroes. Peter wants his readers to minister in a way reminiscent of them. Although powerless, oppressed, and scattered, these Christians communicate through word and action God's mission to the world.

EXPLAIN the Story

In 2:4–10 Peter used vivid OT images of God's people and applied them to his audience. He anchored their identity as "living stones" with Jesus as the chief cornerstone in language taken from the OT. Peter also described his readers as God's elect people, using language from Exodus. Throughout the letter the apostle goes back and forth in encouraging how the Christians should live within an unbelieving society and how they should live with each other. In the passage now before us, Peter exhorts the faithful to live upright lives consistent with their identity as the elect, "peculiar" people (i.e., "God's special possession"; 2:10) while immersed in an unbelieving culture. In the next sections, 2:18–25, 3:1–7, and 3:8–12, the emphasis is on how the Christians ought to relate to one another.

1 Peter 2:11–17 echoes what we've seen in 1:13–21 as well as in 2:1–3 and also anticipates a similar admonition in 4:1–3. For Peter, what makes God's people stand out in a hostile environment is their virtuous behavior. Even though God's people may be victimized, they will also be instruments for the conversion of unbelievers. Indeed, they will be like their Lord Jesus, who suffered at the hands of the unfaithful even though he had done nothing wrong (2:21–23). Peter emphasizes the missional impact of upright behavior: Christians witness to the reality of a resurrected Savior through how they live among those who do not share their faith in Jesus.

There are two main commands in these seven verses, and they address the way God's people witness through upright behavior: first, the command for self-denial ("abstain") governs vv. 11–12, and second, the command to respect secular authorities ("submit yourselves") shapes the argument of vv. 13–17. The first section addresses the "vertical" component of the Christian life, i.e., direct accountability to God, and the second emphasizes the "horizontal" aspect of the faith, i.e., relationships with others. Such dual focus is common in biblical ethics.

Christian Witness through Self-Denial (2:11–12)

With the first two words of this section Peter becomes especially personal with his audience, calling them "dear friends," literally "beloved," *agapētoi*. As a direct address, the term is common in NT letters (e.g., Rom 1:7; 1 Cor 10:14; Phil 2:12; Heb 6:9; Jas 1:16, 19; 2 Pet 3:1; 1 John 2:7; Jude 3); yet the word is rare outside of Christian usage. The next word, *parakalō* ("to urge"), is the first time Peter writes using the first person. He urges his beloved community to be morally and ethically upright.[1] He designates unethical behavior as "sinful

---

1. *Parakalō* can range in meaning from "to comfort" or "to console" (e.g., Matt 5:4; 2 Cor 1:4), to "to urge" or "to exhort" (found in many places, such as Rom 12:1).

desires," literally, "fleshly desires." "Fleshly" signifies that which is not spiritual and is transitory, weak, and corruptible. As with the apostle Paul, the word "flesh" can sometimes depart from a strictly literal meaning (i.e., "skin") to a figurative but neutral meaning (such as 1 Pet 1:24 where physical weakness is in view) or to the moral dimension of sinful flesh. That is the case here in 2:11 (and note also 4:2).

"Desires" are often morally neutral.[2] Yet here, with the modifier "fleshly," Peter focuses on ungodly inclinations. He does not offer an elaborate list of wicked behaviors but has in mind that which was typically found among unbelievers in Greco-Roman society (see 4:3); many of those immoral behaviors would have involved twisted sexual activity.[3] These fleshly desires are depicted as a hostile army doing spiritual battle. Peter's words are akin to the instruction found in other NT passages such as Ephesians 6:12 ("For our struggle is not against flesh and blood, but against the rulers, against the authorities, against the powers of this dark world and against the spiritual forces of evil in the heavenly realms") and James 1:13–14 ("When tempted, no one should say, 'God is tempting me.' For God cannot be tempted by evil, nor does he tempt anyone; but each person is tempted when they are dragged away by their own evil desire and enticed").

Peter urges the Christian believers to "abstain from" evil desires. His advice is similar to what was given at the Jerusalem Council described in Acts 15:1–29, and he uses the same verb "abstain" (*apechō*).[4] The council's letter contained this advice to the new Gentile Christians: "You are to abstain from food sacrificed to idols, from blood, from the meat of strangled animals and from sexual immorality. You will do well to avoid these things" (Acts 15:29). Similarly, Paul the apostle admonishes the Thessalonians: "It is God's will that you should be sanctified: that you should *avoid* sexual immorality" (1 Thess 4:3) and "*reject* every kind of evil" (1 Thess 5:22), both using the verb *apechō*.

Christians should hold out against sinful desires because of their identity as "foreigners" and "exiles" (the word translated as "exiles" was introduced in Peter's opening, 1:2). The people of God, who are God's special possession

---

2. *Epithymia* means "desire" (e.g., Luke 22:15), although it is frequently translated "lust" as context dictates.

3. Moyer V. Hubbard, *Christianity in the Greco-Roman World: A Narrative Introduction* (Grand Rapids: Baker Academic, 2010) notes some egregious behavior found in Greco-Roman society, among them prostitution, pederasty, and the sexual abuse of slaves (pp. 187–93). Also, Everett Ferguson, *Backgrounds of Early Christianity*, 3rd. ed. (Grand Rapids: Eerdmans, 2003) observes, "The numerous words in the Greek language for sexual relations suggest a preoccupation with this aspect of life" (70).

4. The verb *apechō* has a range of meanings spanning from "to receive in full," "to be sufficient," and "to be distant" to "to abstain." This latter sense is found predominately when the word appears in Acts and the Epistles.

(see 2:9–10), simply cannot participate in the same sinful behaviors as the broader society. Consequently, an identifying mark of God's ownership of the Christian community is its distinction, morally, from the rest of those around them. God's people must live qualitatively different lives even while they live in close proximity with those whose values and actions are contrary to God's.

The words "foreigners" and "exiles" may have a literal, geographic significance, indicating those who have made their homes in places other than that of their ancestors; this could have happened through forced relocation or voluntary immigration.[5] In this case, the Christians are not foreigners and aliens merely in a spiritual sense, as if to say that their true home is heaven and they are foreigners on earth. As Elliott well concludes, "the issue is the suffering of believers treated as social-cultural strangers and aliens. The encouragement that our author [Peter] offers is not that the addressees are pilgrims on their way to a heavenly home, but that they have already been granted a home in the household of God."[6]

It is because of their faith in Jesus Christ that Peter's audience is foreign to those around them. "Because all Christians are citizens of God's holy nation, they are to understand themselves as resident aliens and foreigners wherever they may be residing."[7] Foreigners in Peter's time, and in our own as well, are often held at arm's length, as they are typically viewed with suspicion and have an unstable position within the dominant culture. Also, a stranger or foreigner does not know or participate in the customs of the host culture. Such was the case with Peter's audience, particularly with regard to ethics and morality (see 1:13–21). "The moral estrangement Christians experienced in their society was a consequence of not sharing society's values and customs."[8]

The corollary to abstaining from fleshly desires is having praiseworthy conduct.[9] The irony is that the Christian's good conduct—something not common among the pagans (literally "nations" or "Gentiles")—might find approval among unbelievers. It turns out that despite the decadence of ancient Greco-Roman society, some Gentiles appreciated the value of upright behavior. Stephen C. Barton writes that "the moral rigor that attracted pagans to Christianity and Judaism was not without parallel in Greco-Roman society beyond

---

5. Elliott argues at length for this view in both his commentary (*1 Peter*, 476–83) and throughout his sociological study (*Home for the Homeless*), as well as in other writings.

6. Elliott, *1 Peter*, 483. It is unlikely that Peter uses the specialized vocabulary of foreigner (*paroikos*) and alien, or stranger (*parapidēmos*), in a metaphorical way, to suggest that his audience is alienated from their heavenly homeland. Such an idea is found in Heb 11:13–16, using similar vocabulary but with a different point to make than Peter. See Achtemeier, *1 Peter*, 175.

7. Jobes, *1 Peter*, 169.

8. Ibid.

9. The adjective *kalos* (here translated as "good") describes something of exceptional quality or appearance.

the church and synagogue. It needs to be recognized more widely that many pagans converted to Christianity because they found in the Christian groups moral standards that they recognized already as profoundly important for human welfare."[10] Barton illustrates his point with the translation of an inscription dating from the late second- or early first-century BC. Its text describes the behavioral expectations of attendees at a religious meeting dedicated to a pantheon of gods in Asia Minor. Those coming into the *oikos* ("household"), a word common in the NT, included men and women, slave and free, people who were to be honest with one another and avoid the use of abortifacients "or any other thing fatal to children," and who were to be sexually moral—not engaging in adultery (the rule was applied to both men and women) or homosexual acts (these instructions were directed toward the men).[11] Apparently some among the pagans would have been attracted to aspects of Christian ethics and morality. But "many others scorned Christianity because they regarded the behavior of the Christians as reprehensible."[12] Although Peter does not state explicitly what accusations of wrongdoing were levied against the Christians, what we know from some second-century writings suggests there could have been charges such as "cannibalism, incest, and atheism."[13]

Peter does not give a full list of all that constitutes "good conduct," but we can gather from the entire letter that it included self-discipline (1:13; 4:7; 5:8), reverence for God (1:17; 2:17), compassion (3:8), humility (3:8), love for one another (1:22; 2:17; 3:8; 4:8), godly submission (2:18; 3:1; 5:5), respect for secular authorities (2:13–14, 17), nonretaliation (3:9–11), and hospitality (4:9).[14] Additionally, good conduct included the avoidance of sinful activities such as evil desires (1:14; 2:11), community-destroying attitudes (2:1), hedonistic pleasures (4:2–3), and criminal activity (4:15). Peter encourages his readers to maintain their good conduct even in the face of criticism, in the hope that some Gentiles would eventually be converted and be enabled to give glory to God. The Lord Jesus gave similar encouragement in the Sermon on the Mount: "let your light shine before others, that they may see your good deeds and glorify your Father in heaven" (Matt 5:16). The praise that Gentiles will give to God extends all the way to the day of judgment.

Peter refers to the day of judgment as literally the "day of visitation," once again borrowing from the OT, specifically Isaiah 10:3: "What will

---

10. Stephen C. Barton, "Social Setting of Early Non-Pauline Christianity," *DLNTD* 1108.
11. Ibid.
12. Ibid.
13. Achtemeier, *1 Peter*, 177.
14. For a helpful discussion concerning the relationship of good works to the suffering that Peter's readers likely faced, see Travis B. Williams, *Persecution in 1 Peter: Differentiating and Contextualizing Early Christian Suffering*, NovTSup 145 (Leiden: Brill, 2012), 258–97.

you do on the day of reckoning, when disaster comes from afar? To whom
will you run for help? Where will you leave your riches?" The NIV's "day
of reckoning" in the Isaiah passage is virtually the same expression in the
Septuagint that Peter uses here in 2:12. Although readers of the NT might
expect Peter to emphasize the return of the Lord Jesus (see 1:13), Peter
speaks of the day that *God* will visit. His language harks back to the OT
notion of the day of the Lord, a prominent theme in the prophets. This
referred not to a literal twenty-four-hour period but to a cataclysmic series
of events when God's people would be vindicated and God's enemies would
be vanquished.[15] NT writers associated the day of the Lord with the return
of Christ, as in 1 Thessalonians 5:2 ("you know very well that the day of the
Lord will come like a thief in the night"). We should understand the day of
God's visitation of which Peter writes as indistinguishable from the return
of Jesus Christ to the earth. In that time there will be those who praise God
even though they formerly opposed the Lord (see Phil 2:10–11) and accused
God's people of wrong behavior. Such a viewpoint is expressed in the Jewish
book of Wisdom:

> Then the righteous will stand with great confidence in the presence of
> those who have oppressed them and those who make light of their labors.
> When the unrighteous see them, they will be shaken with dreadful fear,
> and they will be amazed at the unexpected salvation of the righteous. They
> will speak to one another in repentance, and in anguish of spirit they will
> groan, and say, "These are persons whom we once held in derision and
> made a byword of reproach—fools that we were! We thought that their
> lives were madness and that their end was without honor." (Wis 5:1–4
> NRSV)

The missional impact of the Christians' behavior (see previous discussion
of 2:4–10) is not diminished even in the event that some unbelievers may not
see their error before the day of judgment. Still, as Joel Green stresses, "This
does not vacate this text of its evangelistic import, however, since on the last
day, both believers and unbelievers will glorify God; the question is whether
they will do so as an extension of their faith or as a contradiction of decisions
made in the present life."[16]

---

15. There are nineteen references to the day of the Lord in the OT. One that aptly illustrates the
judgmental aspect is Isa 24:21 ("In that day the LORD will punish the powers in the heavens above
and the kings on the earth below"). An example that describes the vindication of God's people is
found in Isa 28:5–6 ("In that day the LORD Almighty will be a glorious crown, a beautiful wreath
for the remnant of his people. He will be a spirit of justice to him who sits in judgment, a source of
strength to those who turn back the battle at the gate").

16. Green, *1 Peter*, 70.

Christian Witness by Respecting Secular Authorities (2:13–17)

The second command in this section is in v. 13: "submit yourselves" (*hypotagēte*). The motivation for submission to secular rulers is devotion to the Lord. Peter says that his friends are to submit voluntarily to (i.e., "obey") the governing authorities "for the Lord's sake" (v. 13). This idea is reinforced in the next few verses when Peter says that good behavior is God's will (v. 15), that a proper perspective for the Christians is to view themselves as God's slaves (v. 16), and that a fundamental attitude is to "fear God" (v. 17). The obedience that Christians have to the government is not so much an endorsement of the rulers of this age but an act of devotion to God. Peter echoes the teaching of Paul to Titus: "Remind the people to be subject to rulers and authorities, to be obedient, to be ready to do whatever is good, to slander no one, to be peaceable and considerate, and always to be gentle toward everyone" (Titus 3:1–2); and also to the church in Rome:

> Let everyone be subject to the governing authorities, for there is no authority except that which God has established. The authorities that exist have been established by God. Consequently, whoever rebels against the authority is rebelling against what God has instituted, and those who do so will bring judgment on themselves. For rulers hold no terror for those who do right, but for those who do wrong. Do you want to be free from fear of the one in authority? Then do what is right and you will be commended. For the one in authority is God's servant for your good. But if you do wrong, be afraid, for rulers do not bear the sword for no reason. They are God's servants, agents of wrath to bring punishment on the wrongdoer. Therefore, it is necessary to submit to the authorities, not only because of possible punishment but also as a matter of conscience. (Rom 13:1–5)

Both Peter and Paul show that one's devotion to God is the primary motivation for submission to human government. Elliott makes a good point, observing that "in regard to the civil realm, urging subordination is hardly a call to 'loyalty'... In this context being subordinate to the emperor and his governors is to respect his authority and show him the honor due all persons (v. 17)—nothing more and nothing less."[17] Neither Peter nor Paul openly addresses the question of unjust government; rather, they emphasize that the ideal purpose of government is to keep order in society.[18]

---

17. Elliott, *1 Peter*, 492–93.

18. Joseph A. Fitzmyer, *Romans: A New Translation with Introduction and Commentary*, AB 33 (New York: Doubleday, 1993), 655: "Paul does not envisage the possibility of either a totalitarian or a tyrannical government or one failing to cope with the just rights of individual citizens or of a

Under the emperor, local leaders ("governors") are to punish evildoers and commend, or praise, the upright (v. 14). Peter does not question the existence of the emperor as supreme authority on earth, and his support of the role of human authority shows him to be innocent of treason or any subversion. Therefore, any suffering that he or his people might face should clearly be seen as unjust in the eyes of most people. Consequently, Peter's words could shame the authorities whenever they mistreat people, because Peter has never advocated anything other than good citizenship on the part of his readers.

The community of believers must behave in such a way that any accusations of wrongdoing on their part would be unfounded. By living in such a manner, Peter's readers would be able to dismiss any negative charges against them as "the ignorant talk of foolish people" (v. 15). Without challenging anyone outright, Peter offers pastoral admonition to his people while simultaneously belittling the naysayers. Those who upbraid the Christians are spiritually uninformed and possibly even deceived. The vocabulary of "ignorance" and "foolish" is often used in the LXX as well as in the NT to describe people who do not know God or at least lack spiritual discernment. For example, the non-canonical Jewish book of Wisdom makes this observation: "For all people who were ignorant of God were foolish by nature; and they were unable from the good things that are seen to know the one who exists, nor did they recognize the artisan while paying heed to his works" (Wis 13:1 NRSV). In the NT, Paul verbally chastens the Corinthians with these words: "Come back to your senses as you ought, and stop sinning; for there are some who are ignorant of God—I say this to your shame" (1 Cor 15:34).

Although Peter is critical of the spiritually ignorant, his focus is chiefly on his readers, not on the rest of society. He admonishes his readers to live, paradoxically, as freed slaves. Once again Peter's message reverberates with Paul's writings to the Romans: "For we know that our old self was crucified with him so that the body ruled by sin might be done away with, that we should no longer be slaves to sin—because anyone who has died has been set free from sin" (Rom 6:6–7). And also, "Don't you know that when you offer yourselves to someone as obedient slaves, you are slaves of the one you obey—whether you are slaves to sin, which leads to death, or to obedience, which leads to righteousness? But thanks be to God that, though you used to be slaves to

---

minority group…. Paul is not discussing in exhaustive fashion the relation of Christians to governing authorities." Neither does Peter give an exhaustive discussion of the relationship between Christians and the government, nor does he say what to do when Christians are at odds with local Jewish authorities, as in Acts 5:29: "We must obey God rather than human beings!"

sin, you have come to obey from your heart the pattern of teaching that has now claimed your allegiance. You have been set free from sin and have become slaves to righteousness" (Rom 6:16–18).

At first glance the freedom in 2:16 might seem to contradict the acknowledgment of literal slavery in nearby v. 18. However, the freedom in v. 16 is spiritual. Peter, like Paul, sees Christian believers as free from a life of sin through submission (i.e., slavery) to God. Peter argues that Christian freedom should not be used as a veil that covers over evil activity. This idea is similar to Paul's in Galatians 5:13: "You, my brothers and sisters, were called to be free. But do not use your freedom to indulge the flesh; rather, serve one another humbly in love."

Verse 17 serves as a summary to Peter's present argument and also provides a transition to his discussion of ethical living in 2:18–3:7. The present overarching admonition is: "Show proper respect to everyone." "Everyone" includes those within the church, God, and those outside the church. Those who comprise the church, the "family of believers," must be loved. Love for others in the community is of paramount importance, as it was addressed earlier in 1:22 and will show up again in 4:8. In the next section Peter will deal with the close relationships that were typical within Greco-Roman households.

While the relationship among sisters and brothers within the community is characterized by love, God is to be feared, which suggests a reverential respect and awe rather than terror. And the emperor, as the quintessential example of those outside the community, is to be honored. By living upright lives characterized by love, honor, and respect, Christians will carry out God's will (v. 15), offering a positive testimony for the Lord before the eyes of unbelievers.

LIVE the Story

A Bit More about Hostility toward Early Christian Believers

This section, 2:11–17, is one of several passages that mention the pressure that Peter's readers were under (see 1:6; 3:13–17; 4:12–16). There are other ancient primary sources that describe some of what early Christians endured at the hands of unbelievers. Perhaps the most famous example is found in a letter from Pliny the Younger to Trajan. Trajan was the emperor of Rome, and Pliny the Younger was governor of Pontus and Bithynia from AD 111–13. Note that Pliny writes just a few years after Peter's letter and governed a region where many people in Peter's community lived (see 1 Pet 1:1). In his letter Pliny describes his practice of interrogating and persecuting Christians:

Soon accusations spread, as usually happens, because of the proceedings going on, and several incidents occurred. An anonymous document was published containing the names of many persons. Those who denied that they were or had been Christians, when they invoked the gods in words dictated by me, offered prayer with incense and wine to your image, which I had ordered to be brought for this purpose together with statues of the gods, and moreover cursed Christ—none of which those who are really Christians, it is said, can be forced to do—these I thought should be discharged. Others named by the informer declared that they were Christians, but then denied it, asserting that they had been but had ceased to be, some three years before, others many years, some as much as twenty-five years. They all worshipped your image and the statues of the gods, and cursed Christ.

They asserted, however, that the sum and substance of their fault or error had been that they were accustomed to meet on a fixed day before dawn and sing responsively a hymn to Christ as to a god, and to bind themselves by oath, not to some crime, but not to commit fraud, theft, or adultery, not falsify their trust, nor to refuse to return a trust when called upon to do so. When this was over, it was their custom to depart and to assemble again to partake of food—but ordinary and innocent food. Even this, they affirmed, they had ceased to do after my edict by which, in accordance with your instructions, I had forbidden political associations. Accordingly, I judged it all the more necessary to find out what the truth was by torturing two female slaves who were called deaconesses. But I discovered nothing else but depraved, excessive superstition.[19]

Thus, the expectation was that the emperor be worshipped along with other gods, and according to Pliny's understanding, genuine Christians could not be convinced to do such a thing. There is also a glimpse of church practice in the early years of the movement, after the death of the apostles: Christians worshiped early in the morning, venerating Christ as deity, and making verbal commitments to abstain from sin. These early worshippers also ate together regularly but were willing to cease when government pressure was upon them.

Pliny's letter affirms what Peter writes in 2:12, that some Gentiles accused Christians of doing wrong no matter how blamelessly the Christians lived.

Biblical Examples: Joseph and Daniel

The stories of Joseph (Gen 39–50) and Daniel (esp. Dan 1:1–6:28) illustrate what Peter teaches in 2:11–12. The two narratives are similar, as they recount

---

19. "Medieval Sourcebook: Pliny on the Christians," Fordham University, www.fordham.edu/halsall/source/pliny1.asp.

the events of a faithful courtier serving a foreign, pagan king.[20] We may recall their special abilities to interpret dreams and their upright behavior in the face of temptations. For example, in Genesis 39:1–20 Joseph is sexually harassed by the wife of his employer, Potiphar, but nobly resists the temptation, although at great personal cost. After being dragged into exile in Babylon, Daniel and his companions, considering the royal menu as a source of defilement (Dan 1:8), refused to indulge in the king's food. Consequently, God rewarded their act, which displayed God's faithfulness before the pagan officials (Dan 1:18–20). Joseph and Daniel may serve as inspirational examples for Christians who work in environments where their faith makes them objects of special scrutiny or even scorn. Also, Joseph and Daniel illustrate that faithful workers can give a powerful witness when they honor their irreligious supervisors.

A More Recent Example: The Civil Rights Movement in America

Peter's admonition to his community in 2:11–17 includes the idea that upright behavior—particularly when under pressure—will communicate a positive message to onlookers (vv. 12 and 15), including silencing "the ignorant talk of foolish people." The Civil Rights Movement in America illustrates Peter's point and may serve as a more contemporary example of how God's people witness to the world even when suffering.

One of the things that made the Civil Rights Movement effective was the abuse taken by innocent protestors who did not retaliate. Dr. Martin Luther King Jr., through his studies of theology and of Mohandas Gandhi, embraced and propagated the notion of nonviolent protest. And although there were some who disagreed with his approach, many look back on history and note that his philosophy drove the changes that gradually moved through the United States of America. Yes, there were violent acts on the part of blacks and whites that got the attention of society, and some of those actions prompted some fear among the white majority. But what attracted the sympathy of most white Americans was the harsh treatment that black people faced as they made their cause known. Through television especially, people across the nation saw dogs and hoses turned onto women and young people who were simply marching. News about black and white freedom riders being attacked was broadcast throughout the country. Many felt the horror of four little girls losing their lives when their church was bombed.

---

20. John J. Collins, *Daniel: A Commentary on the Book of Daniel*, Hermeneia (Minneapolis: Fortress, 1993), 39, points out not only the thematic similarity but also that of phrases and expressions. Louis F. Hartman and Alexander A. Di Lella, *The Book of Daniel*, AB 23 (Garden City: Doubleday, 1974), 55–61, call attention to a possible genre of ancient literature focused on the "successful or wise courtier" and discuss figures from within and outside of the Jewish canon, including Esther, Tobit, and Judith.

In his memoir *Walking with the Wind*, Rep. John Lewis describes how the protest in Selma, Alabama on March 7, 1965, in which he participated, was especially impactful in catching the attention of the broader society. Lewis writes:

> ABC Television cut into its Sunday night movie … with a special bulletin. News anchor Frank Reynolds came on-screen to tell viewers of a brutal clash that afternoon between state troopers and black protest marchers in Selma, Alabama. They then showed fifteen minutes of footage of the attack…. The American public had already seen so much of this sort of thing, countless images of beatings and dogs and cursing and hoses. But something about that day in Selma touched a nerve deeper than anything that had come before …. People just couldn't believe this was happening, not in America. Women and children being attacked by armed men on horseback—it was impossible to believe. But it happened. And the response from across the nation to what would go down in history as Bloody Sunday was immediate.[21]

Some of the immediate response came from the federal government, from the Justice Department as well as from President Lyndon Johnson himself. Bloody Sunday serves as an example of how the suffering of innocent people (many of whom could articulate a living faith in Jesus Christ) could shame the perpetrators of evil and "silence the ignorant talk of foolish people."

Honor Everyone

The series of commands in 2:17 start with "show proper respect [i.e., honor] to everyone." Such a command, which might seem superfluous, is important for the witness of God's people in the world. Sadly, some people have legitimate gripes against those who identify themselves as Christians while showing disrespect to others. One stark example is the Westboro Baptist Church of Topeka, Kansas, whose website at the time of this writing is www.godhatesfags.com. One hopes that most Americans are able to make a distinction between this church with its rhetoric and other churches that strive to show proper respect to everyone.

Respect for others can happen in all sorts of ways. For example, I have known of landlords whose positive experiences with Christian believers caused them to be eager to rent to more Christians. As a pastor, I can affirm that we Christians are often trustworthy people, paying our rent on time and taking care of the place where we are staying. We are often known as honest people and good neighbors. We are people eager to help others, especially when they

---

21. John Lewis and Michael D'Orso, *Walking with the Wind: A Memoir of the Movement* (San Diego: Harcourt Brace, 1999), 344–45.

are facing challenges. Christian people have long been the helpful ones in society: building hospitals, schools, and orphanages; caring for the homeless, the helpless, the sick, and the needy of all kinds. Peter points out that it is precisely this kind of behavior that will speak positively to the unbelieving society around us.

Even so, there is an area in which Christians don't have a good reputation. We are often seen as cheap, specifically by not being good tippers. I once was in a restaurant with a pastor friend of mine during a Christian conference. Some others from the conference were there, still wearing their nametags, but they didn't notice my friend and me. The waitress who served us also waited on those other conferees and began to tell us how she dreaded serving "church people." She didn't expect much of a tip from them. I know people who are eager to give servers a gospel tract, but not much of a tip. I believe we should be seen as generous people. While my experience is merely anecdotal, the topic was more scientifically examined by researchers at my alma mater, Cornell University.[22] One conclusion of the study was that "while it is statistically false to say that Christians are bad tippers, it is true that Christians are more likely to stiff their servers than people of other religious (or non-religious) bents."[23] The reputation of Christians in this particular arena even prompted a pastor to start a website called "Sundays are the Worst." Pastor Chad Roberts of Tennessee said, "The two goals we have with this are number one, that Christians would begin to realize that their attitude really matters when they go to eat… The second goal is that particularly unchurched servers would understand that not all Christians are rude, impatient, lousy tippers. That's what we want to communicate."[24]

There are, of course, countless ways besides tipping that Christians by which can honor others, but this area highlights how something that may have been considered insignificant (tipping) can carry a greater weight than first realized. Consequently, we should always be vigilant to look for ways for doing good deeds in society and showing respect to all.

Honor the Emperor

We don't have an emperor in the United States of America; nevertheless, we can find ways to live out Peter's final admonition of 2:17. American politics

---

22. Michael Lynn and Benjamin Katz, "Are Christian/Religious People Poor Tippers?," Tipping Expert, http://tippingresearch.com/uploads/ChristianTippersJASPaccepted.pdf.

23. Terry Firma, "On 'Sundays Are the Worst' Website, a Pastor Tries to Make Amends for Poor Tipping by Christians," Patheos, http://www.patheos.com/blogs/friendlyatheist/2014/03/09/on-sundays-are-the-worst-website-a-pastor-tries-to-make-amends-for-poor-tipping-by-christians/#ixzz39HEqa46g.

24. Ibid.

can trigger cynicism and downright disrespect. Recently, it seems that little gets done in Washington, DC, as the systems are gridlocked due to the inability of elected officials to work together. The headline of a May 2014 article in the Washington Post asserts: "Congressional Gridlock Has Doubled since the 1950s."[25] The general public has grown weary of politics, but we must honor our elected officials by offering them respect and refraining from the rampant negativism associated with our political system. One positive thing that our churches can do, if they are not already, is pray regularly for our elected officials. Our forebears did that and as noted above, they were in a lot worse danger from the government than we are from ours. First Clement, which may have been penned as early as the late first century, contains a prayer that may serve as encouragement even for our times:

> O Master . . . give harmony and peace both to us and to all who inhabit the earth, just as you gave it to our ancestors when they called upon you in a holy way, in faith and in truth; and allow us to be obedient to your all powerful and virtuous name, and to those who rule and lead us here on earth. You have given them, O Master, the authority to rule through your magnificent and indescribable power, that we may both recognize the glory and honor you have given them and subject ourselves to them, resisting nothing that conforms to your will. Give to them, O Lord, health, peace, harmony, and stability, so that without faltering they may administer the rule that you have given to them. (1 Clem. 60:3–61:1).[26]

---

25. Christopher Ingraham, "Congressional Gridlock Has Doubled Since the 1950s," *Washington Post*, May 28, 2014, http://www.washingtonpost.com/blogs/wonkblog/wp/2014/05/28/congressional-gridlock-has-doubled-since-the-1950s/.

26. As referenced in Vinson, Wilson, and Mills, *1 and 2 Peter, Jude*, 116. The authors quote various writings illustrating early Christian attitudes toward government.

1 Peter 2:18-25

 LISTEN to the Story

¹⁸Slaves, in reverent fear of God submit yourselves to your masters, not only to those who are good and considerate, but also to those who are harsh. ¹⁹For it is commendable if someone bears up under the pain of unjust suffering because they are conscious of God. ²⁰But how is it to your credit if you receive a beating for doing wrong and endure it? But if you suffer for doing good and you endure it, this is commendable before God. ²¹To this you were called, because Christ suffered for you, leaving you an example, that you should follow in his steps.

> ²²"He committed no sin,
> and no deceit was found in his mouth."

²³When they hurled their insults at him, he did not retaliate; when he suffered, he made no threats. Instead, he entrusted himself to him who judges justly. ²⁴"He himself bore our sins" in his body on the cross, so that we might die to sins and live for righteousness; "by his wounds you have been healed." ²⁵For "you were like sheep going astray," but now you have returned to the Shepherd and Overseer of your souls.

Listening to the Text in the Story: Deuteronomy 24:14–15, 17–18; Job 31:13–15; Ephesians 5:21–6:9; Col 3:18–4:1.

As soon as we read the opening word of this section, "slaves," we may be tempted to leave Peter's context and move forward through the ages to a time more familiar to us. We may arrive in our minds to the time of the enslavement of Africans by Europeans and those of European descent living in the colonies of the New World and later the United States of America. Or perhaps our mental journey would take us up to the present time when boys, girls, and young adults are trafficked for sexual abuse. We certainly need to discuss such matters, but first we must discern how Peter's address to slaves fits into his overall message and also to appreciate the phenomenon that slaves are addressed at all.

113

The entire community consists of "foreigners and exiles" (v. 11), who are spiritually free through enslavement to God (v. 16). However, Peter now addresses a particular group within the community—literal slaves—who, like everyone else, were in the precarious position of not fitting well into the broader culture because of their lifestyle as followers of Jesus Christ. The slaves needed to be encouraged that even in their miserable place in society, God would honor their ability to follow the example of Jesus. To behave like Jesus when life is supremely unfair is something with which contemporary Christians can identify.

⚒ EXPLAIN the Story

In 1 Peter 2:18–3:7 the apostle addresses the members of the typical Greco-Roman household. Anyone familiar with the teaching of Aristotle would recognize the traditional members of a household (*oikos*), which was the fundamental unit of the state:

> And now that it is clear what are the component parts of the state, we have first of all to discuss household management; for every state is composed of households. Household management falls into departments corresponding to the parts of which the household in its turn is composed; and the household in its perfect form consists of slaves and freemen. The investigation of everything should begin with its smallest parts, and the primary and smallest parts of the household are master and slave, husband and wife, father and children; we ought therefore to examine the proper constitution and character of each of these three relationships, I mean that of mastership, that of marriage, and thirdly the progenitive relationship. Let us then accept these three relationships that we have mentioned.[1]

Craig Keener explains that "Aristotle developed household codes to advise aristocratic men about the various ways they should rule their wives, children, and slaves."[2] The NT contains such household codes, which scholars refer to as *Haustafeln*, the most notable examples being Ephesians 5:21–6:9, Colossians 3:18–4:1, and here at 1 Peter 2:18–3:7. The NT versions of the household codes reflect attempts to use a common rhetorical form to address Christian behavior within a non-Christian society. The goal is for the believers to have the most effective witness among their neighbors without conforming to secular values and expectations.

---

1. Aristotle, *Pol.* 1.1253b, http://www.perseus.tufts.edu/hopper/text?doc=Perseus%3Atext%3A 1999.01.0058%3Abook%3D1%3Asection%3D1253b.
2. Craig S. Keener, "Family and Household," *DNTB* 353.

The household code therefore presented to the Christian community a way of reacting to both internal and external threats that would sacrifice neither missionary role nor central values. On the one hand, to the extent that the household code could be shaped to express Christian values, it could become the focus for internal cohesion through its expression of the mutual interrelationships envisioned by the Christian community. On the other hand, because it also reflected values highly prized by the potentially hostile external culture, the adoption of the household code was capable of reducing tension with Roman society by identifying shared values. Adherence to those values in the Christian's social conduct would thus be a way of avoiding discredit being brought upon the Christian community.[3]

Peter's discussion does not address children but focuses on slaves (2:18–25), wives (3:1–6), and husbands (3:7) before returning to general instructions for the entire community (starting at 3:8).[4] For Peter, the household code "presents examples of groups who, like all Christians, are vulnerable to the dominant forces of secular society but who nevertheless are to maintain appropriate Christian conduct."[5]

Slaves Must Submit to Their Masters (2:18a)

Peter addresses "household slaves" (*oiketai*) with the command to submit to their masters "in reverent fear of God."[6] Just as in 2:1, Peter uses a participle (in this case *hypotassomenoi*) with the force of a command. The participle *hypotassomenoi* comes from the verb *hypotassō* ("to submit"). In the LXX, with which Peter is familiar, words sharing the same *hypotassō* root most often describe how all things are subject to God.[7] The same attitude that the entire community should have toward God (v. 17) must be expressly evident among slaves toward their masters (*despotai*).

Literally, Peter says that submission must be "in all fear." Although the words translated as "reverent" and "of God" do not appear in the Greek text,

---

3. Achtemeier, *1 Peter*, 54; see also Jobes, *1 Peter*, 181–87. David Balch, *Let Wives Be Submissive: The Domestic Code in 1 Peter*, SBLMS 26 (Chico, CA: Scholars Press, 1981), 109, points out that "as a defense, 1 Peter encouraged the slaves and wives to play the social roles which Aristotle had outlined; this, he hoped, would shame those who were reviling their good behavior (3:16; 2:12)."

4. Kelly, *Epistles of Peter and of Jude*, 114–15, proposes that Peter's relatively lengthy section on slavery is because "a large proportion, perhaps the bulk, of his correspondents belong to this class."

5. Achtemeier, *1 Peter*, 55.

6. The more common word, *doulos*, occurs in 2:16 and is used metaphorically for all Christians in service to God. Achtemeier, *1 Peter*, 194, alleges that even though the word *oiketai* refers to household slaves, "it can also be used generically for slaves and is probably to be understood in that way here [1 Pet 2:18]."

7. See Balch, *Let Wives Be Submissive*, 97–99.

the NIV rightly understands the fear in v. 18 to be God-directed awe, as is the case in v. 17. J. Ramsey Michaels notes well that, "Although the word order could suggest that the reverence is directed toward slave masters…, the clear distinction in 2:17 between reverence toward God and respect for the emperor demands that here too *phobos* means reverence toward God and not human masters."[8]

In the "Live the Story" section below, I will discuss the fact that NT authors do not explicitly condemn the institution of slavery (Phlm 15–16 notwithstanding). However, it is a remarkable thing that slaves are even addressed at all. Given the reality that NT letters were read aloud to groups of people, every indication is that some slaves (male and female) and masters (male and female) were together in the same churches when 1 Peter was read. Regardless of the different stations in life, slaves, masters, men, and women are to be considered equal, as we see in Galatians 3:28 ("There is neither Jew nor Gentile, neither slave nor free, nor is there male and female, for you are all one in Christ Jesus"). And as Peter says, all are "God's slaves" (2:16).

The Reaction of Slaves to Unjust Suffering (2:18b–20)

Godly slaves must submit to their masters no matter how kind or how harsh the treatment from those masters might be; Peter assumes it may be severe. This call to submit to injustice will offend our American sense of right and wrong. Our culture readily celebrates the rebellious slave who refuses to bow to the harsh treatment of the master and simultaneously denigrates the "Uncle Tom" who yields to the whip and does not fight back.[9] It must be seen, however, that Peter gives absolutely no validation of harsh treatment by slave masters. His advocacy of nonretaliatory behavior is not an endorsement of slavery and is also not an indication of the weakness of slaves. Peaceful submission to even the harshest of masters is evidence of genuine Christian faith. The point is to grasp what Christlike behavior looks like in one of the most difficult situations imaginable. Slaves, though in a horrible, unenviable position, have the

---

8. Michaels, *1 Peter*, 138.

9. The title character in Harriet Beecher Stowe's *Uncle Tom's Cabin* is on the one hand taken to be a model of Christian faith in the face of suffering, but on the other hand he is viewed as a weak, passive lackey, kowtowing before the master. Indeed, the designation "Uncle Tom" is an insult, often directed by African Americans toward other African Americans who appear to be subservient or too accommodating to the dominant culture. However, it could be argued that Stowe did not intend to describe what should be appropriate *Black* (or *slave*) behavior, per se. She rather intended Tom's Christian witness to be a lesson to all people as to what constitutes virtuous behavior for all people, thereby shaming those who would not denounce the institution of slavery. In that light, Tom is to be seen as Christlike: appearing weak to those who view strength only in limited ways (e.g., military might, physical strength, societal status, etc.), but all the while possessing inner strength—that which is to be more greatly valued.

peculiar honor of serving as living examples of what Jesus is like and modeling those values that are important to God.

God is the one who is most watchful of the slaves' behavior. According to vv. 19 and 20, God will show favor to slaves who are able to endure unjust treatment. To endure, or "bear up under" (*hypopherō*), figuratively describes the tenacity needed when facing troubles, especially persecution, and occurs only three times in the NT. In 2 Timothy 3:11 the word describes Paul's response to persecutions and sufferings, and in 1 Corinthians 10:13 it describes the Christians' tolerance of whatever trial (*peirasmos*) that might overtake them. Despite its rarity in the NT, *hypopherō* appears many times outside of the NT, and Clement uses it to describe the apostle Peter's own response to trials: "There was Peter, who because of unrighteous jealousy endured not one or two but many trials, and thus having given his testimony went to his appointed place of glory" (1 Clem 5:4, Holmes). Clement's example of Peter occurs in a section where other godly heroes, including Paul, are celebrated for their endurance and also eventually given a place of "glory" (see also 1 Clem 5:6–7). Peter's own words here in vv. 19–20 have a similar theme.

In both verses Peter uses the word *charis*, translated here as "commendable," although often translated "grace," to communicate God's favor.[10] The phrase "conscious of God" functions in a similar way as "reverent fear of God" in v. 18. Although slaves may be mistreated by their masters on account of their faith in God, it is precisely that faith which God will reward. Peter is not explicit in what the reward will be, but God will somehow recognize slaves who withstand injustice, including beatings and insults (v. 23).

In v. 20 Peter rhetorically asks if there is any "credit" (*kleos*) for taking a beating for having behaved wrongly. There is no reward for those who are punished because they somehow broke their master's rules, but God is on the side of those who suffer unfairly. *Kleos* occurs only here in the entire NT, and is a word that suggests recognition, or fame.[11] God is ready to honor good behavior in some way; unjust suffering will not go unnoticed (see 1 Pet 5:10).

Joel Green points out that the idea of suffering for doing good "is thematic in 1 Peter (see the repetition of the idea in 3:17; 4:15; 5:10), but this does not mean that Peter advises his Christian audience to call for opportunities to suffer. He is not supporting the equation: the more suffering, the more

---

10. Note the usage in 2 Cor 1:15, for example: "Because I was confident of this, I wanted to visit you first so that you might benefit twice" (the last phrase is literally, "so that you may have grace—*charis*—twice").

11. Not surprisingly, Clement uses *kleos* in the section noted above to describe the apostle Paul's reward for endurance: "After he had been seven times in chains, had been driven into exile, had been stoned, and had preached in the east and in the west, he won the genuine glory for his faith" (1 Clem. 5:6, Holmes).

commendation from God."[12] Indeed, neither the Christian slave, nor anyone else, need go looking for suffering. Peter reminds us that it will find us when we live faithfully among those who do not share our faith.

The Example of Jesus (2:21–25)

Fearing God (v. 17) and being conscious of God in the face of brutal treatment (vv. 18–20) are part of a divine call on the life of Christian slaves (v. 21). The phrase at the start of v. 21, "to this you were called" points back to v. 20. Suffering is not meaningless; it serves a purpose. That purpose is found when considering the suffering of Christ. What Christ went through on earth was for others—even these slaves—and provides an example for encouragement and motivation.

Peter does not spell out here everything that Christ's suffering accomplishes for us (i.e., he does not elaborate on various aspects of salvation, such as in 1:3–10) but focuses upon the inspirational impact that suffering can have. In the same way that Christ serves as an example for Christian slaves because he endured unjust treatment, the attitude of these slaves during the heat of oppression can also be a witness to onlookers (2:15). Slaves are called to follow in the footsteps of Christ, which reminds us of the call that Peter received from Jesus when the Lord walked the earth, as in Matthew 4:19 ("'Come, follow me,' Jesus said, 'and I will send you out to fish for people'"). Slaves are honored as true disciples, similar to Peter and the other eleven who were called by Jesus himself. The notion of discipleship is present in the image of following footsteps but also in the word "example." As Joel Green observes, Peter uses "picturesque language for discipleship," employing the word *hypogrammos*, "pattern," which appears only here in the NT. Green notes that *hypogrammos* "was used otherwise of lines on a page to assist children learning to write."[13]

To reinforce that the suffering Christ is a worthy example, Peter recounts some aspects of the passion of Christ, using the OT as the foundation of his explanation. We have come to expect Peter to cite the OT as part of his argumentation, and here he quotes the LXX version of Isaiah 53:9 and alludes to other verses of Isaiah 53.[14]

Peter's application of Isaiah 53 to Jesus is reminiscent of how Philip the evangelist ministers to the Ethiopian eunuch as seen in Acts 8:26–40. In that passage the Holy Spirit moves Philip to catch up to an official who was reading a scroll of Isaiah, the passage we today know as Isaiah 53:7–8. Philip, creating an opportunity to engage in discussion with the official about the

---

12. Green, *1 Peter*, 81.
13. Ibid., 84.
14. In the order of 1 Pet 2:21–25, Peter cites or alludes to: Isa 53:9, 4, 5, 6.

passage, applies the prophetic words to Jesus: "Then Philip began with that very passage of Scripture and told him the good news about Jesus" (Acts 8:35).

Isaiah 53 is part of the prophet Isaiah's "Servant Songs" and has long been seen as a clear OT picture of the suffering of Jesus that is described in the Gospels. Jesus, Israel's Suffering Servant, received brutal treatment despite having lived a sinless life. Yet during the humiliation of betrayal, beatings, and eventual crucifixion, Jesus did not speak a word to defend himself. For example, in Matthew's depiction of events, Pilate questions Jesus, "but Jesus made no reply, not even to a single charge—to the great amazement of the governor" (Matt 27:14). Instead of retaliating, Jesus entrusted himself to the Father, described by Peter as the one who "judges justly" (2:23), a welcomed contrast to brutal human beings who often judge and act unfairly.

It is clear from 1 Peter 2:24–25 that the suffering of Jesus was redemptive for all who believe.[15] The crucified body of Jesus was the vessel that bore the sins of humanity, making it possible for the followers of Jesus to reject sinful behavior and adopt a righteous way of life (see earlier discussion of 1 Pet 1:14–15 and 2:11). The sacrifice of Jesus was vicarious; he carried our sins so that we could abandon them.[16]

The word translated "die" in v. 24 is the rare *apoginomai*, used only here in the entire NT (and absent from the LXX). Its basic meaning has to do with separation, of having no part of something. Our separation from sin is a radical one, tantamount to death. And by contrast we adopt a new way of life, one characterized by righteousness, behavior that conforms to God's character.

"By his wounds you have been healed" has often been invoked as proof that Christ's death guarantees our physical healing. What Peter actually says is that our sick *souls* are revived on account of the wounds that Jesus suffered. The physical punishment of Jesus has spiritual benefit for the faithful. The spiritual context is made clearer with the allusion to Isaiah 53:6 found in v. 25. Humanity was going astray like sheep that have no supervision, presumably headed toward destruction. But the faithful have returned to God because of the spiritually healing ministry of Jesus.

---

15. For a thoughtful discussion of Peter's Christology, see Jobes, *1 Peter*, 194–96. A more technical discussion of this passage as it relates to Peter's overall teaching of salvation may be found in Williams, *Doctrine of Salvation*, 97–117.

16. Earlier helpful studies on the nature of the atonement of Christ and his vicarious death are found in Morris, *Atonement* and J. R. W. Stott, *The Cross of Christ* (Downers Grove, IL: InterVarsity Press, 1986), 133–63. More recent studies that build upon and challenge these and other works while also examining the appropriateness of penal substitution as an accurate depiction of Christ's work on the cross include James K. Beilby, and Paul R. Eddy, eds., *The Nature of the Atonement: Four Views* (Downers Grove, IL: IVP Academic, 2008) and the massive work by Darrin W. Snyder Belousek, *Atonement, Justice, and Peace: The Message of the Cross and the Mission of the Church* (Grand Rapids: Eerdmans, 2012).

"Return" is a synonym for "repent." It was common for the OT prophets to command the people of God to "turn" or "return." The image is of the people rejecting the way of idolatry and turning back to sincere worship of YHWH.[17] By faith, Peter's audience, no longer wayward sheep, have left the way of sin in order to follow the Shepherd, also known as the Overseer of their souls. The shepherd metaphor logically fits with the image of people as sheep; it provides a welcome contrast to *the human* "master" in v. 18, where *despotēs* is etymologically related to the English "despot."

"Overseer" is a translation of *episkopos*, a word sometimes used to describe a particular role in the church community (e.g., Phil 1:1; 1 Tim 3:2; the KJV translates it as "bishop"). Generally, *episkopos* means "guardian" or "supervisor" and is related to the word translated "visit" in 2:12 (*episcopē*). Because Jesus has born our sins, healing our souls, we are able to reorient ourselves and come under the direct guardianship of the Lord himself.

LIVE the Story

The Difficulty of Dealing with Slavery

A few years ago the Quentin Tarrantino movie *Django Unchained* garnered acclaim as well as some criticism. It depicted a slave, befriended and freed by a German-American bounty hunter, who becomes a bounty hunter himself. The slave violently takes revenge on various people throughout the movie as he searches for the woman he loved who had been taken from him. Despite the far-fetched story line, or perhaps because of it, the film was quite successful, even earning a "Best Supporting Actor" Academy Award for Christoph Waltz, the actor who portrayed the German-American bounty hunter.

Not long after his win, Christoph Waltz was the guest host on the popular *Saturday Night Live* television program and starred in a skit entitled "Djesus Unchained." If you did not see it, you can probably imagine it: a postresurrection Jesus returns to mete out vengeance violently on all who were complicit in his crucifixion. It was, as we might expect, just the opposite of the image of Jesus we see in 1 Peter 2:21–24.

"Djesus Unchained" appeals to our baser instincts, as does *Django Unchained*. The year following the release of *Django Unchained* the film *42* was released, a biopic of Jackie Robinson, the first African American to play Major League Baseball. What stood out for many was Robinson's ability to

---

17. There are many passages that employ a form of the Hebrew command *shub* (e.g., Isa 31:6; Jer 3:14; Ezek 14:6; Hos 14:2), typically translated in the LXX with a form of the word *epistrephō*, the same word that Peter uses in v. 25.

endure the abuse of racist players, coaches, and fans yet still play at such a high caliber.

When I spoke with some young people familiar with *Django Unchained* as well as *42*, there was some disdain for Jackie Robinson because he didn't "fight back." Ironically, the fictional slave who fought back seemed to get more respect than the real person who bravely tackled racism. I could not help to wonder if a "Djesus Unchained" is more appealing to many than the actual Jesus. The thought of revenge—even through violence—can be gratifying.

After all, injustices such as slavery are vicious. I know that some of us cringe reading Peter's (as well as Paul's) commands to slaves, as their words offend our twenty-first century sensibilities. That is why in contemporary preaching the passages about slavery are sometimes just ignored. Jobes points out that "since slavery is not an accepted part of Western society today, modern preaching of 1 Peter 2:18–3:7 (as well as Eph 5:21–6:9 and Col 3:18–4:1) has primarily focused on the instructions addressed to wives and husbands as a type of marriage manual, obscuring its original sociopolitical message and function."[18] When the instructions to slaves are not ignored, modern preaching attempts to downplay slavery through a variety of means: (1) translating *doulos* and *oiketai* as "servants" (e.g., KJV) rather than the harsher sounding "slaves," a smoothing that might distort the actual cultural arrangement;[19] (2) emphasizing differences between Greco-Roman slavery and American slavery, which could have the effect of minimizing the cruelty of the former institution;[20] and (3) treating the master/slave relationship as analogous to the contemporary employer/employee relationship.[21] Certainly it is legitimate and necessary to point out the historical reality of slavery (or anything else)

---

18. Jobes, *1 Peter*, 183.

19. Joseph A. Fitzmyer, *The Letter to Philemon: A New Translation with Introduction and Commentary*, AB 34C (New York: Doubleday, 2000), 19–20, complains that "countless American interpreters of the NT" are reluctant to translate *doulos* as "slave."

20. It is common to read or hear that ancient slavery was "indentured servitude," a phrase offered as an attempt to downplay the demeaning reality of slavery. J. A. Harrill, "Slavery," in *DNTB* 1125, claims that "evidence proves the torture of ancient slaves to have been far more severe than the punishment sanctioned by the law in the slave society of Brazil, the most brutal of the modern world." Also, because ancient slaves could purchase their freedom, some contemporary preachers suggest that slavery was not as harsh. Yet, as Harrill also points out, "Manumission in the Roman context, however, should not be exaggerated. The vast majority of slaves and especially those in agriculture were never freed. Romans saw manumission as the regular reward for the deserving urban slaves. It suited the master's interest and reinforced the institution and ideology of slavery" (p. 1126).

21. Lynn H. Cohick, "Tyranny, Authority, Service: Leadership and Headship in the New Testament," *ExAud* 28 (2012): 83, makes this astute observation: "Given that slavery is illegal in this country, the American church has a tendency either to romanticize the slave metaphor or to quickly redefine the reality of slavery as roughly equivalent to one's employment. Both interpretive options run aground on the shoals of self-determinism. When we sentimentalize the slave metaphor, we retain in our imagination and heart a sense of 'veto power' over God's orders. When we circumscribe

in context, noting similarities and differences. But in our analysis we cannot ignore or soften the dark side of slavery. We must deal with the reality that the early church faced head-on, without the hindsight that history affords.

Despite our discomfort, Peter (and Paul) address slaves directly without explicitly denouncing the institution of slavery.[22] We cannot know for sure why the NT writers did not address the issue in a way that we might desire, but we do know that they laid the groundwork for abolition. Moyer V. Hubbard concludes:

> Slavery in the Roman world was perhaps the most pernicious and pervasive social evil facing the early church, and modern Christians are right to be concerned that slavery was not 'pinged' by the moral radar of the earliest Christians. Yet there are also clear indicators that the Christian faith as articulated by Paul and other NT writers could not coexist with the institution of slavery. Paul's vision of the church as community in which 'slave and free' were obsolete categories (Gal 3:28) was not conducive to the institution of slavery. To the extent that this vision of humanity affected the larger society—and it did—slavery would become increasingly untenable.[23]

The longer the Lord has tarried from returning bodily to earth, the more time the church in the world has to address issues of injustice. In some cases, like slavery, it took hundreds of years, but an understanding of Scripture and faith in Jesus motivated the abolitionists in Europe and America and, one hopes, continues to motivate us. What we have learned gives us fodder to combat modern-day injustices, such as sex trafficking or the exploitation of workers.

Nonretaliation and Protest

As an urban pastor, I'm frequently confronted with the reality of violence. Every summer there are shootings and stabbings near my office as well as near the homes of my church members. It is not a theoretical issue or the story of people "over there." Young people in the United States die regularly through

---

slavery as employment, we ignore the reality that slaves were owned twenty-four-seven, and they were owned sexually. They lacked the freedom to say 'no' and the right to re-locate."

22. Of course we must appreciate Paul's letter to Philemon in which Paul expects Philemon to disregard cultural expectations and take back the estranged Onesimus "no longer as a slave, but better than a slave, as a dear brother" (Phlm 16). Paul's admonition chips away at the brick wall of slavery, even if it falls short of a full denunciation.

23. Moyer V. Hubbard, *Christianity in the Greco-Roman World: A Narrative Introduction* (Grand Rapids: Baker Academic, 2010), 225. Often quoted is F. F. Bruce, *Paul, Apostle of the Heart Set Free* (Grand Rapids: Eerdmans, 1977), 401, from his discussion of Philemon: "What this letter does is to bring us into an atmosphere in which the institution [of slavery] could only wilt and die."

violence. In fact, according to a significant study, "in 2010, the second most frequent cause of death for people between the ages of 15 and 24 was homicide, and 83 percent of those homicides were committed with a gun."[24] Large numbers of our young people have resorted to violence to settle disputes. But I don't think they learned this behavior on their own. We have to help them find ways to settle disputes without violence. And for all of us, even when we are confronted with injustice, we must learn to distinguish personal retaliation from thoughtful protest.

When Peter tells us that Jesus had insults hurled at him yet did not retaliate (2:23), we are forced to consider the quality of our response to personal attacks as well as acts of injustice. What Peter advocates is based on the behavior of Jesus as seen in the Gospels: he never retaliated and at times gave no verbal response to his accusers (Matt 27:14). Jesus practiced as he taught. In the Sermon on the Mount, Jesus rejects the "tit-for-tat" view of justice. He says:

> You have heard that it was said, "Eye for eye, and tooth for tooth." But I tell you, do not resist an evil person. If anyone slaps you on the right cheek, turn to them the other cheek also. And if anyone wants to sue you and take your shirt, hand over your coat as well. If anyone forces you to go one mile, go with them two miles. Give to the one who asks you, and do not turn away from the one who wants to borrow from you. You have heard that it was said, "Love your neighbor and hate your enemy." But I tell you, love your enemies and pray for those who persecute you. (Matt 5:38–44)

The apostle Paul is consistent with the ethics of Jesus when he tells the church at Rome:

> Bless those who persecute you; bless and do not curse.... Do not repay anyone evil for evil. Be careful to do what is right in the eyes of everyone. If it is possible, as far as it depends on you, live at peace with everyone. Do not take revenge, my dear friends, but leave room for God's wrath, for it is written: "It is mine to avenge; I will repay," says the Lord. On the contrary:
> "If your enemy is hungry, feed him;
>   if he is thirsty, give him something to drink.
> In doing this, you will heap burning coals on his head.'"
> Do not be overcome by evil, but overcome evil with good.
>   (Rom 12:14, 17–21)

---

24. Chelsea Parsons and Anne Johnson, "Young Guns: How Gun Violence is Devastating the Millennial Generation," http://cdn.americanprogress.org/wp-content/uploads/2014/02/CAP-Youth-Gun-Violence-report.pdf.

One thing that marks Christians—in ancient times as well as current—is our conformity to the life of Christ. And a witness to Christ that speaks powerfully and remarkably to the broader society is the ability to show restraint and not seek vengeance, even when attacked. One relatively recent example was the kindness shown by the Amish community in Nickel Mines, Pennsylvania, after a gunman killed ten of the community's young daughters in a schoolhouse in 2006. Members of the Amish community reached out to the killer's family, showing love rather than a desire for revenge. Their nonretaliatory behavior received worldwide attention, a level of scrutiny that must have felt strange for that reclusive community.

But even though we do not retaliate in kind, there may be a place for peaceful protest. Civil rights heroine Rosa Park's act of defiance on the bus in Alabama was not retaliation for a personal attack; it was instead a protestation of an unjust policy. Peter does not prohibit Christians from speaking out against what is wrong in society. Consider the words of Peter as recorded in Acts, defending his actions with "we must obey God rather than human beings" (Acts 5:29). Indeed, the nonviolent protests led by Mohandas Gandhi, and then later those of the American Civil Rights Movement, illustrate that retaliation need not be part of a strategy for positive change. Yet, Christians have the ability to protest injustice and make prophetic calls for what is right.

The God of the Oppressed
Peter's descriptions of Jesus in 2:21–24, as well as his terms in 2:23, 25, offer encouragement for all who suffer.

Jesus is the one who is in solidarity with the sufferer. Jesus knows suffering because he also suffered. The writer of Hebrew says that he is able to sympathize with our weaknesses because he "has been tempted in every way, just as we are—yet he did not sin" (Heb 4:15). And the suffering of Jesus was altruistic; he had nothing obvious to gain. The apostle Paul declares, "God made him who had no sin to be sin for us, so that in him we might become the righteousness of God" (2 Cor 5:21). And Peter will return to the topic of Christ's vicarious suffering ("For Christ also suffered once for sins, the righteous for the unrighteous, to bring you to God"; 1 Pet 3:18a). Perhaps we can find some comfort in knowing that Jesus can relate to our suffering, no matter the situation that we might be facing. Of course I can only imagine what slaves went through or what many others face whose suffering is far greater than mine. Yet the NT pictures a savior who shared in some of the most painful aspects of being human so that we could have eternal life. He is one with whom we can relate.

God is called the one who "judges justly." A sufferer may find some peace of mind knowing that the just God is the final arbiter of what is right and wrong and will make things right in the end. But for some people there is little consolation in such words. Over the years, even in Christian circles, there has been a seeming reluctance to discuss life after death. Perhaps out of fear of the accusation of being "so heavenly minded that they're no earthly good," Christians have given a good deal of attention to earthly matters. That has often proved helpful, especially when addressing injustice. But there are matters that no human can make right. We cannot make right the tragic death of a child from cancer, for example. We cannot easily make right the inequities of life in the Western Hemisphere versus that in developing nations. For issues that have no easy or quick solution, we might do well to remember that there's more to life than what meets the eye: God has plans for humanity that transcend our lives on earth.

The NT teaches that there will be life—in physical form—even after our bodies are physically dead. And for believers, that future is awesome. The apostle Paul described it in this way to the church in Corinth: "Listen, I tell you a mystery: We will not all sleep, but we will all be changed—in a flash, in the twinkling of an eye, at the last trumpet. For the trumpet will sound, the dead will be raised imperishable, and we will be changed. For the perishable must clothe itself with the imperishable, and the mortal with immortality. When the perishable has been clothed with the imperishable, and the mortal with immortality, then the saying that is written will come true: 'Death has been swallowed up in victory'" (1 Cor 15:51–54).

But not only can saints look forward to new bodies, they can be assured that God will judge those who have caused our suffering. As Peter noted earlier, there is a day of God's visitation (2:12) and on that day his people will be vindicated and the wicked will be punished.

Jesus is also the shepherd of our souls. He calls himself "the Good Shepherd" in John 10:11, 14, and the image of God as shepherd is common in Scripture. It calls to mind care, protection, and provision, which the suffering soul finds refreshing. Certainly, the famous Psalm 23 may be the best picture we have of God as a shepherd:

> The LORD is my shepherd, I lack nothing.
>   He makes me lie down in green pastures,
> He leads me beside quiet waters,
>   he refreshes my soul.
> He guides me along the right paths
>   for his name's sake.

Even though I walk
    through the darkest valley,
I will fear no evil,
    for you are with me;
Your rod and your staff,
    they comfort me.
You prepare a table before me
    in the presence of my enemies.
You anoint my head with oil;
    my cup overflows.
Surely your goodness and love will follow me
    all the days of my life,
And I will dwell in the house of the LORD
    forever.

Finally, Peter refers to Jesus as "Overseer." As noted above, the term is often used of church officials, sometimes translated as "bishop" (e.g., 1 Tim 3:2; Titus 1:7). The basic usage is that of a guardian, someone who literally "watches over" or "oversees." People who suffer often feel isolated. Whether the suffering is physical, mental, emotional, or otherwise, it is comforting to know that one is not alone. I noted earlier, in my discussion of 1:22–2:3, that the word of God is powerful. Therefore, sharing Scripture (such as Psalm 23) may also be a soothing balm to aching souls. Furthermore, simply being present with someone who is suffering or feeling alienated, even when no words are exchanged, may represent the companionship of Jesus, who is the true shepherd and guardian.

CHAPTER 8

1 Peter 3:1-7

 LISTEN to the Story

¹Wives, in the same way submit yourselves to your own husbands so that, if any of them do not believe the word, they may be won over without words by the behavior of their wives, ²when they see the purity and reverence of your lives. ³Your beauty should not come from outward adornment, such as elaborate hairstyles and the wearing of gold jewelry or fine clothes. ⁴Rather, it should be that of your inner self, the unfading beauty of a gentle and quiet spirit, which is of great worth in God's sight. ⁵For this is the way the holy women of the past who put their hope in God used to adorn themselves. They submitted themselves to their own husbands, ⁶like Sarah, who obeyed Abraham and called him her lord. You are her daughters if you do what is right and do not give way to fear.

⁷Husbands, in the same way be considerate as you live with your wives, and treat them with respect as the weaker partner and as heirs with you of the gracious gift of life, so that nothing will hinder your prayers.

Listening to the Text in the Story: Genesis 12:10–20; 18:12; 20:1–18; Proverbs 31:10–31.

Various pressures weigh upon the people of God, threatening to derail us even as we try to pursue a way of life that conforms to Jesus's plan for us. First Peter 2 addresses several aspects of this pressure:

- The internal pressure to give in to fleshly desires (2:11–12)
- The pressure from governing authorities that would discourage real faith (2:13–17)
- The pressure on household slaves to retaliate against harsh treatment by their masters (2:18–25)

Presently, in 3:1–7 we read of pressures on married people. Peter's focus is on two particular subsets: Christian wives married to unbelieving husbands, and Christian husbands in general. Husbands and wives must adopt behaviors reflecting an upright character, which will bring marital harmony and please God.

EXPLAIN the Story

The household code continues here in 3:1–7. Peter has addressed slaves, who were members of the typical Greco-Roman household. Now the focus is upon wives and husbands. The passages are tied together by Peter's use of the adverb, "in the same way" (*homoiōs*). Christian wives and husbands, just like Christian household slaves, are to act as people who follow the example of the Lord Jesus, who endured evil treatment without retaliating.

The Witness of Christian Wives (3:1–6)

Even though 3:1 focuses on the submission of wives, throughout his letter Peter does not use the word "submit" solely—or even predominately—for women. Submission is offered as a strategic way of life for all men and women. In so doing they could glorify God and simultaneously minimize the conflict that they might face, particularly from those who were above them in the social hierarchy. Balch points out that "'Be submissive' might be viewed as the superscript of the whole code (2:13, 18; 3:1, 5; cf. 5:5). The root is used thirty-one times in the Septuagint, the strongest idea being that all things are subject to God."[1] The word *hypotassō* appears six times in 1 Peter, and all but one appearance is within a command directed to Peter's audience.[2] Two of those occurrences are part of this section (v. 1 and v. 5) and relate to wives and husbands, but it may be helpful to look at the other three occurrences as part of our analysis.

First, *hypotassō* appears in 2:13, where submission to governing authorities could possibly make life easier on the believers. Critics of the Christians, according to 2:15, may be silenced through the discipline of submission practiced by the followers of Jesus.

Second, as we noted in the previous discussion of 2:18–25, Peter urges household slaves to submit, even if their masters are harsh, as there remains the possibility that masters will behave kindly (2:18). Yet even if the masters do not relent, the slaves' submission will bring them reward as well as honor God (2:19). Those masters who have no fear of God and behave unjustly (2:19) will eventually be ashamed and will have to face the judgment of God (see 3:16; 4:3–6, 17–18; 5:5).

---

1. Balch, *Let Wives Be Submissive*, 98.
2. The one exception is found in 3:22, where the participle *hypotagentōn* ("submitting") refers to the supernatural beings—the "angels, authorities, and powers"—that are subject to the resurrected Lord Jesus.

Later, *hypotassō* is found in 5:5 to admonish younger believers to respect the leadership of their elders in the church. After all, God will honor the humility of those who submit, but he will clash with those who will not (see 5:5c).[3]

According to 3:1, wives, just like the household slaves, are to take their behavioral cues from the Lord Jesus. Peter does not suggest any natural inferiority of women to men (3:7 notwithstanding). He does not require that *all* women be submissive to *all* men: Peter's interest is the household unit, wives are to submit to their "own" (*idios*) husbands. Wives can do their part to minimize conflict by adopting a Christlike posture toward their husbands. In fact, such humble behavior may win over the non-Christian husbands.

To say that husbands "may be won over" (*kerdēthēsontai*) stresses that within evangelism there lies an element of persuasion. It is the same way the apostle Paul speaks of communicating the good news in 1 Corinthians 9:19–22:

> Though I am free and belong to no one, I have made myself a slave to everyone, to win as many as possible. To the Jews I became like a Jew, to win the Jews. To those under the law I became like one under the law (though I myself am not under the law), so as to win those under the law. To those not having the law I became like one not having the law (though I am not free from God's law but am under Christ's law), so as to win those not having the law. To the weak I became weak, to win the weak. I have become all things to all people so that by all possible means I might save some.

The same verb that Peter uses in 3:1 (*kerdainō*) is behind the five occurrences of the word "to win" in the Pauline passage. And in a similar way that Paul spells out his plan for winning both Jews and Gentiles to faith, Peter offers his own strategy: wives do not submit solely because society demands it but because it may be evangelistically effective. When evangelizing, actions oftentimes speak louder than words, especially when the evangelist has little societal clout. Jobes explains that "in Greco-Roman society it was expected that the wife would have no friends of her own and would worship the gods of her husband."[4] Furthermore, "the husband and society would perceive the wife's worship of Jesus Christ as rebellion, especially if she worshiped Christ exclusively."[5] In light of their subordinate role in society, the wives must be especially strategic.[6]

---

3. Peter's strategy of *passive* resistance will find its corollary, *active* love, in 3:8–12 and more of its justification in 3:13–4:19.

4. Jobes, *1 Peter*, 203. See also Achtemeier, *1 Peter*, 211.

5. Jobes, *1 Peter*, 203.

6. For more on the role of women in ancient Rome, see Elliott, *1 Peter*, 553–70.

When these wives submit to their husbands it could minimize backlash that might come their way. It would be typical for those with more power in society to dismiss, or even harass, those with less power, especially if they do not share the same beliefs.

The similarity of the argument of 3:1–6 and 2:12–17 is reinforced by Peter's unique vocabulary. It is only in 2:12 and 3:2 that he uses the verb *epopteuō*, a word that occurs nowhere else in the NT; its basic meaning is "to pay close attention." The related noun, *epoptēs*, occurs only once in the NT, in 2 Peter 1:16, with the sense of "eyewitness." Throughout 1 Peter, and particularly in the arguments of chapters two and three, he stresses that the Christian community is under scrutiny by those on the outside. And those on the outside can be hostile.

Yet outsiders may be won to the faith—including husbands who take note of the pure and respectful behavior of their wives. "Pure" indicates moral cleanliness and is reminiscent of Peter's call to the entire community for holiness (1:15). The wives' behavior is also to be done "with reverence," or literally, "in fear." Yet, as we noticed in the earlier discussions of 1:17 and 2:18, "fear" carries the sense of "respect" and "reverence." The question here is, "to whom is a wife's reverence to be directed, to God or to her husband?" In light of the admonition at the end of the section (v. 6), as well as Peter's other usage (1:17; 2:17, 18; 3:14, 16), this is fear that is directed toward God. Unbelieving husbands are witnessing in their wives what a life devoted to Christ might look like.

A wife's wordless witness must rely more on attractive behavior rather than on physical beauty. Despite what has often been preached in American Christianity, Peter does not condemn cosmetics, hairdressing, jewelry, or fine clothing. What he does discourage is the reliance upon such things as part of a wife's evangelistic witness to her husband, which should be based on inner beauty. Recently, it has been common to hear male pastors boasting of their "hot" wives. Such language is undignified and may even undermine efforts to understand Peter's point in this passage. Beauty cannot be only skin deep; it must be an aspect of one's character. A wife's "inner self" should consist of a "gentle and quiet spirit," which is described as having "unfading beauty" and is prized by God.[7]

A gentle spirit does not suggest timidity or any sort of weakness of disposition, nor is it quality that only women should possess. The Greek word *praüs* is typically translated as "gentle" or "meek." In Matthew 11:29 Jesus describes himself as gentle ("Take my yoke upon you and learn from me, for I am gentle

---

7. The expression "inner self" translates an idiom, *ho kryptos tēs kardias anthrōpos*, which the KJV translates literally, "the hidden man of the heart."

and humble in heart, and you will find rest for your souls"). The Lord commends this attribute in Matthew 5:5, the third of the Beatitudes ("Blessed are the meek, for they will inherit the earth"). A gentle spirit is a Christlike spirit and is therefore valuable to God.

God also desires a quiet spirit. Even though the word *hēsychios* (translated "quiet") in 3:4 occurs only one other time in the NT (1 Tim 2:2), it occurs in the LXX at Isaiah 66:2 ("'Has not my hand made all these things, and so they came into being?' declares the LORD. 'These are the ones I look on with favor: those who are humble and *contrite in spirit* (*hēsychios*), and who tremble at my word.'"). Given Peter's frequent use of the OT, he may very well have the Isaiah passage in mind when noting God's appreciation of gentleness and quietness.

With regard to clothing in the first century, "To a degree difficult to fathom today, a person *was* her clothing."[8] This fact helps us to appreciate the irony in vv. 3–4. One expects beauty to be an external quality, observed by the eye, but instead it is really an inner quality. Also, the external elements that are typically thought to bring beauty (i.e., elaborate hairstyles, gold jewelry, and fine clothes) are financially costly but are of little worth to God.[9] What God sees and values cannot be bought and is not visible to the human eye. What Peter says is reminiscent of 1 Samuel 16:7 ("The LORD does not look at the things people look at. People look at the outward appearance, but the LORD looks at the heart").

True inner beauty is described as "unfading" (*aphthartos*), a word that is sometimes translated as "imperishable" (1:23). Elliott observes that "the expression 'imperishable seed' in 1:23 suggests that the imperishable adornment mentioned here likewise is the result of a regeneration from hearing the word of the good news."[10]

As motivational examples for the wives in Peter's audience, he refers to "holy women of the past who put their hope in God." Which women Peter had in mind is not clear, but his continued reliance upon the OT to make his case is clear, as he gives the specific example of Sarah, whose faith is commended in Isaiah 51:2 ("look to Abraham, your father, and to Sarah, who gave you birth. When I called him he was only one man, and I blessed him and made him many"). Sarah held a place of respect for Jews and later for Christians as well (see Heb 11:11).[11] Her story is found in Genesis 12–23, and

---

8. Green, *1 Peter*, 98 (emphasis original).

9. Michaels, *1 Peter*, 172, does well to caution that "Peter's warnings against jewelry and extravagant dress in this passage do not necessarily mean that the women, and therefore the Christian communities in Asia Minor to which they belonged, were of the wealthy class."

10. Elliott, *1 Peter*, 565–66.

11. Achtemeier, *1 Peter*, 216, writes that Sarah was idealized for her beauty and wisdom.

in Genesis 18:12 LXX she indirectly refers to her husband Abraham as *kyrios* ("lord"): "So Sarah laughed to herself as she thought, 'After I am worn out and my lord is old, will I now have this pleasure?'" Peter probably does not have any one OT passage in mind but is likely reflecting on tradition. "In Jewish tradition Sarah is a virtuous woman, and virtuous women are understood to be obedient to their husbands."[12]

Regarding the honorific, *kyrios*, it has the meaning of "master," or "owner." Sometimes it communicates basic respect, as conveyed by the English word "sir," such as in Matthew 25:11 ("Later the others also came. 'Lord, Lord,' they said, 'open the door for us!'") and John 20:15 ("Thinking he was the gardener, she said, 'Sir, if you have carried him away, tell me where you have put him, and I will get him'"). In the case of Abraham and Sarah, Abraham held greater status in their culture and Sarah acknowledged that in how she addressed her husband. The issue is one of respect for Abraham's societal role. It may be helpful to realize that Sarah was addressed by the similar title, *kyria*, the feminine equivalent of *kyrios* (Gen 16:4, 8 LXX). Compared to her slave Hagar, Sarah was in a relatively higher position and Hagar honored Sarah by calling her *kyria*.

Sarah also showed respect to Abraham when she "obeyed" him. The point once again is that she respected Abraham's position in society. It certainly is not to suggest that husbands are always right and wives simply must do as their husbands say. Indeed, in the stories of Abraham attempting to pass off Sarah as his sister instead of his wife (Gen 12:9–20; 20:1–18), it is clear that Abraham did not do the right thing, but it is also clear that Sarah's position in society afforded her few options. Rather than view Sarah as weak, we are to see her as strong enough and faithful enough to keep peace with her husband and submit to God's plans.

Contemporary Christian wives are daughters of Sarah, which is to say that they become like her if they imitate her admirable character and do what is good, which is the very same admonition that Peter gave to the entire community in 2:15 (see also 2:14, 20; 3:10–12, 17; 4:17). These daughters of Sarah are also known for being fearless in the face of threats. The NIV's rendition of 3:6, "do not give way to fear," translates an expression that literally reads, "not fearing anything *intimidating* (*ptoēsis*)," yet another rare word. It occurs only here in the NT, but Homer's *Odyssey* uses the word to refer to "women frightened by a superior figure." It may be that Peter understands how unbelieving husbands might be intimidating to Christian wives, but one should not assume that Peter advocates women becoming voluntary victims

---

12. Jobes, *1 Peter*, 206.

of abuse; the emphasis is on the active demonstration of good behavior. Christian wives are to have faith that their conduct can win over even potentially hostile husbands.

The Witness of Christian Husbands (3:7)

Verse 7 opens with "in the same way" (*homoiōs*), which is also how 3:1 begins, and as I noted at the outset, is the word that connects 2:18–25 with 3:1–7. Christian husbands are to take their behavioral cues from Christian wives, who in turn take *their* cues from slaves. The submissive actions of the slaves follow the righteous example of the Lord Jesus who endured torturous treatment without retaliation. In each case—Jesus, slaves, wives, husbands—the emphasis is on respect, consideration, and the resisting of one's vindictive or heavy-handed urges.

A Christian husband is to be considerate toward his wife, which is to say that he must pay attention to the reality of his wife's situation. The expression, "be considerate" is literally, "according to knowledge" (*kata gnōsin*). Husbands must not be ignorant of their wives and must understand their physical capabilities as well as their equality in Christ.

With the phrase "weaker partner," Peter does not suggest that women are naturally inferior to men but notes that men are generally physically stronger than women. Jobes, while acknowledging that "the weaker vessel is primarily understood as physical weakness," makes the significant observation that "the immediate context makes it clear that the female is also weaker in the sense of social entitlement and empowerment."[13] The Greek text refers to the wives as weaker "vessels" (using the word *skeuos*). The NIV, however, chooses to use the word "partner," perhaps emphasizing the reality that Christian husbands and wives "live together" (*synoikeō*) and share a common faith.[14] Although some in the prevailing Greco-Roman culture broadened the weakness of women to include mental and moral deficiencies, Peter does not share that chauvinistic viewpoint. He is, however, warning Christian husbands against bullying their wives. In a way that counters the possibility of "fear" in v. 6, Christian husbands should not use their greater physical strength or superior position in society to take advantage of their wives.

The proper attitude for husbands toward their wives is one of respect or honor (both words are typical translations of *timē*). Interestingly, what Paul advises Christian wives to give their husbands in Ephesians 5:33, namely "respect," is essentially the same charge that Peter gives Christian husbands here.

---

13. Jobes, *1 Peter*, 209.
14. Most commentators take 3:7 to refer to Christian husbands with believing wives. Jobes, *1 Peter*, 207, however, suggests that the wife could possibly be an unbeliever.

The husband's display of honor is described using the verb *aponemō*, which occurs only here in the NT. It has the meaning "to grant that which is appropriate in a relationship" and often occurs in extrabiblical literature with the same noun, "honor" (*timē*). For example, 1 Clement 1:3 has the following: "Submitting yourselves to your leaders and *giving* to the older men among you the *honor* due them" (Holmes, emphasis added). Consequently, even if wives are physically weaker than their husbands, they are not spiritually inferior in any way.

The honor that Christian husbands are to show to their Christian wives comes from the knowledge that these wives share in the same salvation that the husbands look forward to. They too are "heirs with you of the gracious gift of life." The new birth that Peter praises God for in 1:3, as well as the inheritance that is anticipated (1:4), is provided equally to women and men. The readers are reminded that new life is a result of God's grace—a gift freely given. Perhaps there is subtle counsel that one's greater position in society or physical strength does not factor into one's status before God. Men may be physically stronger than women and may have enjoyed culturally greater prestige, but in the eyes of God women have no disadvantage.

Indeed, the way that Christian husbands treat their wives is according to spiritual values and not cultural ones: if Christian husbands do not live with their wives with appropriate knowledge of their relatively weaker physical strength along with their equal status as fellow believers in Jesus, then God may not respond to those men when they pray! Their prayers will be hindered, which is not to say that the men will be reluctant to pray but that their prayers will not have their intended consequences.

LIVE the Story

Over the course of more than thirty years of marriage, my wife, Susan, has sometimes playfully teased me by responding to various favors I've asked of her with "Yes, my lord!" Her words are meant to razz me because she knows 1 Peter 3:6 but also knows that I reject the patriarchy and sexism that many of our peers held on to. Our two adult sons and two adult daughters have been raised in a much different environment than my wife and I were, especially with regard to gender roles. And so the questions that many Christians often ponder today go something like: "Are our more progressive views regarding gender roles contrary to what the Scriptures teach?" Or, "Are we simply giving in to societal pressure and not obeying the word of God?" The answers to such questions are complex; let us try to think through Peter's teaching, at least in outline form.

A Hermeneutical Challenge: Applying the Biblical Household Codes Today

Popular—and sometimes controversial—author and blogger Rachel Held Evans wrote a substantial piece on the household codes and how we might view them today.[15] Among her observations, she notes the inconsistency of some Christians of applying the household codes in our contemporary context. For example, many will focus on the supposed role of women, and as I noted in my discussion of 1 Peter 2:18–25, will ignore the issue of slavery. "If Christians are to use these passages [household codes] to argue that a hierarchal relationship between man and woman is divinely instituted and inherently holy, then, for consistency's sake, they must also argue the same for the relationship between master and slave."[16] Even though many used the household codes to justify the enslavement of Africans by Europeans and Americans, such views are anathema in our times. But traditional views regarding the submission of women have outlasted that older understanding of slavery.

In dealing with master/slave or husband/wife relationships found in the NT household codes, it may be helpful to consider the historical function of these codes, as that may give us insight as to how we might apply them today. At the beginning of the previous section, 2:18–25, I noted the missional role that the household code played in the early church's life. I pointed out how adherence to some of society's views—albeit with Christian values always at the fore—would allow the early Christians to avoid problems with the greater society. Indeed, Balch refers to the "apologetic function of the household code in 1 Peter," noting the Christian community's precarious situation, being subjected to the suspicions of the dominant culture.[17] As part of his conclusions, Balch points out that "the [household] code has an apologetic function in the historical context; the paraenesis [ethical exhortation] is given in light of outside criticism."[18]

Our forebears struggled to live as witnesses for Christ in whatever context they found themselves. We have the same challenge in our pluralistic and postmodern context. We should consider the household codes in light of our witness in the world, which is fundamentally a question of hermeneutics. William J. Webb is among those who tackle the hermeneutical question, particularly with regard to historically difficult topics for the church: slavery, the role

---

15. Rachel Held Evans, "Submission in Context: Christ and the Greco-Roman Household Codes," *Rachel Held Evans Blog*, June 5, 2012, http://rachelheldevans.com/blog/mutuality-household -codes?buffer_share=49970.

16. Ibid.

17. Balch, *Let Wives Be Submissive*, 81–116.

18. Ibid., 109.

of women, and homosexuality. His approach is what he calls a "redemptive-movement hermeneutic," which he contrasts with a "static hermeneutic."[19] The former model "encourages movement beyond the original application of the text in the ancient world," while the latter method "understands the words of the text aside from or with minimal emphasis upon their underlying spirit and thus restricts any modern application of Scripture."[20]

With regard to slavery, as we see in 1 Peter 2:18–25, Webb asserts that, "a static hermeneutic would not condemn biblical-type slavery, if that social order were to reappear in society today."[21] However, "in addition to the complete removal of slavery, a redemptive-movement hermeneutic proposes quite a different way of applying the household codes in our modern context. A redemptive-movement hermeneutic does not argue that the Modern Christians apply the household codes through submitting to and obeying their employers. Such an application not only neglects the element of movement to a more fully realized ethic but overlooks fundamental difference between slavery and modern employee-employer relations."[22]

Regarding the role of women, as we see here in 1 Peter 3:1–6, Webb argues for a similar movement which entails a "softening of patriarchy" and movement "within Scripture to a more improved expression for gender relationships."[23] Webb goes on to make some specific observations of the texts that concern submission, which is germane to our discussion of 1 Peter 3:1–6. He concludes: "It is important to note that a wife's submission is explicitly linked to purpose statements about evangelism and Christian mission…. Today, unilateral-type submission and obedience of a wife toward her unbelieving husband, adorned by her addressing him as 'master/lord,' generally fails to fulfill the mission statements within the biblical text."[24]

Much of what Webb suggests is helpful in applying the household codes to our time. Indeed, Jobes takes a similar hermeneutical approach. Citing James E. Crouch, she notes that "the significance of a NT household code 'derives from its original situation and at the same time transcends the historically conditioned form of its exhortations,' calling believers to live out the gospel in the givenness of the historical moment into which they have been placed."[25] Consequently, "Christian men and women are called by the household codes

19. William J. Webb, *Slaves, Women and Homosexuals: Exploring the Hermeneutics of Cultural Analysis* (Downers Grove, IL: InterVarsity Press, 2001), 30–66.
20. Ibid., 30–31.
21. Ibid., 30.
22. Ibid., 37.
23. Ibid., 39.
24. Ibid., 107.
25. Jobes, *1 Peter*, 211.

to live out their marriages in a way that honors the gospel in today's social order.... Therefore, the specific expressions of appropriate submission must be culturally defined."[26]

Power and Position vis-à-vis the Household Codes

I noted earlier in my discussion of 1 Peter 2:11–17 that the Civil Rights Movement in the United States made significant progress after people within the dominant culture were motivated to make changes. One can even state as a principle, that the onus for change rests upon those who possess the greater social capital. In my response to an article by Lynn Cohick, reflecting on her discussion of the hermeneutical principle of reciprocity, I noted that "it seems more radical to challenge the member of society with greater status, but it is that challenge that is more likely to lead to social change (cf. Phlm 15–16)."[27] The biblical household codes are unique in that they address both those with power and status and at the same time those who had no such power.

Much of what Richard B. Hays writes regarding the household code in Ephesians is also applicable to 1 Peter:

The formal structure of the code is unusual in its pattern of addressing the subordinate persons in the social order (wives, children, and slaves) as moral agents who must *choose* to 'be subject.' More typically, ancient *Haustafeln* address the holders of power and instruct them on their duties toward those who are subject to them ... the household code is notable for its reciprocity. It does not merely call upon the less powerful to submit ... it equally charges the more powerful (husbands, fathers, and masters) to act with gentleness toward and concern for the those over whom they exercise authority.[28]

This reciprocity of which Cohick and Hays write must be stressed when we go to apply the biblical household codes to our times. Those in the more vulnerable position should receive greater respect than they would normally otherwise receive outside the church, and those in the more powerful position are given a responsibility to behave more justly. There are all sorts of implications for our modern context. As one example, we cannot do as some have attempted and justify domestic violence using this passage, berating the battered wife (*She must have done something to provoke her husband!*), while not holding the husband to account for his actions (*After all, he is the head of*

---

26. Ibid., 211–12.
27. Dennis R. Edwards, "Response to Cohick," *ExAud* 28 (2012): 93.
28. Richard B. Hays, *The Moral Vision of the New Testament: Community, Cross, New Creation* (San Francisco: HarperOne, 1996), 64–65.

the house!). If we want to claim that we defer to the Bible's household codes, then we must apply them with consistency. We should also take into account Peter's context: Christian wives, from their lowly position in society, had the honorable task of trying to win their unbelieving husbands to Christ; meanwhile, Christian husbands had to forfeit heavy-handedness and honor their wives as sisters in Christ.

CHAPTER 9

1 Peter 3:8–12

 LISTEN to the Story

⁸Finally, all of you, be like-minded, be sympathetic, love one another, be compassionate and humble. ⁹Do not repay evil with evil or insult with insult. On the contrary, repay evil with blessing, because to this you were called so that you may inherit a blessing. ¹⁰For,

"Whoever would love life
  and see good days
must keep their tongue from evil
  and their lips from deceitful speech.
¹¹They must turn from evil and do good;
  they must seek peace and pursue it.
¹²For the eyes of the Lord are on the righteous
  and his ears are attentive to their prayer,
but the face of the Lord is against those who do evil."

Listening to the Text in the Story: Psalm 34:12–16; Matthew 5:1–13, 38–42; Romans 12:14–21.

The sideways glances, insults, and dismissive attitudes that Christians sometimes face in our North American context are far from what might be called persecution, but they can still hurt. The way that we respond to those who demean us says much about the nature of our faith. When we respond well, we display the character of our Lord Jesus himself. Responding well means taking a "high road" when bullied and not retaliating in kind. Peter echoes the OT, which proves that God will bless those who pursue peace and refrain from vengeance. Such virtuous action is of course best modeled in the life and teachings of Jesus, particularly in his Sermon on the Mount.

But Peter would not have us think that we face opposition alone. Since we are part of a community, we are called on to do what it takes to enhance our unity as fellow disciples. And by developing the character of Christ, we will be better equipped to face opposition—and to do so with sisters and brothers equally committed to the same peacemaking goals.

We will also remember those sisters and brothers in faraway places who face actual violence and cruel opposition and who have little experience of the freedom we in the United States have to share in the life of Christian faith. Peter's words are true for them as well, and if they are difficult for us, imagine how hard it must be for them and, for that matter, for Peter's original audience. It is right and fitting for us to pause and pray for our sisters and brothers near and far and to honor the memories of those who have gone on before us.

EXPLAIN the Story

Peter begins to wrap up his exhortations regarding how Christians should behave within a hostile environment. He has discussed personal ethics (2:11–17), then the role of household members: slaves (2:18–25), wives (3:1–6), and husbands (3:7). Peter now returns to addressing the entire community ("all of you," v. 8) with some pointed words in order to encourage unity and peacemaking in the face of persecution.

Peter's readers are vulnerable to the verbal and physical attacks of a society that hates Christians. Although some non-Christians will be appreciative of the fact that believers do not retaliate, others will not, and this latter group of haters will make life miserable for the faithful. In order for the Christian community to thrive it must grow in unity with one another, have a strategy for dealing with offensive people, and continue to look to Jesus for motivation.

Attitudes That Foster Unity (3:8)

Verse 8 focuses on those characteristics that promote unity. What appears in the NIV as a command ("*be* like-minded," etc.) is in the original a string of adjectives that describe healthy Christian community: like-minded (*homophrōn*), sympathetic (*sympathēs*), mutually loving (*philadelphos*), compassionate (*eusplanchnos*), and humble (*tapeinophrōn*).

Once again Peter uses words that are rare within the NT. His vocabulary is similar to Paul's in Philippians, but the adjectives *homophrōn* and *sympathēs* occur only here. The former term describes unity of spirit or harmony and literally means "same-thinking." Paul's letter to the Philippians stresses similar themes: "then make my joy complete by being like-minded, having the same love, being one in spirit and of one mind" (Phil 2:2). When the Christian community is united, it is better equipped to stand up against opposition, a point Paul also makes: "Whatever happens, conduct yourselves in a manner worthy of the gospel of Christ. Then, whether I come and see you or only hear about you in my absence, I will know that you stand firm in the one Spirit, striving together as one for the faith of the gospel without being frightened in any way by those who oppose you" (Phil 1:27–28a). As the Philippians stand together in unity, they are able to face their challengers without fear; Peter's community must do the same.

The next trait is *sympathēs*, which describes an understanding disposition or the ability to put oneself in another's place. In 4 Maccabees the writer states that mothers have a higher degree of natural sympathy for their children than do the fathers since the mothers have given them birth: "In what manner might I express the emotions of parents who love their children? We impress upon the character of a small child a wondrous likeness both of mind and of form. Especially is this true of mothers, who because of their birth pangs have a deeper sympathy (*sympathēs*) toward their offspring than do the fathers" (4 Macc 15:4 NRSV). Peter urges that every member of the Christian community have that kind of affection. This sympathy is related to the next term, *philadelphoi*.

The adjective *philadelphoi*, which literally means, "loving one's sister/ brother," echoes the description of purified, obedient believers, found in 1:22 (see the discussion there).[1] Once again, 4 Maccabees may give us some background in its description of the noble Jewish mother and her seven sons:

> You are not ignorant of the affection of family ties, which the divine and all-wise Providence has bequeathed through the fathers to their descendants and which was implanted in the mother's womb. There each of the brothers spent the same length of time and was shaped during the same period of time; and growing from the same blood and through the same life, they were brought to the light of day. When they were born after an equal time of gestation, they drank milk from the same fountains. From such embraces brotherly-loving souls are nourished; and they grow stronger from this common nurture and daily companionship, and from both general education and our discipline in the law of God.
>
> Therefore, when sympathy and brotherly affection had been so established, the brothers were the more sympathetic to one another. Since they had been educated by the same law and trained in the same virtues and brought up in right living, they loved one another all the more. (4 Macc 13:19–24 NRSV)

Just as blood-related siblings might develop an indissoluble bond that gets nurtured over time, Christians are to grow in their emotional connection for one another, one based upon their common faith.

---

1. The adjective *philadelphos* occurs only here in the NT; in a few other places one finds the cognate noun *philadelphia*, brotherly love (Rom 12:10; 1 Thess 4:9; Heb 13:1; 2 Pet 1:7).

Since emotional reactions, such as those described here in 3:8, are often accompanied by physical sensations, "gut feelings," we can understand the Greek idiom that uses "intestines" (*splanchnon*) to denote feelings of great affection (here *eusplanchnos*).[2] These are the kinds of feelings that the Lord Jesus had when he viewed the needy crowds (e.g., Matt 9:36; 14:14; 15:32); so too did the Good Samaritan who happened upon a victim of a violent assault (Luke 10:33). True affection is more than intellectual; it is felt. Those feelings of affection are part of what makes up compassion, and compassion results in kindly actions, and kindly actions will help foster unity.

The final adjective, *tapeinophrōn*, occurs only here in the NT but is one of a family of words that speak of humility (see 1 Pet 5:5). This is voluntary submission, and it stands in contrast to boastfulness or self-aggrandizement. "In the highly competitive and stratified world of Greco-Roman antiquity, only those of degraded social status were 'humble,' and humility was regarded as a sign of weakness and shame, an inability to defend one's honor."[3] Humility was not a virtue in ancient Greco-Roman society, but it is trait that God commends. Such is the case in Proverbs 29:23 ("Pride brings a person low, but the lowly in spirit gain honor"), as well as in subsequent Christian literature, e.g., 1 Clement 21:8 ("Let our children receive the instruction that is in Christ: let them learn how strong humility is before God, what pure love is able to accomplish before God, how the fear of him is good and great and saves all those who live in it in holiness with a pure mind," Holmes).

The great Old Testament hero Moses is described as "more humble than anyone else on the face of the earth" (Num 12:3) at a time when he faces criticism and his role as prophet is being called into question. The Lord Jesus himself is humble. For example, in the moving invitation that the Lord gives in Matthew 11:28–30, he describes himself as "gentle and humble in heart." And returning to Philippians, a letter that encourages unity, the Christ Hymn (called *Carmen Christi*) found in chapter 2 offers Jesus as a model for the Christian community, the same Lord who "humbled himself" (Phil 2:8).

The constellation of adjectives Peter employs in 3:8 draws us inward to examine the types of character traits that promote unity within the Christian community. But Peter also urges right behavior toward those outside of the church, even to those who are downright hostile. His words are countercultural, urging nonretaliation in the face of insult and injury.

---

2. Other Greek words include the noun *eusplanchnia* ("benevolence") and the verb *splanchnizomai* ("to have pity").

3. Elliott, *1 Peter*, 605.

Behaviors That Counter Hateful Attacks (3:9–12)

The five adjectives in v. 8 are qualities that foster unity, and the actions of v. 9 comprise some of the difficult choices that contribute to peacemaking. Not only are Christians admonished to be nonretaliatory when facing threats; they must go further than that! They must repay evil deeds and insults with a blessing, an act that "calls down God's grace," a translation of the Greek *eulogia*, "blessing." In fact, the language of v. 9 is reminiscent of the Sermon on the Mount. Matthew 5:38–42 reads: "You have heard that it was said, 'Eye for eye, and tooth for tooth.' But I tell you, do not resist an evil person. If anyone slaps you on the right cheek, turn to them the other cheek also. And if anyone wants to sue you and take your shirt, hand over your coat as well. If anyone forces you to go one mile, go with them two miles. Give to the one who asks you, and do not turn away from the one who wants to borrow from you."

In a Jewish context, the Torah allowed for a response in kind when one is violated, i.e., a retaliatory act that is consistent with the infraction, hence the allusion that Jesus makes to Exodus 21:24, Leviticus 24:20, and Deuteronomy 19:21. Old Testament justice attempted to ensure that the offender and the one offended suffer equivalent losses.[4] However, Jesus demanded more than equalizing; he required grace, a favor that the offender does not deserve. The disciple must go further toward making peace, giving when asked and even offering more than what was required. These teachings of Jesus are echoed throughout the NT. For example, in Romans Paul writes: "Bless those who persecute you; bless and do not curse. Rejoice with those who rejoice; mourn with those who mourn. Live in harmony with one another. Do not be proud, but be willing to associate with people of low position. Do not be conceited. Do not repay anyone evil for evil. Be careful to do what is right in the eyes of everyone. If it is possible, as far as it depends on you, live at peace with everyone" (Rom 12:14–18).[5] Peter says that such gracious action is part of the "calling" that Christians have received.

As noted earlier, "calling" is important for Peter, a theme that begins with his opening designation of his audience as "elect" (1:1) and runs throughout the letter.[6] Peter has also said that his readers are called to be holy (1:15),

---

4. The "eye for an eye/tooth for a tooth" form of justice is known as the *lex talionis*. According to *The Jewish Study Bible: Jewish Publication Society Tanakh Translation*, ed. Adele Berlin and Marc Zvi Brettler (Oxford: Oxford University Press, 2004), 154, it is a "measure-for-measure punishment by which the law strives to make punishment for death or injury fit the crime perfectly." The idea was to avoid vengeance so that the punishment "may not exceed the original injury."

5. These verses from Romans also contain similar ideas as found in 1 Pet 3:8. In fact, Michaels, *1 Peter*, 174, juxtaposes 1 Pet 3:8–9 and Rom 12:9–18 in columns, emphasizing parallel ideas and vocabulary.

6. See the earlier discussions of 1:1–2 and 1:15.

called out of darkness (2:9), and even called to suffer unjustly (2:20–21). Here in 3:9, Peter's people are "called" to respond to evil with a blessing. These heirs of God will receive an inheritance by virtue of their new birth (see 1:3–4), and there is an inheritance destined for those who practice peacemaking; the two themes are interconnected.

At the end of v. 9 Peter points out that the reaction of believers, offering blessing instead of cursing, will result in them inheriting a blessing from God. The language of inheritance connected to nonretaliation is also reminiscent of the Sermon on the Mount, particularly the beatitude in Matthew 5:9 ("Blessed are the peacemakers, for they will be called children of God").

The apostle does not describe what kind of "blessing" Christians give; it most likely is a spoken one. The basic meaning of "blessing" (*eulogia*) is speaking a favorable word or offering praise.[7] In 3:10 Peter expands on what that means by citing Psalm 34:12–16 as proof that there is a blessing for those who bless others.[8] God will give favorable treatment to those who refrain from evil—especially evil speech—and who show that they are peacemakers by their good deeds.

God's blessing means an enhanced quality of life for those who bless others (v. 10). This is a remarkable promise for people who are facing persecution (and one cannot help but to think of what these words might mean for those obedient slaves of 1 Pet 2:18–21). It is a life under God's benevolent eye and his attentiveness to his people's prayers (3:12). This does not mean that his people will not suffer. Quite the contrary: Jesus made the offer of an "abundant" life (John 10:10) along with the acknowledgment that his disciples will suffer (e.g., Matt 5:11–12); Peter is in agreement. And as for the evildoers, they are destined for judgment (see 1 Pet 2:8).

LIVE the Story

I suspect every human being, let alone every Christian, would appreciate being part of a community that possesses the values Peter recommends in 3:8. Our society has a high need for genuine connection. The way of Jesus offers the potential for authentic community here and now; we do not have

---

7. The meaning of words is not determined by etymology but by usage in a given context. Yet even so it is interesting that our English word eulogy, which is typically used for the speech delivered at a funeral, is derived from *eulogia* and etymologically is formed from a prefix meaning "good" (*eu*) and the verb "to speak" (*legō*).

8. Jobes, *1 Peter*, 220–23, offers a detailed analysis of Peter's use of Psalm 34 (Psalm 33 in the LXX). Jobes points out, "Peter's extensive allusions to that psalm indicate that it is an important scriptural foundation for his thinking about Christian ethics" (p. 220).

to wait for Christ's return to experience a foretaste of ultimate connectedness with God and others.

Missional communities experience a growing sense of connection to God and to each other. Such communities attract the interest of the isolated, alienated, and unloved. God's transformational love can touch such people when they interact with those who are working to build genuine Christian community.

Yet arguably the most countercultural aspect of genuine community is a willingness to pursue peace in the face of insult or assault. Such behavior is so rare that it seems that we can only imagine what such peacemaking might look like today. I can give a positive example: I have had the opportunity to minister in Rwanda on more than one occasion and have gotten acquainted with several Rwandese Christians. The memories of the 1994 genocide are still fresh, yet many Christians there are actively pursuing peace. Even though colonialism bears much of the responsibility for the tensions that existed in Rwanda, the Christians are still willing to work with believers from outside of their country. The tribalism that was exacerbated by colonialism is now practically nonexistent, as Christians are key in promoting a newfound spirit of unity in the country.

The Need for Genuine Community

Despite the advent of Facebook and Twitter and other social media, people in North America do not appear to be well-connected. In the church that I serve as senior pastor, one of our toughest challenges is helping people to connect with others; I know other pastors who report the same struggle. Nor do I think that our experiences are merely anecdotal: there is evidence that in the greater society, people find it difficult to make connections, even when they have the desire to do so.

In 2000, Robert D. Putnam wrote *Bowling Alone: The Collapse and Revival of American Community*.[9] He followed up three years later with *Better Together: Restoring the American Community*, which aims to highlight examples of creative efforts to build or restore community.[10] Putnam wrote before the idea of "virtual community" was fully developed, but his analyses are still relevant.

The trend over recent decades, Putnam argues, has been toward a reduction in community engagement. Fewer people have chosen to become connected to others, not just through church, but in most segments of society.[11]

---

9. New York: Simon and Schuster, 2000.

10. Coauthored with Lewis M. Feldstein (New York: Simon and Schuster, 2003).

11. David T. Olson, *The American Church in Crisis* (Grand Rapids: Zondervan, 2008), 16, concludes, "The church in America is not booming. It is in a crisis. On any given Sunday, the vast majority of Americans are absent from church. Even more troublesome, as the American population continues to grow, the church falls further and further behind. If trends continue, by 2050 the percentage of Americans attending church will be half the 1990 figure."

"Civic disengagement appears to be an equal opportunity affliction. The sharp, steady declines in club meetings, visits with friends, committee service, church attendance, philanthropic generosity, card games, and electoral turnout have hit virtually all sectors of American society over the last several decades and in roughly equal measures."[12]

In the absence of civic engagement or genuine community, some neighborhoods fall prey to entropy (i.e., a gradual decline toward chaos), spiraling downwards with a host of problems. Peter Block offers a description of healthy community.[13] He writes, "To improve the common measures of community health—economy, education, health, safety, the environment—we need to create a community where each citizen has the experience of being connected to those around them and knows that their safety and success are dependent on the success of all others."[14] Even though his work focuses on "secular" community, his observations are in sync with what Christians should desire.

People feel the need to make genuine connections. For example, there are atheist groups who meet on Sunday to sing together and commit themselves to doing good deeds. People are looking for connections that the church has the ability to provide. I argue elsewhere that through small groups that practice genuine community, people will discover new connections that can lead to the transformation of families and even neighborhoods.[15]

The Power of Genuine Community

Churches ought to strive to live the virtues of 1 Peter 3:8: being like-minded, sympathetic, loving, compassionate, and humble. In so doing we would not only help one another to live more abundantly (see John 10:10), we would also be a powerful witness to those who do not have faith in Jesus. Stanley Hauerwas admonishes churches that they must, "above all, be a people of virtue—not simply any virtue, but the virtues necessary for remembering and telling the story of a crucified savior. They must be capable of being peaceable among themselves and with the world, so that the world sees what it means to hope for God's kingdom…. The church must learn time and time again that its task is not to *make* the world the kingdom, but to be faithful to the kingdom by showing to the world what it means to be a community of peace."[16]

---

12. Putnam, *Bowling Alone*, 185.

13. Peter Block, *Community: The Structure of Belonging* (Cleveland: Berrett-Koehler, 2008).

14. Block, *Community*, 5.

15. Dennis R. Edwards, "Good Citizenship: A Study of Philippians 1:27 and its Implications for Contemporary Urban Ministry," *ExAud* 29 (2013): 74–93.

16. Stanley Hauerwas, *The Peaceable Kingdom: A Primer in Christian Ethics* (Notre Dame: University of Notre Dame Press, 1983), 103, emphasis original.

Erland Waltner traces the idea of a peaceable community through the entire letter of 1 Peter.[17] As he sees it, the Petrine community is a "witnessing community":

> Out of their living hope, grounded on God's act of raising Jesus, not only salvation but nonretaliating, peacemaking love has become possible. Their mission begins with becoming a community of hope in the midst of a hostile world, a community of forgiving love in a violent world, and a community of witness and service in the midst of those who misunderstand, misinterpret, and mistreat them. They are not to remain silent or inactive in such a world but are to speak, to proclaim, to confront evil with truth and love, even as they turn from it. They live and witness in a spirit and manner that is congruent with the nonretaliating, peacemaking love of Jesus Christ.[18]

Such authentic Christian community can seem illusive. Sometimes the Amish are held up as the standard, in particular the story from 2006 of how the Amish community in Pennsylvania treated the family of a man who shot ten Amish girls before killing himself. It is well documented how Amish people invited the widow of the shooter to attend the funerals for the girls who were killed, raised money for that widow, and even attended the funeral of the shooter. Such nonretaliatory behavior prompted one writer to ask, "What if the Amish were in charge of the war on terror?" She also muses, "Maybe we should ask them to take over the Department of Homeland Security."[19]

We need not be Amish to conform to what Peter asks of us, but we certainly do need to work at it. Christena Cleveland, a Christian social psychologist, identifies the forces that keep Christians from experiencing the kind of community that the NT describe.[20] She focuses largely on cultural factors but comes to emphasize that Christians must view themselves as part of a family:

> The act of adopting a common identity that supersedes all other identities is a daunting, even painful one. However, research shows that it is the key to true unity. It is consistent with Jesus' teachings that the household of God is to take precedence over all other households.... To embrace our identities in this new, common family, we must engage in the difficult

17. Erland Waltner, "Reign of God, Mission, and Peace in 1 Peter," in *Beautiful Upon the Mountains: Biblical Essays on Mission, Peace, and the Reign of God*, ed. Mary H. Schertz and Ivan Friesen (Eugene, OR: Wipf & Stock, 2008), 235–48.

18. Ibid., 247.

19. Shane Claiborne and Chris Haw, *Jesus for President: Politics for Ordinary Radicals* (Grand Rapids: Zondervan, 2008), 275–76.

20. Christena Cleveland, *Disunity in Christ: Uncovering the Hidden Forces That Keep Us Apart* (Downers Grove, IL: InterVarsity Press, 2013).

process of lessening our grip on the identities that we have idolized and clung to for far too long. In many ways this process will jar our souls, wreaking havoc on the satisfyingly homogeneous existence in which we were rooted. At first it will feel painfully unnatural because we have lived outside of our true identities for so long that the truth seems wrong.[21]

Again, theologian Miroslav Volf, reflecting on the Lord's Supper, challenges us to seek radical transformation among Christian communities. He asserts, "We would most profoundly misunderstand the Eucharist, however, if we thought of it only as a sacrament of God's embrace of which we are simply the fortunate beneficiaries…. Having been embraced by God, we must make space for others in ourselves and invite them in—even our enemies."[22]

Mary Johnson keeps a low profile, but she has earned the respect of many; Mary is from my neighborhood here in Minneapolis. Her story is a remarkable one. Her only son was killed as the result of gun violence. Yet rather than seek revenge, Johnson started a group called "From Death to Life" for women who have suffered the loss of loved ones killed through violence. But even more radical was how she reached out to the very man who killed her son: "From Death To Life was founded by Mary Johnson-Roy in 2005, shortly before she came to forgive Oshea Israel, the young man who took her only son's life twelve years earlier. She now claims Oshea as her 'spiritual son' and together they share their inspiring story of healing and reconciliation in the community."[23] When a woman in my congregation lost her son to gun violence, I helped to connect her to Mary Johnson, and it proved to be of tremendous help. I've met Mary Johnson and Oshea Israel and know that they both confess faith in the Lord Jesus Christ. They are examples of the power of forgiveness, a virtue that is vital for healthy Christian community.

21. Ibid., 190.
22. Miroslav Volf, *Exclusion and Embrace: A Theological Exploration of Identity, Otherness, and Reconciliation* (Nashville: Abingdon, 1996), 129.
23. Oshea Israel and Mary Johnson, "Our Mission," From Death to Life, http://www.fromdeathtolife.us/home.html.

CHAPTER 10

1 Peter 3:13-17

 LISTEN to the Story

> [13]Who is going to harm you if you are eager to do good? [14]But even if you should suffer for what is right, you are blessed. "Do not fear their threats; do not be frightened." [15]But in your hearts revere Christ as Lord. Always be prepared to give an answer to everyone who asks you to give the reason for the hope that you have. But do this with gentleness and respect, [16]keeping a clear conscience, so that those who speak maliciously against your good behavior in Christ may be ashamed of their slander. [17]For it is better, if it is God's will, to suffer for doing good than for doing evil.

Listening to the Text in the Story: Proverbs 25:22; Isaiah 8:12–13; Matthew 5:10–12.

The world puts us Christians on the defensive with questions about what we believe. We in the North American church may not face outright persecution, but we see a range of opposition, from snide remarks all the way to organized actions to suppress Christian witness. This pushback sometimes comes as a surprise, in part because Christians have long enjoyed cultural hegemony, a dominant influence in the culture. However, in our pluralistic society Christian views are not always in the mainstream. To complicate matters, we Christians are not united in our viewpoints, which leads to arguing with one another in public forums. Furthermore, some of us adopt an arrogant tone with unbelievers in a way that is unbecoming of those who claim to be followers of Jesus.

Consequently, we Christians need to be eager to be agents for good, and to be prepared at all times to represent Jesus with respect toward others. If we do so, at least some of our accusers will be brought up short by the voice of their conscience.

EXPLAIN the Story

Christians must remain steadfast, no matter how much abuse they take. But they must also be able to make a case for the validity of their faith through their deeds and their speech. By doing what is good in the world, they have an opportunity to silence their critics. And when questioned, they are to explain respectfully why they follow Jesus. It is in the next section that Peter offers motivation for these believers to maintain their faithful outlook no matter what criticism and abuse they may face; that motivation is the person of Jesus himself.

Do Not Fear Accusers, But Revere Christ Instead (3:13–15a)

There is a symmetrical structure to vv. 13–17 in that v. 17 recapitulates the ideas of vv. 13–14, noting the benefit of unjust suffering. Suffering for doing what is right, which is described as a blessing in v. 14, is affirmed in v. 17 as "better" than facing the negative consequences of evil actions.

Verse 13 is a rhetorical question that causes some problems for interpretation: "Who is going to harm you if you are eager to do good?" It appears that the answer to the question should be "No one." However, the thrust of Peter's entire letter shows that suffering is a possibility; so does the "if you should suffer" in v. 14. Consequently, many commentators argue that "'harm' means inward harm and reflects a trust in God's ultimate salvation, not a belief that Christians will not suffer persecution."[1] But it seems strained to make the "harm" of v. 13 different from the "suffer[ing]" of vv. 14 and 17. A better interpretation is to say that Peter is offering a generality in v. 13, in the same vein as many of the Proverbs in the OT—*as a rule* people will not abuse them for doing good.

Peter may also be emphasizing that evil people might dole out starkly different treatment than God does. To examine v. 13 more deeply, the NIV does not directly translate the conjunction *kai* at the start of v. 13. *Kai* is often translated "and," but here it is better understood as "then," making the connection to v. 12 more explicit. Peter's logic in vv. 12–13 would then be something like: "God looks favorably upon the righteous but rejects the wicked. Who, then, is the one who will harm you when you are doing what is good?" The answer to this question is now, "Certainly not God!" This is why Donelson writes, "The force of the question cannot be found in the simple response of 'no one.' Perhaps the point is that it is unrighteous humans, and not God, who 'do bad to you.' The power of humans to inflict harm is nothing

---

1. Davids, *First Peter*, 129.

compared to what God can do…. The question is an indirect reminder of the power and promise of God to protect those who do good."[2]

Peter stresses the importance of blameless behavior, regardless of how his people may be treated, and urges them to be "zealots of the good." The noun *zēlōtēs* describes one who is eager to perform some action or who may be an enthusiastic adherent to a cause.[3] Peter's readers, therefore, do not do good accidentally, but purposefully. The world should respect their intentionality, but there remains the possibility that not all observers will find the Christians' behavior to be praiseworthy; in fact, the believers might suffer.[4]

Peter goes on to show (v. 14) that Christians will be blessed even if they do suffer, as long as their suffering is a result of their good behavior; this is similar to how he advised slaves in 2:19–20. So, whether or not the community of faith gets persecuted, they are to be living upright lives. These words reinforce the teaching of the previous section, especially vv. 9–12, as Peter offers a beatitude (or macarism), a pronouncement of divine favor. God's blessing helps to alleviate suffering at the hands (or mouths) of other humans. And in what we have come to see as typical of the author, Peter reinforces his point with an allusion to the OT, Isaiah 8:12.[5]

Instead of fearing their enemies, believers are to revere Christ as Lord. The imperative in 3:15 is *hagiasate*, which can be translated, "consecrate," "separate," or "make holy"; its cognate adjective is *hagios*, "holy." What is unusual is that people are to sanctify Christ, when typically it is God who does the sanctifying, not people.[6] However, in the OT, there are frequent commands for individuals as well as groups to "sanctify" or "consecrate" something. For example, Isaiah 8:13, the verse immediate following the one that Peter has just alluded to, says, "The LORD Almighty is the one

---

2. Lewis R. Donelson, *I and II Peter and Jude: A Commentary*, NTL (Louisville: Westminster John Knox, 2010), 103.

3. In the NT *zēlōtēs* is used twice to describe the other apostle Simon—not Peter (Luke 6:15; Acts 1:13). In those cases, the term is used with a technical sense, used of Jewish nationalists.

4. Verse 14 exhibits an instance of the optative mood, rare in the NT (see *plēthyntheiē* in 1:2). There is yet another at 3:17 (*theloi*). The optative mood of a verb indicates possibility. *Paschoite* ("you should suffer") here in 3:14 may reflect the historical circumstance of sporadic hostilities toward Christians rather than systematic oppression that would later come under Nero and other emperors (see Jobes, *1 Peter*, 227; Achtemeier, *1 Peter*, 230–31).

5. The text of the last part of 1 Pet 3:12 is nearly identical to that of Isa 8:12 LXX, hence the quotation marks in the NIV. The LXX has a singular pronoun ("do not fear his fear") while 1 Peter has plural ("do not fear their fear").

6. The verb *hagiazō* is used about twenty-five times in the NT and the vast majority of the times it is used of objects or people being sanctified by God (e.g., John 17:17; Heb 2:11). A notable exception is found in 1 Cor 7:14, where somehow a believing spouse "sanctifies" the unbelieving one.

you are to regard as holy, he is the one you are to fear, he is the one you are to dread."[7] Peter may very well have had Isaiah 8:13 in mind when he admonishes his readers to do for Christ what Isaiah's audience was to do for YHWH: set him apart as holy.

Christ, who is set apart as holy, is deserving of one's ultimate allegiance; he is "Lord." "Lord" (*kyrios*) is a very common word in the NT, ranging from something akin to the English "sir" all the way to a designation for YHWH, the divine name for God. Peter seems to be using *kyrios* in that latter sense, as a way to equate Christ with the God of the OT.[8] Additionally, Peter may be implying that even though the emperor is deserving of honor (2:13, 17), it is Christ alone who must be set apart for the purpose of worship.

Respond to Accusations with a Good Conscience (3:15b–17)

The believers must defend their Christian faith. Behind the NIV's "answer" in 3:15b is the Greek word *apologia*, which is typically translated as "defense." In most of its NT occurrences *apologia* refers to making a verbal argument for the Christian faith before people who are antagonistic toward its claims.[9] Despite the fact that *apologia* is sometimes a specialized term, indicating a response to charges such as in a legal trial, we need not understand the term to have such formality here. Peter is admonishing his readers to be ready to defend their beliefs, using words as their weapons, by giving reasons why they have hope. He has already described the Christian faith as a "living hope" (1:3) and as hope in God (1:21) and in both instances bases this hope on the resurrection of Jesus Christ. Perhaps Peter is urging his readers to be ready to discuss the ministry of Jesus—particularly the resurrection—whenever they are questioned. This is what Peter himself did: in his defense of the faith at Pentecost (Acts 2:14–40), he focused upon the ministry of Jesus with special attention to his resurrection (2:22–36).

Even so, Peter does not share any specific recommendations of what the Christian *apologia* should entail; instead, he focuses on the motivation and manner in which that defense is to be made. Any justification for the Christian faith should be made with gentleness, which is something like the humility described in 3:8 and is also an attribute of the Lord Jesus himself, as seen in Matthew 11:29 ("Take my yoke upon you and learn from me, for I am gentle and humble in heart, and you will find rest for your souls") and 21:5 ("Say to

---

7. The second-person plural imperative *hagiasate*, which is found in the NT only at 1 Pet 3:15, is frequent in the OT. It is used in the Isa 8:13 passage noted above.

8. Peter does a similar thing in 1:25 and 2:3. Other NT writers also associate Christ with YHWH using *kyrios* (e.g., Phil 2:11).

9. See Acts 22:1; 25:16; 1 Cor 9:3; 2 Cor 7:11; Phil 1:7, 16; 2 Tim 4:16.

Daughter Zion, 'See, your king comes to you, gentle and riding on a donkey, and on a colt, the foal of a donkey'"). Christians need not be argumentative when offering a case for what they believe.

Along with gentleness, or humility, is "respect" (*phobos, 3:15*).[10] Christians, who already fear God (2:17), must also show respect to their questioners, giving no grounds for offense. And just as importantly, their coolheaded responses are an indicator that the believers have pure motives, i.e., "a clear conscience."

"Conscience" (*syneidēsis*) is typically found in Pauline literature, but Peter seems to use the term in a similar fashion here in 3:16 and later in 3:21.[11] *Baker's Evangelical Dictionary of New Testament Theology* describes conscience as "a God-given capacity for human beings to exercise self-critique."[12] Furthermore, "The conscience does not dictate the content of right or wrong; it merely witnesses to what the value system in a person has determined is right or wrong. In this regard, conscience is not a guide but needs to be guided by a thoroughly and critically developed value system."[13] A Christian whose conscience is shaped according to the virtues of Jesus will know what is a righteous response to criticism.

The interaction between believers and unbelievers goes along these lines: The Christian community eagerly performs good works, which may invite hurtful words (and possibly actions) by hostile onlookers, accompanied by questions about why the Christians behave as they do (see 4:4), followed in turn by a respectful apologetic offered by the Christian believers. What comes after may very well be regret on the part of the accusers. Verse 16 is reminiscent of Paul's admonition in Romans 12:20 ("On the contrary: 'If your enemy is hungry, feed him; if he is thirsty, give him something to drink. In doing this, you will heap burning coals on his head'"), which in turn cites Proverbs 25:21–22. When Christians act with good consciences and respond respectfully to their accusers, the bullies may feel twinges of guilt for tormenting people who have done nothing wrong.

Verse 17 returns to the ideas of vv. 13–14. In the spirit of a "better proverb," Peter offers a summarizing maxim to explain that if suffering must come

---

10. *Phobos* ("fear") is used here, but again with the sense of "respect" and "honor" as we have seen earlier (i.e., 1:17; 2:18; 3:2).
11. Of the twenty-nine occurrences of *syneidēsis*, five are found in Hebrews (9:14; 10:2, 22; 13:18), three in 1 Peter (2:19; 3:16, 21), two in Acts related to the ministry of Paul (23:1; 24:16) and the rest in Pauline letters. In 1 Pet 2:19 *syneidēsis* is used in the sense of "awareness."
12. Gary T. Meadors, "Conscience," in *Baker's Evangelical Dictionary of Biblical Theology*, Bible Study Tools, http://m.biblestudytools.com/dictionaries/bakers-evangelical-dictionary/conscience.html.
13. Ibid.

then it is nobler to suffer unjustly than to be denounced for genuine wrong-doing.[14] After all, that is the way of Christ.

Random Acts of Kindness?

It is common to see a bumper sticker or some meme encouraging "random acts of kindness." There is certainly nothing wrong with that. The Good Samaritan (Luke 10:25–37) is a story that teaches the power of such acts; kindness is the essence of being a neighbor. Yet, as a pastor I have found it helpful not only to encourage random acts but also to help create deliberate efforts for good.

Of course, the content and manner of the good things that Christians do depends upon our context. Our situation in the West is different from that of the growing Christian movements in the non-Western world, and certainly different from what Peter's readers faced. Yet, we are all called to be agents of good in the world. For those of us in the West, we have long enjoyed a certain social hegemony, or dominant position in the culture; I touched on this in my discussion of 1 Peter 2:4–10. It was popular, for example, to hear people refer to the USA as a "Christian nation." That understanding of our country impacted our laws as well as our social conventions. I'm old enough to recall how rare it was to shop for just about anything on a Sunday because so-called blue laws restricted certain transactions, and the culture made Sunday a Sabbath day. Christians thus felt free to adopt confrontational forms of evangelism and to influence legislation. During part of my nearly eighteen years of ministry in Washington, DC, I regularly passed by or visited 100 Maryland Avenue NE, the address of The Methodist Building, "the only non-government building on Capitol Hill."[15] The Methodist Church bought the property, which is along the same street as the Supreme Court building, across from the US Capitol, in order to lobby for the prohibition of alcohol.

But in our pluralistic world, Christians debate our role in society. We question if our strategy should still include trying to influence society from the centers of power. It may be that we can take a cue from our forebears as

---

14. "Better" or "better than" sayings are a common form of proverb. For example: Prov 16:8, 19, 32. In fact, Prov 16:32 seems apropos of Peter's discussion here ("Better a patient person than a warrior, one with self-control than one who takes a city"). See T. Hildebrandt, "Genre of Proverb," in *Dictionary of the Old Testament: Wisdom, Poetry and Writings*, ed. Tremper Longman III and Peter Enns (Downers Grove, IL: IVP Academic, 2008), 534.

15. "History of United Methodist Building," General Board of Church and Society of the United Methodist Church, http://umc-gbcs.org/about-us/the-united-methodist-building.

well as our fellow believers in the non-Western world. Their contexts require Christians to be agents of good not from a position of relative privilege but rather from the margins of society.

In wrestling with the role of religion in the public sphere, Miroslav Volf addresses the context in which early Christians tried to impact the world:

> For those familiar with the early history of the Christian church—and for careful observers of young and vibrant Christian communities in the non-Western world—there is something odd about the present sense of crisis in the West. The early Christian communities were not major social players at all! They were not even among the cheering or booing spectators. Slandered, discriminated against, and even persecuted minorities, they were at most a bit of a thorn in society's flesh. Yet, notwithstanding their marginality, early Christian communities celebrated hope in God and proclaimed joyfully the resurrected Lord as they endeavored to walk in the footsteps of the crucified Messiah.[16]

Volf's description of the early Christians is apropos of Peter's readers. And perhaps we can learn from the perspective of our marginalized forebears. Volf goes on to write, "We in the West … are already alarmed about diminished influence. In the midst of fierce opposition, early Christians celebrated and embodied a way of life—life that they experienced as God's gift and that was modeled on Christ, a paragon of true humanity. In contrast, living in freedom and economic prosperity, many churches in the West, primarily in the United States, bemoan the loss of influence and scheme how to regain it by acquiring political power."[17] Volf states the goal of his book this way: "I want to make Christians communities more comfortable with being just one of many players, so that from whatever place they find themselves—on the margins, at the center, or anywhere in between—they can promote human flourishing and the common good. Under different circumstances, they may then reacquire the vibrancy and confidence of the early churches."[18]

From my vantage point as an urban pastor, I have to agree with Volf. Some Christians are able to work for good through political means, being direct influencers of those in the seat of power. However, many of us do not have that opportunity. But we can work for the general welfare of our society, much like Peter's readers and also like the Israelite exiles in the prophet Jeremiah's time. Some of his words to the exiles, found in chapter 29, have become

---

16. Miroslav Volf, *A Public Faith: How Followers of Christ Should Serve the Common Good* (Grand Rapids: Brazos, 2011), 78.
17. Ibid., 79
18. Ibid.

famous to Christians because of their upbeat tone: "'For I know the plans I have for you,' declares the LORD, 'plans to prosper you and not to harm you, plans to give you hope and a future'" (Jer 29:11). But we may often forget that these words come on the heels of the sobering words that the Israelites would be in exile for many years. And during that time they were to continue on with their lives, building homes, farming, and having their children marry. Furthermore, they were to "seek the peace and prosperity of the city to which I have carried you into exile. Pray to the LORD for it, because if it prospers, you too will prosper" (Jer 29:7). The Israelites were to work for and pray for the well-being—the *shalom*—of their enemies, the Babylonians.

To live with this perspective requires deliberation and not just random acts of kindness. The strategic witness of Christians working together for good can carry great weight in our culture. The efforts of churches within a denomination to address achievement gaps in education or the collaboration of churches and others in the Christian Community Development Association (CCDA) to combat the devastation of poverty are examples of how Christians can impact society in good ways and possibly deflect the criticism of the unbelieving world (1 Pet 3:13).

Christian Apologetics

Defending the Christian faith is as old as the faith itself. One might consider Peter as the first Christian apologist: in his sermon in Acts 2:14–40 he responded to genuine questions as well as ridicule from those who observed the effects of the Holy Spirit's visit on the Day of Pentecost (Acts 2:12–13). The book of Acts continues with accounts of the apostle Paul defending the beliefs of the nascent church. Since the time of the apostles, several NT texts, certainly including 1 Peter 3:15, have provided impetus for the ministry of apologetics for Christianity. Avery Dulles gives the goal for his work on apologetics as "to tell the story of the various ways in which thoughtful Christians, in different ages and cultures, have striven to 'give a reason for the hope that was in them' (cf. 1 Pt 3.15)."[19]

Simply put, apologetics is "the attempt to defend a particular belief or system of beliefs against objections."[20] The goals and practice of apologetics has morphed throughout the years. "The earliest apologists were primarily concerned with obtaining civil toleration for the Christian community—to prove that Christians were not malefactors deserving the death penalty."[21] Such a

---

19. Avery Dulles, *A History of Apologetics* (New York: Corpus, 1971), xx.
20. James K. Beilby, *Thinking About Christian Apologetics: What It Is and Why We Do It* (Downers Grove, IL: IVP Academic, 2011), 11.
21. Dulles, *Apologetics*, xx.

statement fits the situation of Peter's readers. Dulles notes, however, that the emphasis prior to AD 125 was on "establishing the faith and discipline of the Christian community rather than with attempting to demonstrate the credibility of the Christian faith."[22] Yet, "after the first quarter of the second century," Dulles continues, "apologetics became the most characteristic form of Christian writing."[23]

In light of the changes the world has undergone over the years, some Christian thinkers have questioned the role and the value of apologetics. For example, Myron Bradley Penner, an Anglican priest and scholar, introduces his book on apologetics by writing, "This is a book about apologetics. Or, more precisely, it is a book *against* apologetics."[24] Penner presses for a different way of witnessing for the faith, based upon his dismissal of apologetics as "the Enlightenment project of attempting to establish rational foundations for Christian belief."[25] He argues that in our postmodern context Christians should witness through their lifestyles: "The proof of Christian witness is always in the pudding. The pudding in this case is our *lives* as witnesses—our overall pattern of action and behavior (including our thoughts, feelings, and dispositions)."[26] Few would disagree with the positive point that Penner is making. But rather than an either/or attitude about apologetics, we should adopt a both/and approach, offering rational arguments for the faith when possible while always living in such a way as to demonstrate the authenticity of Christian faith.[27]

Peter's words at the end of 3:15 are as relevant today as they were when written: "Do this [apologetics] with gentleness and respect." Sadly, "too often, Christians have been condescending, arrogant and dismissive in their apologetic encounters."[28] Apologetics, then, is one expression of being "eager to do good" (3:13), as discussed above. As Harink admonishes, "Our apology must be an account of Christ's story, and that account cannot be given apart from the living testimony of the messianic people … the church's apologia for its hope must take the form of witness of the work of Christ; it is therefore characterized not by proud arguments and clever proofs, but by 'humility' (*prautētos*), reverence, and a good conscience (3:16)."[29]

22. Ibid., 27.
23. Ibid.
24. Myron B. Penner, *The End of Apologetics: Christian Witness in a Postmodern Context* (Grand Rapids: Baker Academic, 2013), 4 (emphasis original).
25. Ibid., 7.
26. Ibid., 124.
27. See Beilby, *Christian Apologetics*, 157–84.
28. Ibid., 157.
29. Harink, *1 and 2 Peter*, 94–95.

CHAPTER 11

1 Peter 3:18-22

 LISTEN to the Story

¹⁸For Christ also suffered once for sins, the righteous for the unrighteous, to bring you to God. He was put to death in the body but made alive in the Spirit. ¹⁹After being made alive, he went and made proclamation to the imprisoned spirits—²⁰to those who were disobedient long ago when God waited patiently in the days of Noah while the ark was being built. In it only a few people, eight in all, were saved through water, ²¹and this water symbolizes baptism that now saves you also—not the removal of dirt from the body but the pledge of a clear conscience toward God. It saves you by the resurrection of Jesus Christ, ²²who has gone into heaven and is at God's right hand—with angels, authorities and powers in submission to him.

Listening to the Text in the Story: Genesis 6–9; 1 Corinthians 15:3–8; Philippians 2:5–11; 1 Timothy 3:16.

Apart from a few powerful stories in the Gospels, we know very little about the activities of Jesus immediately after his resurrection. We get one glimpse when the apostle Paul quotes the young church's creed:

> For what I received I passed on to you as of first importance: that Christ died for our sins according to the Scriptures, that he was buried, that he was raised on the third day according to the Scriptures, and that he appeared to Cephas, and then to the Twelve. After that, he appeared to more than five hundred of the brothers and sisters at the same time, most of whom are still living, though some have fallen asleep. Then he appeared to James, then to all the apostles, and last of all he appeared to me also, as to one abnormally born. (1 Cor 15:3–8)

The appearance of Christ to over five-hundred believers at one time is a tradition not found in the canonical Gospels. Peter here offers yet another perspective on the activities of Jesus after his resurrection, but his words have long proved cryptic to interpreters.[1] Despite this, Christians have based certain doctrines on this passage, "and these doctrines have been warmly cherished in the Church and might seem to have much of their foundations cut away if this or that interpretation were adopted."[2]

We will not wade through the variety of interpretations; rather, we will underscore how Peter employs a particular Jesus tradition in vv. 18–20 as an explanation for why it is better to suffer for doing good than for doing evil (v. 17).

EXPLAIN the Story

Once again, Christ is the main example of one who suffered unjustly (see 2:21–25). Yet here the focus is not so much on the demeanor of the one suffering but on the reality that victory follows apparent defeat, just as resurrected life follows death. The passage ends with a focus on salvation that has been secured by a savior who was raised from the dead and possesses authority over all celestial beings.

The Passion and Resurrection of Christ (3:18)

We begin with a straightforward affirmation of the redemptive work of Jesus (v. 18). The verse reads like a creedal statement, an affirmation of the suffering, crucifixion, and resurrection of Christ. The fact that Christ "also" suffered places him in solidarity with Peter's readers, who suffer too. This solidarity also connects that community with one who was raised from the dead and is victorious over all.

Therefore, Peter's words of encouragement are not only about pain but also hope. Christ not only suffered and was put to death; he was made alive in the Spirit. With respect to the "body" or "flesh," which refers to the state of human limitations and suffering, Christ did indeed die. Even so, in the spiritual realm, the sphere of the Holy Spirit's life-giving power, Christ was brought back to life.[3] Peter's readers too can be assured that their suffering will one day come to an end and they too will experience life in a spiritual realm.

---

1. For a detailed discussion of 1 Pet 3:18–22, including a survey of various views throughout the history of interpretation, see William J. Dalton, *Christ's Proclamation to the Spirits: A Study of 1 Peter 3:18–4:6*, 2nd rev. ed., AnBib 23 (Roma: Editrice Pontifico Istituto Biblico, 1989).

2. E. G. Selwyn, *First Epistle of St. Peter: The Greek Text with Introduction, Notes and Essays* (New York: Macmillan, 1947), 314.

3. The expressions "put to death in the flesh (*sarx*)" and "made alive in the Spirit" are syntactically parallel. No prepositions are used, so one must supply one based upon the Greek dative case. Peter does not seem to describe agency (i.e., "put to death by flesh and made alive by the Spirit") but respect, or quality. "The emphasis is not between the agents of the action but between the two states of Christ's existence" (Jobes, *1 Peter*, 240). This is the view of many modern commentators.

Christ's suffering is the way for people to have access to God. Peter's use of "bring" (*prosagō*) is related to the "access" or "approach" (*prosagōgē*) to God found in these three Pauline texts:

"Through [Christ] we have gained access by faith into this grace in which we now stand. And we boast in the hope of the glory of God." (Rom 5:2)
"For through him we both have access to the Father by one Spirit." (Eph 2:18)
"In him and through faith in him we may approach God with freedom and confidence." (Eph 3:12)

Just as a subject may be brought before a king on his throne, the unrighteous are granted access to God by virtue of Christ's death and resurrection.

Proclamation by the Risen Lord (3:19–20)

The debate over these verses includes these three questions:

1. "When did Christ make his proclamation?"
2. "To whom did he make his proclamation?
3. "What did Christ proclaim?"

Question (1) may be answered by the opening phrase of v. 19. The prepositional phrase "in which" (*en hō*) refers back in some way to "Spirit," the last word of v. 18. There are different ways the prepositional phrase may be understood, as evidenced by the NIV's marginal reading "in which also" as opposed to "after" (the phrase "being made alive" is not in the Greek text but helps to make clear that Peter may be describing a sequence of events).[4] Since *en hō* most likely has a temporal sense, Peter refers to when Christ was made alive, that is, his resurrection. In the spiritual realm, after having been raised from the dead, Christ made a proclamation. Even though the "days of Noah" are mentioned, one need not imagine Christ being present at that time, preaching through Noah. This was the view of Augustine, but few modern commentators hold this view.[5] This view gained popularity with the Reformers because it appears better than the competing interpretation that Christ descended to hell and evangelized those already dead, which raises the possibility of postmortem conversion.

---

4. The prepositional phrase *en hō* could be viewed with regard to location (i.e., "in the realm of the Spirit"), with regard to means (i.e., "in the power of the Spirit"), or with regard to timing (i.e., "when made alive in the Spirit ..."). Most commentators interpret *en hō* with this latter, temporal sense, which is the NIV's preferred reading, but one can see how all three senses are related and may be simultaneously applicable to the passage: "At the time he was made alive by the power of the Spirit, in the realm of the Spirit he proclaimed ..."

5. Wayne Grudem devotes forty-seven pages of his 239-page commentary—20 percent of the entire work—to explaining how Christ preached through Noah. See Grudem, *First Peter*, 165–74, 211–48.

The rest of v. 19 says that the proclamation was made to "the imprisoned spir-its," further described in v. 20 as "those who were disobedient long ago when God waited patiently in the days of Noah." Discovering the identity of the imprisoned spirits will answer our question (2) from above. One traditional interpretation is that Christ went to hell, the abode of the dead, to preach a message of salvation to those who had died earlier, particularly those who lived during Noah's time. This view, sometimes referred to as *descensus ad inferos* and touched on in the Apostle's Creed, appears to have originated with Clement of Alexandria.[6] According to this view, the proclamation is an evangelistic message, and the imprisoned spirits are taken to be deceased humans. These deceased humans would have committed this disobedience during the time Noah was constructing the ark.[7]

Consequently, it has become common for people to offer imaginative accounts of Noah pleading for his wicked neighbors to repent as well as responding to naysayers who mocked his construction project. Several years ago the comedian Bill Cosby offered a hilarious rendition of Noah's story, includ-ing conversations that might have taken place between Noah and his confused onlookers. More recently, the movie *Evan Almighty* portrayed a modern-day "Noah" who spent much of his time warning others and responding to critics, in addition to building his ark. But while the biblical account of the great flood in Genesis describes the wickedness of humanity (Gen 6:11–12), it does not say anything about Noah interacting with others or preaching to them.

Because of Peter's vocabulary, as well as his clear reliance upon Jewish tradition, most modern commentators take the imprisoned spirits to refer to fallen angels, not dead human beings; in that case, Christ's proclamation is a cry of victory and not a message of salvation. As for his vocabulary, the fol-lowing observations are helpful:[8]

- Peter never speaks of a "descent," although some assume Christ must have descended in order to fill out their picture of him going to hell.
- Peter makes no mention of hell (Hades, Tartarus, or Sheol).
- The abode of dead people is not called a "prison" in the NT.
- Christ "proclaims" (*kēryssō*), which simply means to make a pro-nouncement rather than "evangelizes" (*euangelizō*).[9]

---

6. Dalton, *Proclamation*, 28–41. Elliott, *1 Peter*, 693–710, gives detailed comments regarding the passage, including some of the doctrinal implications of the *descensus ad inferos* view.

7. See Gen 6:9–9:19. Green, *1 Peter*, 127–34, offers a defense for the *descensus ad inferos* view and reviews some of the literature that builds upon it.

8. Dalton, *Proclamation*, 143–64, discusses the vocabulary of vv. 19–20a, also Achtemeier, *1 Peter*, 252–62.

9. In several instances *kēryssō* has an evangelistic sense (e.g., Matt 4:23; Acts 9:20; Rom 10:14). My point here is that one need not assume such a sense, especially when the identity of the recipients of the message is debated.

- The language of "spirits" who are imprisoned is more naturally taken to refer to supernatural beings rather than humans (see 2 Pet 2:4; Jude 6).[10]

Beyond this consideration, modern exegesis takes into account the extra-biblical tradition found in 1 Enoch. To be sure, the church fathers did not read this passage through the lens of that book; William Dalton offers help for explaining that omission:

> And if one asks why scholars had to wait until modern times to understand the text of 1 Pet 3:19–20, a satisfactory reply is at hand. While *1 Enoch* had profound influence on the books of the New Testament, we have already seen that, early in the church's tradition, it fell into disrepute and finally disappeared completely, only to emerge into the world of western scholarship in comparatively recent times.[11]

Even so, many of us are not familiar with Jewish writings like 1 Enoch. Jobes points out that "the language and imagery of 1 Enoch are so bizarre and unfamiliar to modern readers that while it no doubt provides the background to 1 Peter 3:19–20, it hardly resolves the mystery of these verses. The original readers, likely more familiar with the Enoch traditions than we, would probably not have been so mystified."[12] First Enoch elaborates upon Genesis 6:1–4, where angels take wives and produce a race of giants. At one point, God calls upon Enoch to deliver a message to these fallen angels, also known as Watchers:

> And He answered and said to me, and I heard His voice: Fear not, Enoch, thou righteous man and scribe of righteousness: approach hither and hear my voice. And go, say to the Watchers of heaven, who have sent thee to intercede for them: You should intercede for men, and not men for you: Wherefore have ye left the high, holy, and eternal heaven, and lain with women, and defiled yourselves with the daughters of men and taken to yourselves wives, and done like the children of earth, and begotten giants (as your) sons And though ye were holy, spiritual, living the eternal life, you have defiled yourselves with the blood of women, and have begotten (children) with the blood of flesh, and, as the children of men, have lusted after flesh and blood as those also do who die and perish. Therefore have I given them wives also that they might impregnate them, and beget children by them, that thus nothing might be wanting to them on earth. But you were formerly spiritual, living the eternal life, and immortal for

---

10. Achtemeier, *1 Peter*, 255.
11. Dalton, *Proclamation*, 172. See chapter 7, "Light from the Book of Enoch."
12. Jobes, *1 Peter*, 243.

all generations of the world. And therefore I have not appointed wives for you; for as for the spiritual ones of the heaven, in heaven is their dwelling. And now, the giants, who are produced from the spirits and flesh, shall be called evil spirits upon the earth, and on the earth shall be their dwelling. Evil spirits have proceeded from their bodies; because they are born from men and from the holy Watchers is their beginning and primal origin; they shall be evil spirits on earth, and evil spirits shall they be called. (1 En. 15:1–9, Charles)

If 1 Enoch is the background for Peter's remarks, as most commentators agree, then the resurrected Christ gave his message to fallen angels who were imprisoned because of the wickedness they brought to earth in the days of Noah.

With regard to the final question (3), Peter does not disclose the content of the Lord's proclamation. However, given that he is pictured in v. 22 in a victorious position of authority at God's right hand, with "angels, authorities and powers in submission to him," it seems that what Christ announced was his victory and their defeat.[13]

Before we move on, let's summarize our answers to the three questions prompted by vv. 19–20:

4. "When did Christ make his proclamation?" Answer: Sometime after the resurrection.

5. "To whom did he make his proclamation? Answer: Angels who are in prison, awaiting final judgment, due to their disobedience during the days of Noah. They are mentioned in Genesis 6:1–4, but elaborated upon in a Jewish work known as 1 Enoch.

6. "What did Christ proclaim?" Answer: His victory as well as the defeat and condemnation of those fallen angels.

The end of v. 20 returns to information we remember from the Genesis account: eight people (i.e., Noah, his wife, their three sons, and their sons' wives) were saved through water by being in the ark. The image of salvation through water prompts Peter to offer a comparison to Christian baptism: the waters of the great flood are a symbol, or representation, of the waters of baptism.[14] Water, in both cases, is an agent of salvation. For Noah and his family,

13. Kelly, *Epistles of Peter and of Jude*, 156, offers a helpful summary: "This mysterious figure, who had 'walked with God' and whom 'God took' (Gen. v. 24) was for [Peter], it would appear, a type of Christ, and his allotted task had been to declare, not forgiveness, but doom to the apostates. Viewing Christ as the new Enoch, he must have understood His proclamation to the spirits as His announcement that their power had been finally broken."

14. Peter uses the word *antitypos*. Its only other occurrence in the NT is in Heb 9:24.

even though water was a threat to their lives, it was simultaneously the means through which they were rescued.

Peter sets up a contrast between what baptism is and what it is not. When Peter says baptism does not remove dirt from the body, it may seem at first glance that he is emphasizing the obvious—that baptism is not an ordinary bath. However, it seems unlikely that Peter's readers would have confused baptism with bathing. What seems more likely is an association of ritual cleansings and purification rites of various religions.[15] Peter is saying that baptism does not provide the elimination of immorality.

Peter refers not to the physical body (*sōma*) but to flesh (*sarx*), which typically is used in the NT with a moral sense (note discussion above on v. 18). "Flesh" suggests human frailty, weakness, and carnality. Also, the word translated "dirt" (*rypos*) is yet another of Peter's rare words, used only here in the NT. It is often translated outside of the NT (as in the LXX) as "filth," carrying an ethical sense.[16] And as for "removal" (*apothesis*), Peter has already used its cognate (*apotithēmi*) in 2:1 to refer to the believers' responsibility in "taking off" evil behaviors. In light of Peter's vocabulary, he seems to be saying that baptism does not remove moral filth from a believer; that is something that must be consciously part of the Christian's daily life.

Consequently, upon their baptism people are pledging their dependence upon God, something they do out of a "clear conscience."[17] The picture is likely that of baptismal candidates being asked about their faith and commitment to God.[18] Their response is their pledge, borne out of an awareness, or consciousness, of God's moral standards. Peter reminds his readers that they made a pledge to maintain upright lives, even if they may be struggling to do so, given their hostile environment. Peter does not teach that baptism regenerates; it does not in itself bring about new birth (1:5). However, since salvation for Peter is a process and not a onetime act, baptism serves as part

---

15. Vinson, Wilson, and Mills, *1 and 2 Peter, Jude,* 178.

16. Note the related word *ryparia,* found in Jas 1:21 ("Therefore, get rid of all moral filth and the evil that is so prevalent and humbly accept the word planted in you, which can save you"). Also, the James passage employs the verb *apotithēmi* and is semantically parallel to 1 Pet 2:1–2 and 3:20.

17. The interpretation of 1 Pet 3:18–22 is notoriously difficult, not only because of the unfamiliar background noted earlier but also due to its awkward syntax, especially in v. 21. My interpretation here is consistent with the textual reading of the NIV, but there is a marginal reading: "but an appeal to God for a clear conscience." Behind that reading is the fact that "pledge" translates *eperōtēma,* a word that can also mean "request" or "appeal." Achtemeier, *1 Peter,* 270–72, details the reasons why *eperōtēma* should be taken as "pledge." Also, Vinson, Wilson, and Mills, *1 and 2 Peter, Jude,* 179, provide a helpful and non-technical discussion of the various ways that *syneidēseōs agathēs* may be understood. They conclude, "Baptism was only the beginning—the sign of their [Peter's readers] commitment, either the commitment of their conscience to God or a commitment to God from a conscience already fixed on God."

18. See Davids, *First Peter,* 145; Jobes, *1 Peter,* 255.

of Christian commitment. The act of baptism depends on the resurrection of Jesus as believers pledge their commitment to the Lord.

Peter concludes the section with the climactic affirmation that the resurrected Lord Jesus is seated in a place of prestige and authority. In writing that Jesus "has gone" to God's "right hand," Peter echoes the event described in v. 19 (*poreuomai*, "to go," is the same verb used to describe the movement of Jesus in v. 19). The "right hand" symbolized power, and to be at someone's "right hand"—particularly that of a king or of God—is to enjoy a place of honor (see Ps 110:1). The Lord Jesus owns such a position, having authority over all the messengers of heaven (i.e., angels), as well as over all creatures, human or spiritual (see Eph 1:21; Heb 8:1; 10:12; 12:2). Peter's reference to "authorities and powers" is reminiscent of Pauline language to describe the forces working against God's people. One foundational passage is Eph 1:21, where four entities are named: "rule" or "principality" (*archē*), "authority" (*exousia*), "power" (*dynamis*), and dominion (*kyriotēs*). These entities are "a spiritual dimension of the created order … who, being inimical to Christ and his church, were in some way opposed and either neutralized or conquered by Christ."[19] These spiritual beings somehow have influence over human beings and human institutions. Therefore, the "authorities and powers" could broadly be said to include the local Roman rulers as well as the emperor (1 Pet 2:13, 17). Consequently, Peter's readers should be assured that just as Jesus suffered innocently and went on to hold a place of honor, they too might suffer physically yet in the spirit will receive a position of honor despite the injustice that was shown them.

LIVE the Story

First Peter 3:18–22 is among the most confusing parts of the NT. In reference to vv. 19–22, Martin Luther says, "A wonderful text is this, and a more obscure passage perhaps than any other in the New Testament, so that I do not know for a certainty just what Peter means."[20] Similarly, Edward G. Selwyn observes, "There are few passages in the New Testament which have exercised commentators more, or given rise to greater variety of interpretation, than I Pet. iii. 18–22."[21] Therefore, to try to interpret this passage is a lesson in humility. Even so, it is possible to work out some practical implications of our interpretation as well as how our situation might mirror that of Peter's readers.

---

19. Daniel G. Reid, "Principalities and Powers," *DPL* (Downers Grove, IL: InterVarsity Press, 1993), 747.
20. Luther, *Peter and Jude*, 166.
21. Selwyn, *First Peter*, 314.

The "Harrowing of Hell" and the Apostles' Creed

My interpretation coincides with that of most modern commentators, yet I wonder if many people in the pews can accept the possibility that Peter is reflecting on the Jewish tradition found in the pseudepigraphal book known as 1 Enoch. I have sat under preachers who enthusiastically exclaim "Christ went to hell for you" with such rhetorical flair that we wanted to believe it, even if Peter does not clearly teach such a thing! The *descensus ad inferos* interpretation, that Christ went to hell between his crucifixion and resurrection, fueled the "harrowing of hell" idea, popular in the Middle Ages: "Christ's storming of the stronghold of Hades; his overthrow of Satan, his minions, and death; and his release of the captives."[22] Those captives were said to be people who died before Jesus ministered on earth. Furthermore, the descent-to-hell view typically includes the doctrine that Christ preached in hell, evangelizing the dead, offering them an opportunity for salvation. This line of reasoning, of postmortem conversion, can lead to the doctrine of universalism—the notion that no one need suffer for eternity, as God will grant salvation to all.[23]

One struggles to understand Peter's teaching in this section, but with regard to universalism at least, we must keep in mind the broader teaching of the NT regarding the consequences of rejecting Jesus. There are numerous passages that speak of damnation or some form of eternal judgment, and we need look no further than 1 Peter itself. "If it is hard for the righteous to be saved, what will become of the ungodly and the sinner?" (4:18). Even though some contemporary scholars suggest that Peter implies that unbelievers will get some sort of second chance at salvation (or that even the "imprisoned evil powers" may be converted), the NT offers little indication of this.[24]

It is the harrowing-of-hell view that may be harder for some to let go. The picture of Christ defeating death is a powerful one; my suggestion as a pastor is that we offer a modification of the harrowing-of-hell perspective: that Christ defeated death (1 Cor 15:55), dealt a blow to Satan (Rev 20:2), and also proclaimed victory to the imprisoned fallen angels. We should also point out that Jesus made his proclamation upon his resurrection, helping people to move away from picturing Christ in hell but rather seeing him as standing tall and victorious, risen from the dead.

What Peter Teaches about the Days of Noah

Noah figures in both Petrine epistles. In addition to our present passage, 2 Peter 2:5 reads: "if he did not spare the ancient world when he brought the

22. Elliott, *1 Peter*, 708.
23. See Jobes, *1 Peter*, 247–51, who elaborates on the implications of the *descensus* view.
24. See Vinson, Wilson, and Mills, *1 and 2 Peter, Jude*, 183.

flood on its ungodly people, but protected Noah, a preacher of righteousness, and seven others." The "days of Noah" (1 Pet 3:20) is a time reference that provides a helpful parallel to the situation of Peter's readers, as Wayne Grudem has pointed out.[25] Noah, like Peter's readers, was part of a minority of righteous people who witnessed boldly for God, knowing that judgment is sure to come. Noah and his family were the only few to be saved, and similarly Peter's people, though relatively few in number, will also experience ultimate salvation, as Jesus has secured the victory (v. 22).

Christ is the Victor

Ultimately Christ himself is the focus of 3:18–22; we cannot let him be lost in the confusing details. He is the hero, securing salvation of humanity, bringing his followers to God, modeling what it means to suffer for doing good, but also experiencing ultimate vindication. In some ways Peter's rendering of the Christ event is like Philippians 2:6–11, where Christ is humbled and subsequently super-exalted (*hyperypsoō*). His experience is offered as a model for the rest of us (Phil 2:5). I began this section with 1 Corinthians 15:3–8, a creedal reflection on the death and resurrection of Jesus, so it is fitting to end with another from the NT, 1 Timothy 3:16:

> Beyond all question, the mystery from which true godliness springs is great:
>> He appeared in the flesh,
>>> was vindicated by the Spirit,
>> was seen by angels,
>>> was preached among the nations,
>> was believed on in the world,
>>> was taken up in glory.

---

25. So Grudem, *First Peter*, 168. Grudem's interpretation of 3:19–21, that Christ preached through the mouth of Noah, is held by very few and seems unlikely; still, most of his analysis of the days of Noah compared to the days of Peter's audience is helpful. In fact, Jobes, *1 Peter*, 258, reproduces Grudem's entire list, except for his fifth point (of seven), that in the unseen spiritual realm Christ preached to unbelievers through Noah.

CHAPTER 12

1 Peter 4:1–6

 LISTEN to the Story

⁴:¹Therefore, since Christ suffered in his body, arm yourselves also with the same attitude, because whoever suffers in the body is done with sin. ²As a result, they do not live the rest of their earthly lives for evil human desires, but rather for the will of God. ³For you have spent enough time in the past doing what pagans choose to do—living in debauchery, lust, drunkenness, orgies, carousing and detestable idolatry. ⁴They are surprised that you do not join them in their reckless, wild living, and they heap abuse on you. ⁵But they will have to give account to him who is ready to judge the living and the dead. ⁶For this is the reason the gospel was preached even to those who are now dead, so that they might be judged according to human standards in regard to the body, but live according to God in regard to the spirit.

Listening to the Text in the Story: Romans 12:1–2; Galatians 5:16–26.

While I was working on this commentary, our entire church community tackled the topic of emotionally healthy spirituality, as presented by Peter Scazzero.[1] Within our Wednesday evening discussion group on the section on "enlarging your soul through grief and loss," I heard one participant exclaim: "We Christians don't expect to suffer; we see it as an interruption to our lives." Her observations sparked a lively discussion about the prevalence and role of suffering. Can there be anything encouraging about it?

Peter's first letter urges us to see that suffering is part of the Christian experience, not least because it is part of the human experience. Yet Christians can learn to see that suffering is not the result of random hostility caused by a capricious god but is an opportunity for our faith to be worked, like a muscle, and consequently grow stronger. Suffering for our faith allows us to connect

---

1. Peter Scazzero, *Emotionally Healthy Spirituality: Unleash a Revolution in Your Life in Christ* (Grand Rapids: Zondervan, 2006).

with Jesus, the one who suffered unjustly, having never done anything to deserve the abuse he endured.

EXPLAIN the Story

I noted in the previous section, 3:18–22, that the example of Jesus proves that victory follows suffering. Consequently, there is hope because Peter's readers will experience ultimate salvation at some future point (see 4:7a). However, the present reality for Peter's readers is that suffering is part of life; this letter has made that clear right from the start (1:6). There is suffering that comes from the hands and voices of nonbelievers because Christians refuse to participate in the hedonism of their previous lifestyles. Such forms of suffering, particularly verbal abuse, comes from foolish people (2:15).

Arguably the most encouraging aspect about suffering is that it puts Christian believers in solidarity with their Lord. Christ as the suffering servant is our model in 2:21–24. If we ready ourselves with the same attitude that Christ had, we can be assured of future vindication.

The Motivation to Break from Sin (4:1–3)

With an opening "therefore" Peter refers to the example of Christ in 3:19–22, using it to reinforce his earlier point that Christians must live a purer lifestyle than those who have no faith in Jesus.[2] Employing military imagery (as in 1:13), Peter commands his readers to have the same mindset that the Lord had, one that will help them to prepare for suffering and resist sinful behavior.[3]

Since the Lord's physical suffering brought redemption (3:18), Peter offers what amounts to a maxim: "Whoever suffers in the body is done with sin." This verse is somewhat difficult to understand because of the impression it gives that any human being could bring a stop to sinning simply by enduring physical suffering.[4] Supporters of this view may find Peter in line with Romans 6:7 ("anyone who has died has been set free from sin"). But while on the surface Peter and Paul seem to be making the same point, the contexts are quite different. Paul uses death metaphorically in association with baptism while Peter addresses actual physical suffering. Also, for Paul sin is a power under which humans fall victim, whereas Peter writes of sinful behaviors.[5]

---

2. Peter has made similar points throughout the letter, such as in 1:14–18, 22; 2:1, 11; 3:10–11.

3. The verb *hoplizō* ("arm oneself") is used only here in the entire NT. However, the related noun *hoplon* ("weapon") is one time used literally (John 18:3), but in all its other occurrences is used metaphorically by Paul of spiritual warfare (Rom 6:13; 13:12; 2 Cor 6:7; 10:4).

4. E.g., Selwyn, *First Peter*, 209.

5. See Elliott, *1 Peter*, 716, and Kelly, *Epistles of Peter and of Jude*, 168–69, for more on this passage and Romans 6.

Our daily experience does not confirm the idea that physical suffering eliminates sinful behaviors, and neither does the rest of the NT.[6] To resolve the difficulty, it is attractive to take the expression, "he who suffers" (*ho pathōn*) to refer to Christ, especially since it would be a parallel to the beginning of the sentence (i.e., "Christ suffered in the body ..." and then, "the one who suffers in the body ...").[7] In this case, Christ would not only serve as the model for sinless behavior, he would stand alone as the only one whose suffering led to the cessation of sin—presumably any personal acts of sin. Yet this view raises other questions, such as, "Was there ever a time when Christ ceased from sinning?" This would seem to imply that he had sinned previously, and this would not jibe with the biblical witness concerning Christ.

It seems more likely that 4:1 is saying that, those who have suffered on account of their faith are the same people who have already renounced sinful behavior and therefore are "done" with sin. As Martin Williams notes, "Peter is calling upon believers to arm themselves with a mental readiness to suffer, because if, like Christ, they are committed to following God's will, then, like Christ, they too will suffer. Suffering, then, is a sign of their solidarity with Christ, and for that reason they must be prepared to suffer."[8]

Verse 2 helps us to understand that being done with sin is more about renunciation than about a state of sinless perfection. The result of being done with sin is that one will desire to follow God's will rather than human lusts. As for living "the rest of their earthly lives," Peter literally says, "to live the rest of the time in the flesh." By combining the word for chronological time (*chronos*) with the rare verb *bioō* along with the phrase "in the flesh," Peter stresses day-to-day human existence and behaviors.[9]

Those who have renounced sin and live for the will of God will not join in the sorts of activities that they may once have participated in. However much time was spent previously in such activities is enough! Although Peter has previously referred to lustful desires as characteristic of unbelievers (e.g., 1:14; 2:11), this is the first time where he is specific in naming particular sins; he gives a "vice list," a device common in Greco-Roman writings.[10]

6. See, for example, 1 John 1:8, 10.

7. Among commentators who state that *ho pathōn* refers to Christ are Michaels, *1 Peter*, 226–29; Davids, *First Peter*, 149. The 1984 version of the NIV simply stated, "he who has suffered," which is ambiguous enough to apply to Christ or to humans generically.

8. See Williams, *Doctrine of Salvation*, 213; Jobes, *1 Peter*, 265.

9. The verb *bioō* is used only here in the entire NT. However, the noun *bios* ("life") occurs ten times and typically with the sense of "goods," or "means of subsistence." The more common expression for life in the NT is *zoē*. Although the meanings of *bios* and *zoē* overlap, the latter term is more comprehensive, relating to the fullness of being alive while the former term relates more to the way people carry out their *zoē*. Consequently, a loss of *bios* does not mean the end of *zoē*.

10. E.g., see Daniel G. Reid, "Virtues and Vices," *DLNT* 1190–94.

The first item on Peter's list, "debauchery" (*aselgeia*), sets the tone for his emphasis on hedonistic sins. *Aselgeia* is a broad term that does not focus on any one particular action but is fundamentally a lack of self-constraint. Debauchery is frequently linked to sexual deviance (e.g., *porneia* in 2 Cor 12:21 and Gal 5:19). In Ephesians 4:18–19 the apostle Paul observes that debauchery is the result of insensitivity due to hard-heartedness and alienation from God.

As noted earlier (in my discussions of 1:14 and 2:11), *epithymia*, the second item in the list, describes lustful desires here (and most elsewhere in the NT), even though the term itself can refer to neutral desires; in fact, the NIV translates it simply as "desires" one verse earlier, in 4:2.

The next three terms, *oinophlygia*, *kōmos*, and *potos*, paint a picture of the excessive partying that was part of pagan religious festivals. *Oinophlygia* ("drunkenness") occurs only here in the NT, but the cognate verb is used in the LXX (Deut 21:20). In extrabiblical literature *oinophlygia* is associated with excess. Drunkenness is prohibited elsewhere in the NT with the noun *methē* and the related verb *methyskō* (e.g., Rom 13:13; Eph 5:18). The NIV translates *kōmos* as "orgy" in Galatians 5:21 as well as here in 1 Peter. In Romans 13:13, the only other occurrence of the word, it is translated as "carousing." The celebrations in honor of the Greek god Dionysus (counterpart of the Roman god Bacchus) were known as *kōmoi tō Dionysō* ("Festivals of Dionysus"). Such festivals involved much wine consumption since Dionysus was considered to be its inventor. These festivals were also the site of sexual promiscuity.[11] The next term, *potos*, another word that occurs only in 1 Peter, is translated as "carousing" and in extrabiblical literature could refer to banquets held by the social elite, dinner parties that might also feature intellectual discussion. Plenty of wine was served at these gatherings as well.

The final behavior, "idolatry" (*eidōlolatria*), is the only term with a modifier: it is "detestable" (*athemitos*), behavior that is unacceptable according to tradition or custom, even if not the law of the land. The only other occurrence of the term in the NT is found in Peter's interactions with Cornelius (Acts 10:28), where Jewish traditions of ceremonial cleanliness are in the foreground. Similarly, the LXX uses the term with regard to that which is unclean according to Jewish law (2 Macc 7:1; 10:34; 3 Macc 5:20). Peter, therefore, seems to be describing idolatry with respect to his Jewish sensitivities yet showing its offensiveness in a way that Christians too would understand.

The struggle that Christians face in a pagan society is similar to the oppression Israel faced at the time of the Maccabees. Peter and others of Jewish background may have been familiar with this passage:

11. See John M. Dillon, "Dionysus," *ABD* 2:201–2.

Harsh and utterly grievous was the onslaught of evil. For the temple was filled with debauchery and reveling by the Gentiles, who dallied with prostitutes and had intercourse with women within the sacred precincts, and besides brought in things for sacrifice that were unfit. The altar was covered with abominable offerings that were forbidden by the laws. People could neither keep the Sabbath, nor observe the festivals of their ancestors, nor so much as confess themselves to be Jews. On the monthly celebration of the king's birthday, the Jews were taken, under bitter constraint, to partake of the sacrifices; and when a festival of Dionysus was celebrated, they were compelled to wear wreaths of ivy and to walk in the procession in honor of Dionysus. (2 Macc 6:3–7 NRSV)

Although the Christian believers had a prior history in paganism, they have now become strangers to the pagan way of life (see 1 Pet 1:14, 18; 2:11). However, rather than being celebrated for their morally upright behavior and freedom from decadence, the Christian community is instead being verbally abused.

The Backlash Due to Breaking from Sin (4:4)

The Gentile unbelievers, or "pagans" (v. 3), are not able to comprehend why the Christians do not run with them. By coincidence the English idiom "run with," meaning to join in the activities of others, is similar to the Greek term *syntrechō*.

The pagans view the Christians as odd for abstaining from what they consider normal activities. Interestingly, the word for "they are surprised" (*xenizō*) can in other contexts mean "to show hospitality" or "to receive a guest" (Acts 10:6, 18, 23, 32; 21:16; 28:7; Heb 13:2: "Do not forget to show hospitality to strangers, for by so doing some people have shown hospitality to angels without knowing it"). However, the word can also refer to being surprised at a new or strange idea, as it does in Acts 17:20 ("You are bringing some strange ideas to our ears, and we would like to know what they mean") as well as a few verses later in 1 Peter 4:12 ("Dear friends, do not be surprised at the fiery ordeal that has come on you to test you, as though something strange were happening to you"). The notion of self-restraint seems strange to the pagans; consequently, they denigrate the Christians.

These aforementioned sins are described as "what pagans choose to do," literally, it is "the will of the pagans" (*to boulēma tōn ethnōn*). Peter has already challenged the believers to live according to God's will (v. 2) instead of the will of unholy humans (v. 3). It is reminiscent of the apostle Paul's admonition to reject society's norms of thinking and doing: "Do not conform to the pattern of this world, but be transformed by the renewing of your mind. Then you will be able to test and approve what God's will is—his good, pleasing and perfect will" (Rom 12:2).

Divine Judgment upon the Living and the Dead (4:5–6)

It might have come as some consolation to Peter's readers to learn that the unbelievers would not go unpunished. These slanderers, who literally "blaspheme," will have to "give an account" (*apodidōmi*) of their actions to God. This is a common NT expression indicating judgment on the last day, and Peter echoes the words of Jesus found in Matthew 12:36: "But I tell you that everyone will have to give account on the day of judgment for every empty word they have spoken." God is the one to whom account is given and he is described as the judge of the living and the dead.

Peter goes on to say that it is because of future judgment that the gospel was preached "to the dead." "Dead" in v. 6 should be taken literally as it surely is in v. 5, a verse that points to the universality of God's judgment. The dead ones should be understood, as the NIV translation correctly has it, to be those who are "now dead" (the word "now" is not in the Greek text but may be inferred). These people heard the gospel message during their lifetimes but died prior to the writing of this letter.[12] Otherwise, v. 6 could sound as if the gospel was preached (presumably through Jesus) to some long-dead people who did not get to hear about Jesus during their lifetimes. This view developed in conjunction with the interpretation of 3:19–20 that says that Jesus preached to dead people between the time of his crucifixion and resurrection.

Others have taken the dead of v. 6 to be "spiritually" dead people, i.e., "pagans," who heard the gospel through Jesus or a Christian evangelist. But it seems most natural to take the dead in v. 6 as believers, as they are said to receive life. These dead ones faced judgment from human adversaries when they were alive (literally "in flesh"), but the judgment of God results in future life in the spirit, resurrection life, like that of Christ (3:18).

 LIVE the Story

Self-Mortification and Martyrdom

The controversial bestselling novel (and subsequent movie), *The Da Vinci Code*, contained a mysterious character who was a member of Opus Dei, a group within the Roman Catholic Church. He was depicted as a "flagellant," someone who inflicted physical pain upon himself as punishment for failure

---

12. See Williams, *Doctrine of Salvation*, 216–25.

and also as a way toward moral purity. Christian history—as well as the history of other religions—does include such practices. For example, the church historian Eusebius notes how the early church father Origen, taking the words of Matthew 19:12 literally, went ahead and castrated himself.[13]

The flagellants of the Middle Ages were members of ascetic movements who punished themselves, much like Silas in *The Da Vinci Code*. Such activity apparently flowed from the early church's emphasis on martyrdom as part of a theology of suffering. Among the early church fathers, according to William J. Webb, "interest in martyrdom eclipses all other discussion about suffering. Early martyrs became the supreme standard and example of suffering for all Christians to follow."[14] Our letter, 1 Peter, with its emphasis on the suffering of Christ, influenced the theology of martyrdom among the church fathers. "At its core, martyrdom was imitation and participation in the sufferings of Christ."[15] This theology of martyrdom may be traced back to "a tradition in Second Temple Judaism whereby the suffering and death of martyrs reverses God's judgment on Israel."[16] For example, consider 2 Maccabees 7:37–38 NRSV: "I, like my brothers, give up body and life for the laws of our ancestors, appealing to God to show mercy soon to our nation and by trials and plagues to make you confess that he alone is God, and through me and my brothers to bring to an end the wrath of the Almighty that has justly fallen on our whole nation."

Israel's wisdom literature teaches that suffering may have a purifying effect.[17] The book of Proverbs is full of examples, such as Proverbs 23:13–14 NRSV: "Do not withhold discipline from your children; if you beat them with a rod, they will not die. If you beat them with the rod, you will save their lives from Sheol." Divine discipline may well involve pain as part of our spiritual maturity (e.g., Heb 12:5–11), but this is not Peter's topic here.

Let us make clear that 1 Peter does not encourage any morbid desire to receive pain at the hands of others nor advocate the need to inflict pain upon oneself in order to achieve moral purity. Peter's goal is to prepare believers for suffering at the hands and mouths of others as a consequence of his readers' prior renunciation of sin. His readers lived within a pagan culture that expected them to participate fully in its life, which included the very behaviors denounced in 4:3. "The problem for Christians consisted in the fact that

---

13. Matthew 19:12 reads: "For there are eunuchs who were born that way, and there are eunuchs who have been made eunuchs by others—and there are those who choose to live like eunuchs for the sake of the kingdom of heaven. The one who can accept this should accept it."
14. William J. Webb, "Suffering," *DLNT* 1140.
15. Ibid.
16. Helyer, *Life and Witness*, 176.
17. Elliott, *1 Peter*, 716–17.

their new way of life no longer allowed them the kind of full participation in the religio-cultural activities that was expected of all people living within the Roman Empire, a participation they had enjoyed prior to their conversion. Such participation was impossible principally because every public festival involved to one extent or another religious activities that Christians could only regard as idolatry."[18]

Teetotalism?

Does 1 Peter 4:3 speak to whether or not believers may consume alcoholic beverages? I grew up in a church that regularly denounced alcohol consumption, and most of my Christian experience as an adult has been within denominations or educational institutions that either prohibited alcohol or strongly discouraged it. But I also knew that certain branches of Christianity had no problem with alcohol consumption, and that some used wine as opposed to grape juice in the communion service. As one non-Christian friend said to me regarding her perception of the church's view of alcohol, "The church seems to encourage it!" When I teach in ecumenical settings, I sometimes hear the joke—a riff on Matthew 18:20—told by members of different denominations about their use of alcohol: "Wherever two or three [fill in the name of the denomination] are gathered, there's a fifth!" The reference to "a fifth" is to a fifth of a gallon, a common size of liquor bottle. On the other hand, I had other students who refused to believe that Jesus actually turned water into wine, incredulous that *methysthōsin* in John 2:10 can be translated as "have become drunk" on what was served at the wedding at Cana. Christianity in America has not always known what to do about alcohol.

Various Christian groups took the lead in the Temperance Movement of the early 20th century. Because of the negative impact alcohol was having on society, they successfully lobbied for a constitutional amendment "eliminating the businesses that manufactured, distributed, and sold alcoholic beverages."[19] This 18th Amendment to the US Constitution was ratified in 1919, and alcohol consumption did decrease, although organized crime grew more common. On December 5, 1933, the 21st Amendment to the US Constitution was ratified, repealing the 18th Amendment; the Prohibition Era was over.

Alcohol consumption is now legal (for those over twenty-one years of age), and Christians today face some of the same concerns that Americans had a hundred years ago. The National Institutes of Health (NIH) cites alarming

---

18. Achtemeier, *1 Peter*, 284–85.
19. "Why Prohibition?," The Ohio State University: Temperance and Prohibition, https:// prohibition.osu.edu/why-prohibition.

statistics regarding alcohol consumption in the USA, such as the fact that "nearly 88,000 people (approximately 62,000 men and 26,000 women) die from alcohol related causes annually, making it the third leading preventable cause of death in the United States."[20] Alcohol abuse takes a huge toll on families as well as the country's economy and health care system.[21]

Christians in Europe may be facing similar challenges. Some have assumed that Europe's more liberal attitude toward alcohol consumption would mean that alcoholism and related problems are less evident among young people. But "recent data from representative surveys provide no evidence that young Europeans drink more responsibly than their counterparts in the United States."[22]

Whether or not one's denomination provides guidelines for alcohol consumption, we do well to practice moderation. Clergy have an important task of setting a good example, and due to social media we must be aware that our private lives are on public display. We can teach our people about Christian liberty by not unnecessarily condemning all alcohol consumption while simultaneously pointing out the dangers of overconsumption.

Of course, alcohol consumption is but one of the long list of ethical issues facing Christians. The partying of 4:3 is excessive, yet the church of my childhood forbade attendance at any secular party. Such prohibition seems unnecessary, especially in light of the NT picture of Jesus: "The Son of Man came eating and drinking, and you say, 'Here is a glutton and a drunkard, a friend of tax collectors and sinners'" (Luke 7:34). However, discernment is needed in how we demonstrate and communicate our faith, as noted in my discussion of apologetics (3:13–18). We must exercise wisdom regarding which activities that could promote godliness versus those that merely reflect self-centeredness and hedonism.

The Judgment of God

As a young man I was invited to minister at the oldest rescue mission in America, the McAuley Water Street Mission (now known as New York City Rescue Mission). For some years I led a monthly worship service and sometimes preached. One man who worked along with me wanted every sermon we preached to touch on the topic of hell. His advice to me at one point was

---

20. "Alcohol Facts and Statistics," National Institute on Alcohol Abuse and Alcoholism, June 2016, http://www.niaaa.nih.gov/alcohol-health/overview-alcohol-consumption/alcohol-facts-and-statistics.

21. Ibid.

22. "Comparison of Drinking Rates and Problems in European Countries and the United States," US Department of Justice, Office of Juvenile Justice and Delinquency Prevention, www.mdt.mt.gov/visionzero/docs/taskforces/ojjdp_feb01.pdf.

"preach about sin." I recall how one evening I opted to allow the men present to offer brief words of testimony. One man stood up describing how he got out of prison just that morning. My partner interrupted him and said, "I bet I know the first place you went!" The assumption was that the newly freed man had gone straight out to visit a prostitute. My fellow preacher was eager to pronounce judgment. But the hurting man stood there telling us all something different from that. All he did was walk around the city for hours, trying to figure out what he would do with his life. I'll not elaborate on what I thought concerning my partner, who stood self-righteously on the platform of the mission's chapel that evening, but I recall how much my heart ached for the man who was bold enough to offer his testimony.

In some circles the central message is divine judgment, punishment in hell. At the opposite extreme of these "fire and brimstone" preachers are those who avoid the topic of divine punishment altogether. N. T. Wright observed, "The merest mention of final judgment has been squeezed out of Christian consciousness in several denominations."[23] Perhaps people are afraid of alienating anyone who has not yet made a commitment to follow Christ; perhaps they base their theology on how they read the NT; perhaps they just want to avoid the old stereotypes. It is helpful for all of us to recall that divine punishment is part of the NT and has long been part of the church's teaching. Indeed, the Apostles' Creed contains the words of 4:6: Jesus will "come again to judge the living and the dead."[24]

Divine judgment is part of God's work in the world. "Judgment is necessary—unless we are to conclude, absurdly, that nothing much is wrong or, blasphemously, that God doesn't mind very much."[25] In 1 Peter, importance is given to one particular aspect of judgment, that of vindication.[26] Michael Bird point out that God's final judgment "is more than a distribution of rewards and punishments. Judgment is the vindication of Christ and his people."[27] Those who have faced injustice will appreciate that God's judgment includes their vindication. In my years of ministry, I have met many people who have hungered and thirsted for justice (see Matt 5:6) but have had to conclude that the system works against them. There are people who have been incarcerated, but when they are released, having supposedly paid their debt to

23. N T. Wright, *Surprised by Hope: Rethinking Heaven, the Resurrection, and the Mission of the Church* (New York: HarperOne, 2008), 178.

24. Even though the creed mentions the role of Jesus, Peter seems to refer to God the Father as the judge.

25. Wright, *Surprised by Hope*, 179.

26. Bird, *Evangelical Theology*, 301–8, has a good basic discussion of divine judgment. His bibliographic references are helpful for more detailed study.

27. Bird, *Evangelical Theology*, 304.

society, they are confronted with all sorts of barriers that make transition back into mainstream society nearly impossible. These people need to know that God is not merely about punishment, but about vindication. For oppressed people, it is good news to know that God sees their plight. It is good news to know that "God is utterly committed to set the world right in the end."[28]

---

28. Wright, *Surprised by Hope*, 179.

CHAPTER 13

1 Peter 4:7-11

 LISTEN to the Story

> [7]The end of all things is near. Therefore be alert and of sober mind so that you may pray. [8]Above all, love each other deeply, because love covers over a multitude of sins. [9]Offer hospitality to one another without grumbling. [10]Each of you should use whatever gift you have received to serve others, as faithful stewards of God's grace in its various forms. [11]If anyone speaks, they should do so as one who speaks the very words of God. If anyone serves, they should do so with the strength God provides, so that in all things God may be praised through Jesus Christ. To him be the glory and the power for ever and ever. Amen.

Listening to the Text in the Story: Psalm 39:12–13; Proverbs 10:12; Romans 12:3–13; 1 Corinthians 12:1–31.

During an American football game, the teams get a "two-minute warning" at the end of each half of play. A whistle sounds and it often seems that both teams put forth an extra effort when the end of the half is near; the offense tries desperately to score points and the defense is especially cautious in not giving ground to their opposition. Years ago, while a friend and I were watching a team make a noticeable surge after the two-minute warning, my friend asked, "Why don't they always play like there's two minutes left?"

If this is true for football, perhaps we too need to ask, "How would I live if I knew I only had a short time left on earth?" Peter reminds his readers that the end was drawing near. And just like modern footballers, Peter's people are not to give up or relax in their efforts to live faithful lives. On the contrary, they are to keep the focus on their vertical relationship with God, through prayer, and also on their horizontal relationships, through Christian community.

EXPLAIN the Story

Peter's teaching about God's judgment in 4:5–6 leads to his assertion that "the end of all things is near." Peter not only refers to the end of the sufferings his people have had to endure but more broadly to the end of time. In doing so he returns to ideas that he put forth earlier in his letter related to the return of Christ (e.g., 1:5–6, 13, 20; 2:12).

End-time Ethics (4:7a)

The NT repeatedly affirms that Christ will return and that his return is "near" (e.g., Heb 10:25; Jas 5:8). To be "near" is a translation of *engizō*, the word used in the preaching of Jesus (e.g., "The kingdom of God has come near. Repent and believe the good news!," Mark 1:15). For NT writers, particularly of the General Epistles, awareness of the end of time provides additional motivation for upright behavior:

> The later NT writings see the moral life in the light of the end. The early proclamation of Jesus and the earliest proclamation about Jesus, of course, had announced the end … when the later NT writings appropriated the Christian tradition, they appropriated certain convictions about the end. They knew the end of the story, and when they thought about the con- duct and character appropriate to Christians thought about their conduct and character in the light of the end.[1]

Peter is an example of those NT writers who emphasizes the proper pos- ture for believers in light of the fact that time is drawing to a close.

The Vertical Dimension of Last-Day Living (4:7b)

With his call to prayer (v. 7) along with his commands for love, hospital- ity, and service (vv. 8–11), Peter touches on what might be called vertical and horizontal aspects of Christian life. That is to say that communication with God—prayer—nurtures our vertical, or upward life. And the horizontal dimension is our life with others, our communal life. As one of my seminary professors said in regards to 1 Peter 4:7–11, "Christians live on the hypot- enuse, balancing the vertical and the horizontal." As an engineering major and then later a math teacher, I appreciated and have long remembered that I heard a reference to the hypotenuse of a right triangle in a seminary class!

Perhaps this upward and outward balance of life is related to the notion of cruciformity, a term literally related to being "cross-shaped," that has

---

1. Allen D. Verhey, "Ethics," *DLNT* 348.

become increasingly popular in Christian theology and ethics, thanks largely to the writings of Michael J. Gorman. With respect to Pauline theology, he writes:

> Cruciformity is cross-shaped existence in Christ. It is letting the cross be the shape, as well as the source, of life in Christ. It is *participating in* and *embodying* the cross. It may also be described, more technically, as non-identical repetition, by the power of the Holy Spirit, of the narrative of Christ's self-giving faith and love that was quintessentially expressed in his incarnation and death on the cross.[2]

Peter's ethical perspective resonates with Gorman's description of Paul's. Christ's life and death have already provided examples for Peter's readers (e.g., 2:21–25; 3:17–18). And in this present section Peter focuses upon the horizontal and vertical dimensions of Christian life, which are also cross-shaped, or cruciform.

Stressing purpose (i.e., "so that you may pray"), Peter exhorts God's people to be alert (*sōphroneō*) and sober minded (*nēphō*). With the use of *nēphō* Peter returns to an earlier theme in his letter of vigilance in light of the impending *parousia* of Christ (see the earlier discussion of 1:13) and simultaneously prepares us for the closing of his letter (see 5:8). Peter's language of sobriety is in contrast to the descriptions of drunkenness and associated behaviors in 4:3. Yet Peter refers to something deeper than simply not being intoxicated; he speaks of a spiritual alertness where attention is given to the signs of the times. Correspondingly, *sōphroneō* "describes the ability to see things clearly for what they are, and hence to act in a way appropriate to the prevailing circumstances."[3] Peter need not command his people to pray; he assumes that they know what prayer is (the word translated "pray" is *proseuchas*, the plural form), as well as the importance of offering prayers. He does, however, get at the attitude that provides motivation for prayer.

The Horizontal Dimension of Last-Day Living (4:8–11)

As a good pastor, Peter has encouraged and challenged his readers in their beliefs as well as their behaviors. Many of Peter's instructions concerning proper behavior relate to the impression the Christians should strive to make toward outsiders. But Peter has also directed these followers of Jesus in how they are to treat those within the community (e.g., 1:22; 2:1; 3:7, 8). He does so using phrases that indicate reciprocity: 4:8 *eis heautous* ("each other"), v. 9

---

2. Michael J. Gorman, *Reading Paul*, Cascade Companions (Eugene, OR: Cascade, 2008), 146–47 (emphasis original).

3. Achtemeier, *1 Peter*, 294.

eis allēlous ("to one another"), and v. 10 *eis heautous* ("others"). Peter focuses on love, the practice of hospitality, and the use of spiritual gifts.

Peter has been emphasizing that love be paramount. In 1:22 he urges the community to love "deeply" using the adverb *ektenōs*, and the related adjective *ektenēs* appears here in v. 8. Such intense love is demonstrated in concrete acts more than in words. As the writer of 1 John puts it, "let us not love with words or speech but with actions and in truth" (1 John 3:18).

Intense love helps to foster unity, something especially needed when the community is threatened by outside forces. Peter once again has the OT in mind, alluding to Proverbs 10:12b.[4] While the phrase "love covers over a multitude of sins" is axiomatic, applying even to divine forgiveness through Christ's sacrifice, in this context the saying best relates to that which preserves the bonds of fellowship. That is to say that love between the community members allows personal offenses to be readily forgiven.

With regard to "offer hospitality" (4:9), in the ancient Mediterranean world hospitality was a manifestation of the system of honor and shame (see the discussion of 2:6–8). Stephen C. Barton explains that in contrast to our contemporary Western, individualistic concept of hospitality where we think mostly of entertaining friends and family, "hospitality was a public duty toward strangers where the honor of the community was at stake and reciprocity was more likely to be communal rather than individual."[5] Itinerant missionaries characterized the early days of Christianity, and our forebears met in private homes for worship, instruction, and fellowship (e.g., Acts 2:46; 16:15, 31–34; Phlm 2). Consequently, the growing movement depended upon the hospitality that could be found among fellow believers who were scattered from town to town.[6]

We know from the Didache, a postapostolic Christian writing of the second century, that the practice of hospitality was subject to abuse. Note the following passages:

> Let every apostle who comes to you be welcomed as if he were the Lord. But he is not to stay for more than one day, unless there is need, in which case he may stay another. But if he stays three days, he is a false prophet. (Did. 11:4–5, Holmes)

> Everyone "who comes in the name of the Lord" is to be welcomed. But then examine him, and you will find out—for you will have insight— what is true and what is false. If the one who comes is merely passing

---

4. Peter does not cite the LXX, but is closer to the Hebrew text, as is Jas 5:20.
5. Stephen C. Barton, "Hospitality," *DLNT* 501.
6. Elliott, *1 Peter*, 752–53.

through, assist him as much as you can. But he must not stay with you for more than two or, if necessary, three days. However, if he wishes to settle among you and is a craftsman, let him work for his living. But if he is not a craftsman, decide according to your own judgment how he shall live among you as a Christian, yet without being idle. But if he does not wish to cooperate in this way, then he is trading on Christ. Beware of such people. (Did. 12:1–5, Holmes)

Even though travelers could take advantage of their hosts, Peter acknowledges that hospitality should be provided "without grumbling."[7] He understands the reality that offering hospitality could be burdensome, yet under the umbrella of love for others (v. 8), visitors should be welcomed gladly and not grudgingly.

Many readers of the NT will notice that v. 10 is reminiscent of the apostle Paul's teaching concerning gifts that come from the Holy Spirit, for example: "We have different gifts, according to the grace given to each of us" (Rom 12:6a). *Charisma* ("gift") is only found in the writings of Peter and Paul and both authors are explicit in attributing *charisma* to its cognate *charis* ("grace"), God's favor.

Both Peter and Paul point out that each believer receives divine *charisma* (e.g., 1 Cor 12:7), and both authors are clear in admonishing believers to go ahead and put their gifts into practice (see Rom 12:6–8). Peter views the employment of spiritual gifts as good stewardship.[8] A steward (*oikonomos*) was a household manager or administrator (see Luke 16:1). The steward "was often, but not necessarily, a slave born in the household (= Hebrew *ben bayit*, 'a son of the house' [Gen 15:3]) … who was especially trained and tested in the supervision of a farm-estate."[9] Just as a good household manager acts in the best interest of the entire household, the members of the church are to use their gifts for the benefit of all.[10] Indeed, they are to serve (*diakoneō*) each other.

If the readers of Peter's letter encounter a variety of trials (1:6), they also experience varieties of God's grace (v. 10). The apostle acknowledges that there are different kinds of spiritual gifts, but unlike Paul, Peter does not itemize specific gifts; rather, he divides them into two categories: speaking and serving. Those who speak would include teachers and preachers, and Peter

---

7. The guttural *gongysmos* literally refers to tones made in a low voice, i.e., mumbling or muttering as a form of complaining.

8. The NIV translates *kalos* as "faithful." *Kalos* has a broad range of meanings, including "beautiful," "good," "useful," "blameless," and other such words indicating high quality.

9. Joseph A. Fitzmyer, *The Gospel according to Luke X–XXIV: Introduction, Translation, and Notes*, AB 28A (Garden City: Doubleday, 1985), 1099.

10. See Achtemeier, *1 Peter*, 298.

may also refer to others within the Christian community, such as prophets and evangelists. Yet the admonition need not refer to any particular leader or group within the congregation, since Peter refers to "anyone" who speaks (v. 11). Jobes notes that Peter likely refers to those "who teach about Christ and offer counsel in his name."[11] Such a description might apply to any member of the community at some time or another.

Those who speak must communicate the oracles (*logia*) of God. *Logia* is rare in the NT (only in Acts 7:38; Rom 3:2; Heb 5:12, with the latter two references having "of God" as part of the expression, as Peter does here). The expression suggests "weighty words or promises originating with God."[12] This refers to Scripture and other words that are in sync with Scripture.

All spiritual gifts are a form of service, and anyone who serves must do so with awareness that God empowers his people; God provides the strength necessary for his people to serve. Peter uses yet another rare word, *chorēgeō* ("to provide"; it occurs also in 2 Cor 9:10), which frequently referred to the generous provision of a benefactor. As the apostle Paul wrote, God is the one who energizes (Phil 2:13) and who provides divine strength for our lives of service (Phil 4:13).

The purpose of offering spiritual gifts through divine inspiration and empowerment is to bring glory to God. God is the giver of all gifts (see Jas 1:17), and their use should bring him praise. Such praise comes "through Jesus Christ," as he serves as the one who makes it possible for human beings to praise God "in all things." In all that the Christian community does through prayer and service flowing out of love—even as the end draws near—God is glorified.

Peter concludes this section with a doxology, a prayer of praise, ascribing glory and power "to him." It is not clear if "him" refers to God or Jesus Christ. The proximity of the words "Jesus Christ" to the pronoun *hō* ("to whom") suggests that Peter's praise is directed toward Jesus. However, with few exceptions (e.g., 2 Pet 3:18) the vast majority of doxologies in the NT are directed to God. Even though scholars debate the object of the doxology, the ambiguity may simply follow from Peter's understanding that the Father and Jesus Christ are each worthy of praise and glory (see 3:22; 4:13).

LIVE the Story

The Irony of Seeking Christian Community
Earlier in my discussion of 3:8–12, I pointed out the need for Christian community. The importance of community comes up again in this present

---

11. Jobes, *1 Peter*, 282.
12. Elliott, *1 Peter*, 759.

passage, but with a degree of irony. The irony stems from the reality that while being alienated from the broader society is painful, it is precisely from that place on the margins that believers are best able to focus on what makes for true fellowship with one another.

Any group facing the shame of being on the margins needs to draw together around its common values in order to reinforce a sense of community. Dr. Martin Luther King Jr. often spoke and wrote about the notion of a "beloved community." For example, "Our goal is to create a beloved community and this will require a qualitative change in our souls as well as a quantitative change in our lives."[13] Similarly, Peter has written about qualitative and quantitative changes in our lives throughout his letter.

As he approaches the end of his letter, Peter gets at some basic topics that touch on much of what genuine Christian community is about: prayer, mutual love, service, and respect for the word of God. But even when they know how to define true fellowship, Christians seem to have struggled perennially with how best to experience it.

Throughout the history of Christianity, believers strived to practice their faith in the way of the earliest followers of Jesus.[14] Real Christian community has been the goal from the earliest monastic movements, to the communes of the 1960s and 70s, up to the intentional communities that we have seen burgeoning recently in Western Christianity. One such community is called The Simple Way. That community, as well as others, has been part of a revival of sorts. Many young people, in particular, have been drawn to intentional communities, leading to what observers refer to as The New Monasticism. Ironically, it appears that once Christians were no longer on the margins, as Peter's readers were, there developed a need to be intentional in getting back on the margins of society. Some have concluded that it is nearly impossible to live in the way of Jesus while experiencing the distractions of contemporary society. Peter's call to be "alert and of sober mind" (v. 7) is increasingly difficult in a noisy world in which Christians find themselves living no differently than the rest of society.

As an African-American urban pastor, I have witnessed and participated in the struggle for fellowship in the way that Peter describes. I have served in Chicago, New York, Washington, DC, and Minneapolis. In every one of those cities I have met young adults who crave a deeper sense of community, becoming willing to share life with possessions and spaces in common.

---

13. Martin Luther King Jr., "Nonviolence: The Only Road to Freedom," speech delivered May 4, 1966.

14. See "The Amazing Growth of Christian Communities," Beliefnet, www.beliefnet.com/Love -Family/2000/08/The-Amazing-Growth-Of-Christian-Communities.aspx?p=1.

However, some of us have noted that most of the young adults drawn to such intentional community are part of the majority Anglo culture. Minorities (and I speak largely from an African-American context) and poorer people have less interest in communal living in the way of the New Monastics. Perhaps minorities and poorer people already find themselves on the margins of society—often even among other Christians—and the established church has already been an alternative to the way of the world.

I do see, however, that as minority Christians become more connected to the broader society, and as some Christians break from the shackles of poverty, they also struggle with how to live their Christian faith honestly and consistently. Peter is showing us that Christians on the margins need to focus on what makes for genuine Christian community, and the irony is that we may all have a better chance at achieving such fellowship when we are willing to embrace our status as peculiar people (see 1 Pet 2:9) who are not fully at home in this world.

Hospitality: A Lost Art?

One particular aspect of Christian community that may be in need of a revival is hospitality. Hospitality is popularly thought of as mere "entertaining." Theologian Arthur Sutherland faults such a view. He explains how the song "Be Our Guest" in the movie *Beauty and the Beast*, with its singing and dancing household utensils, illustrates how contemporary culture equates being a guest with having fun. Hospitality, however, is not entertainment, but something much deeper. "Hospitality is the practice by which the church stands or falls."[15] He defines Christian hospitality as "the intentional, responsible, and caring act of welcoming or visiting, in either public or private places, those who are strangers, enemies, or distressed, without regard for reciprocation."[16] If hospitality is as important as Sutherland suggests, then it may be helpful to consider how Peter's audience likely thought about and practiced hospitality.

Christine D. Pohl, in her thorough and helpful book on hospitality, observes that, "In a number of ancient civilizations, hospitality was viewed as a pillar on which all morality rested; it encompassed 'the good.'"[17] Indeed, hospitality was ingrained in the culture. Our Christian forebears inherited the practice of hospitality first of all from the Jews: "For the people of ancient Israel, understanding themselves as strangers and sojourners, with responsibility to care for vulnerable strangers in their midst, was part of what it meant

---

15. Sutherland, *I Was a Stranger*, 83.
16. Ibid., xiii.
17. Christine D. Pohl, *Making Room: Recovering Hospitality as a Christian Tradition* (Grand Rapids: Eerdmans, 1999), 5.

to be the people of God."[18] In addition, early Christians had models in the institution of hospitality among the Greeks. "The early Christians took over, in some sense, a Greek institution of considerable antiquity."[19] Pohl takes into account both hospitality traditions but concludes that "a distinctively Christian understanding of hospitality developed in the early centuries of the church."[20]

The meaning of the NT term for hospitality, *philoxenia* (see also *philoxenos*, "hospitable"), is closely connected to its etymology; the word combines *philos*, a general word for love or affection, with *xenos*, the word for "stranger." There are only a few NT texts employing *philoxenia* and *philoxenos* (Rom 12:13; 1 Tim 3:2; Titus 1:8; Heb 13:2). These references do not allow us to paint an exhaustive picture of the practice of hospitality, but Hebrews 13:2 does include the element that it involved taking in strangers, which might include fellow Christians who had been traveling ("Do not forget to show hospitality to strangers, for by so doing some people have shown hospitality to angels without knowing it").

Even after the writing of the NT, hospitality remained a key component of Christian faith and practice. For example, in the Shepherd of Hermas, a second-century writing, hospitality is placed alongside other familiar virtues: "serving widows, looking after orphans and those in need, delivering God's servants from distress, being hospitable (for the practice of hospitality results in doing good)" (Herm., Mand. 8:10, Holmes). Also in the second century, Justin Martyr writes about hospitality toward strangers: "And they who are well to do, and willing, give what each thinks fit; and what is collected is deposited with the president, who succors the orphans and widows and those who, through sickness or any other cause, are in want, and those who are in bonds, and the strangers sojourning among us, and in a word takes care of all who are in need" (*1 Apol.* 67:6, *ANF*).

There were four aspects of early Christian hospitality: (1) shared meals, (2) care for traveling evangelists, (3) care for worshipers who met in homes, and (4) understanding that its practice was one sign of fitness for leadership (1 Tim 3:2; Titus 1:8). Pohl elaborates on these elements but notes that as society changed, hospitality became more commercialized and bureaucratized so that "in the churches, hospitality had little moral, spiritual, and physical significance."[21]

I suggest that we orient ourselves toward biblical hospitality by choosing to simplify our lives; it is the busyness of contemporary life that prevents us

18. Ibid.
19. Donald W. Riddle, "Early Christian Hospitality: A Factor in the Gospel Transmission," *JBL* 57 (1938): 143.
20. Pohl, *Making Room*, 17.
21. Ibid., 35.

from entering into the lives of others through the practice of hospitality. For example, we can serve those who may struggle because of poverty or physical limitations. Again, I cite the wisdom of Christine Pohl: "Hospitality will not occur in any significant way in our lives or churches unless we give it deliberate attention. Because the practice has been mostly forgotten and because it conflicts with a number of contemporary values, we must intentionally nurture a commitment to hospitality."[22]

A Word of Caution about Hospitality

Along with my plea for reviving the practice of hospitality, a word of caution is in order. We must nurture our own lives with an appropriate rhythm of work and rest lest we grow bitter in serving others. Some people have been known to take advantage of hospitable servants. I have seen many of my colleagues in urban ministry grow cynical, burn out, or simply give up from being overwhelmed by the needs of others. Dr. Chanequa Walker-Barnes addresses this very issue, noting, "Christian leaders laboring in under-resourced communities often endorse and embody a theological understanding of selfhood that predisposes them to neglect themselves and their families for the sake of ministry."[23] I noted above in the "Explain the Story" section that the early Christian document Didache ("Teaching") addressed the possibility that some Christian visitors could wear out their welcome. The fact that a gracious host could be taken advantage of seems also to be behind Peter's admonition in v. 9. He commands that hospitality be practiced, but "without grumbling." There are limits to what we can do, and even in the benevolent work of hospitality we must practice adequate self-care.

There are greater dangers than the occasional annoying visitor. We make ourselves vulnerable to theft or other danger. I have a dear friend who was molested as a child by a youth minister who stayed in his family's home for a time. We must exercise discernment and also stay connected to others in the Christian community, since hospitality can often involve more than the solo effort of the homeowner.

---

22. Ibid., 171.
23. Chanequa Walker-Barnes, "Love Yourself: Urban Ministry and the Challenge of Self-Love," *ExAud* 29 (2013): 98.

CHAPTER 14

1 Peter 4:12-19

 ## LISTEN to the Story

¹²Dear friends, do not be surprised at the fiery ordeal that has come on you to test you, as though something strange were happening to you. ¹³But rejoice inasmuch as you participate in the sufferings of Christ, so that you may be overjoyed when his glory is revealed. ¹⁴If you are insulted because of the name of Christ, you are blessed, for the Spirit of glory and of God rests on you. ¹⁵If you suffer, it should not be as a murderer or thief or any other kind of criminal, or even as a meddler. ¹⁶However, if you suffer as a Christian, do not be ashamed, but praise God that you bear that name. ¹⁷For it is time for judgment to begin with God's household; and if it begins with us, what will the outcome be for those who do not obey the gospel of God? ¹⁸And,

"If it is hard for the righteous to be saved,
    what will become of the ungodly and the sinner?"

¹⁹So then, those who suffer according to God's will should commit themselves to their faithful Creator and continue to do good.

Listening to the Text in the Story: Psalms 31:5; 66:10–12; Proverbs 27:21.

My personal journey of faith includes many interactions with so-called Prosperity Theology or the Prosperity Gospel. Even before I knew it had a name, I heard preachers exclaim that we should "name it and claim it" with regard to our personal desires for wealth, health, and happiness. Believers are entitled to experience only good things, I was taught, and suffering is incompatible with Christian faith. Consequently, if one suffers—at the hands of others or even from sickness—it is because faith is lacking. If we had more faith, we would not suffer.

Even apart from the Prosperity Gospel, ordinary Christians may fall prey to the notion that suffering is a sign of divine disapproval. There is a tendency to blame victims who suffer, assuming that God is punishing them (e.g., Job 4:7–9). Perhaps this is a uniquely Western perspective since here we enjoy relative prosperity when compared to Christians in developing nations.

For Peter's readers suffering was part of the community's experience. Ironically, it was their faith that was to blame, in a manner of speaking, and not their lack of faith. What I mean is that the Christian believers faced hostility from their neighbors precisely because of the differences in allegiances.

Even though Peter has already addressed the topic of suffering, he returns for a final word of admonition and encouragement as he nears the conclusion of his letter.

EXPLAIN the Story

Reading Peter's body closing, 4:12–5:11, we may be struck immediately by its similarity to earlier parts of the letter. The structure mirrors that of 2:11–4:11, which is the heart of the letter and contains the core of Peter's teaching on suffering while living within a pagan society. Both sections open with *agapētoi*, literally, "beloved" (2:11; 4:12), and close with a doxology (4:11d; 5:10–11). Several images and topics from earlier in the letter appear in the last main section. For example:[1]

- Fire as a metaphor (1:7; 4:12a)
- Following a suffering Christ (2:19–23; 4:13)
- Joy through suffering (1:6; 4:16)
- Suffering unjustly because of faith in God (3:16–17; 4:4–5; 5:10)
- The coming end of the age, judgment, and Christ's return in glory (1:13; 2:12; 4:5, 7, 17–18)

Also, as Peter presses toward the end of his letter a sense of urgency may be detected in his amassing of commands:[2]

- Do not be surprised (4:12)
- Rejoice (4:13)
- Let no one suffer (4:15)
- Do not be ashamed (4:16)
- Glorify God (4:16)
- Let them commit themselves (4:19)
- Shepherd the flock (5:2)
- Submit yourselves (5:5)
- Humble yourselves (5:6)

1. My list is adapted from Achtemeier, *1 Peter*, 301–2.
2. Adapted from Green, *1 Peter*, 149.

- Be alert (5:8)
- Be sober-minded (5:8)
- Resist (5:9)

In the present passage under consideration, 4:12–19, Peter recapitulates the major themes that he treated earlier in the letter, notably Christian conduct within the community (2:18–3:7) and the suffering from outsiders (3:8–4:11). Although Peter's references to the Holy Spirit are uncommon in this letter (see 1:2, 11, 12), it is the Spirit's presence that is a source of blessing while God's people are being maligned.

Blessed through Suffering (4:12–16)

Peter's direct address, "dear friends" (*agapētoi*, "beloved"), should be taken as more than a casual greeting or word of transition; rather, it is a message of comfort to those who are feeling the heat of harassment, marginalization, and other forms of oppression. Peter reminds his readers that they are not alone but are connected to one other, to Peter, and to the larger Christian community through the bonds of love. However, Christians are not immune to suffering, and when it comes it should not be surprising. As noted in the earlier discussion of 4:4, "surprised," translates a verb (*xenizō*) that is a cognate with the word for "strange" (*xenos*), found later in v. 12.

Peter does not here elaborate on the nature of the suffering that his readers faced. However, 1:6–7 served to foreshadow the topic of suffering using the image of refining fire and now the same image is used as a flashback. Between these two references to a smelter's fire (1:6–7 and 4:12, see Prov 27:21), we read of what this might include: accusations of wrongdoing (2:12), physical abuse (2:18–20), insults (2:23; 3:9), threats (3:14), and verbal abuse (4:4). Peter likens that to a fire that will lead to cleansing. Such cleansing is a testing of faith that allows impurities to be burned away (see discussion of 1:6–7). Psalm 66:10–12 expresses a similar sentiment with regard to Israel's history: "For you, God, tested us; you refined us like silver. You brought us into prison and laid burdens on our backs. You let people ride over our heads; we went through fire and water, but you brought us to a place of abundance."

Such words, taken in isolation, might not seem comforting. But Peter goes on to command his readers to rejoice while in the midst of their pain. There is no joy in the act of suffering (as we noted in our discussion of 4:1), but there can be joy when believers understand how suffering puts them in solidarity with Christ. First Peter 4:13 is reminiscent of Paul's letter to the Philippians, which handles the theme of rejoicing along with the idea of fellowship, or sharing, using forms of the word *koinōnia*. Philippians 3:10 even uses the phrase "participation in his [Christ's] suffering." Paul is not saying that he endured crucifixion like Christ did, and neither is Peter saying that his readers must withstand the exact same crucifixion. However, these followers of Christ suffer as the Lord suffered—facing abuse from hostile critics because of faith in God. Joy, even while in the throes of persecution, is a foretaste of the ecstasy that will accompany Christ's return. At the *parousia* Christ's status as the one who was elected (2:4), resurrected (e.g., 1:3), and vindicated (3:22) by God will be made known to all. Those who share in Christ's sufferings will also share in his glorification (see 2 Tim 2:12).

A section of the Sermon on the Mount, Matthew 5:10–12, contains thematic and linguistic parallels to 1 Peter 4:13–14, in particular Peter's use of a beatitude (or macarism, as in 3:14) as well as the words "righteousness" (Matt 5:10) // "righteous" (1 Pet 4:18), "insult" (Matt 5:11) // "insulted" (1 Pet 4:14), and "rejoice and be glad" (Matt 5:12) // "rejoice … be overjoyed" (1 Pet 4:13).[3] Peter's teaching is consonant with the Lord's own teaching. In picking up the Lord's own words, Peter emphasizes the connection between their suffering and Christ's.

Verse 14 contains a beatitude, and "beatitudes in Judaism, the New Testament, and early Christianity tend to be directed toward people who on the surface do not appear to be blessed."[4] What is true in the Sermon on the Mount is surely true here in 1 Peter. Peter explains this irony with an allusion to the OT. And using what is likely a reference to the Holy Spirit's presence on God's Messiah, Peter makes another association between his people and the Lord Jesus Christ. The "Spirit of glory and of God" resting upon those who suffer harks back to Isaiah 11:2: "The Spirit of the LORD will rest on him—the Spirit of wisdom and of understanding, the Spirit of counsel and of might, the Spirit of the knowledge and fear of the LORD." As Jobes has well said, "Peter claims that the same Spirit of God predicted to rest upon the Messiah also rests on the believer who is willing to suffer for Jesus Christ."[5]

Reproach toward the Christian community is likely and Peter's grammar in v. 14 stresses that reality.[6] He is speaking about *when* insults occur, not *whether or not* they will happen. And when those insults come, the believers should consider themselves to be blessed, because of the Holy Spirit's presence, provided that the Christians are indeed defamed because of Christ. The Christians must not be guilty of heinous offenses such as murder, theft, or other criminal

---

3. See Green, *1 Peter*, 156.
4. Donelson, *I and II Peter and Jude*, 136.
5. Jobes, *1 Peter*, 288.
6. The Greek construction of a conditional sentence using the particle *ei* ("if") along with a verb in the indicative mood indicates a situation that may be assumed to be true for the sake of the argument. The elaborations found in vv. 15 and 16 should be considered as part of the condition introduced in v. 14.

activity (literally "as an evildoer," see 2:12). Neither should anyone be a "meddler." That final term, *allotriepiskopos*, is yet another word that only Peter uses. In fact, the word occurs nowhere else in Greek literature. Consequently, Elliott, among others, suggests that the term is a "Petrine coinage" used to describe "one who meddles in the affairs of others," i.e., a busybody (see 1 Thess 4:11).[7] Such meddling might involve an air of moral superiority as Christians, engaging in evangelistic efforts, censure the behaviors of unbelievers.

We do not know if Peter's readers were guilty of the behaviors noted in v. 15 or if they were falsely accused of them, but Peter removes any ambiguity about their appropriateness. Such behaviors must not be found among God's people (see 1 Cor 6:9–11).

According to v. 16, suffering is a reason for praising God, provided that the suffering is because of one's identity as a Christian. The use of the epithet "Christian" in v. 16 is parallel to the expression, "name of Christ" in v. 14. The term is rare in the NT (apart from here, only in Acts 11:26; 26:28) and was most likely initially a derogatory expression hurled at some of the first followers of Jesus. Peter notes that among all the insults dumped onto his readers, this particular one—Christian—should not be a cause for dishonor. As noted in our discussion of 2:4–10, honor and shame were important values in the world of the ancient Mediterranean. Shame involved a loss of social status. Peter points out, as he did in 2:6, that followers of Jesus need not bear the weight of shame. Their loss of status in the eyes of their accusers could in no way jeopardize their status in God's eyes. Instead of shame, the believers are to "glorify God" because of the name "Christian." Furthermore, Christians can glorify God since God's judgment has begun.

The Judgment of God (4:17–19)

Peter returns to the topic of judgment, which he had raised earlier in vv. 5–6. Some may not be comfortable with the idea of God judging Christians. After all, didn't Paul say that, "there is now no condemnation for those who are in Christ Jesus" (Rom 8:1)? Based on that passage and others like it, we may think that Christians will bypass God's judgment. However, we do well to keep in mind that judgment does not necessarily mean "condemnation"; the term *krima* and its cognates may simply refer to the action of a judge who pronounces guilt as well as innocence. All people—including believers—will face the scrutiny of God the Judge (see 2 Cor 5:10). It is one's relationship to Christ that will determine the outcome of God's judgment. Peter's argument in vv. 17–18 is that if believers suffer in light of God's judgment—which

7. Elliott, *1 Peter*, 785–88.

judgment has already begun—they should know that the outcome for unbelievers would be much worse.

"Time" (*kairos*) often refers to a critical, decisive moment as opposed
to chronological time (*chronos*). The word frequently appears within eschatological contexts (e.g., Mark 13:33; Luke 21:8; Acts 1:7; Rev 1:3; 22:10).
Throughout his letter Peter uses *kairos* to refer to God's appointed time in
his redemptive acts (see 1:5, 11; 5:6). Previously, Peter asserted that the end
is near (4:7), and now he stresses that God's final judgment has begun. The
suffering that Peter's readers face is part of that judgment.

The OT teaches that God's people within the community are judged prior
to those outside of the community (e.g., Jer 25:29; Zech 13:7–9). Similarly,
Peter says that judgment starts with the church but with similar picturesque
language as he used in 2:4–5. Furthermore, the NT declares that God's people
will face suffering prior to the end of time (e.g., Mark 13:19–20; 1 Thess
3:3–4; 2 Thess 1:5–10; Rev 2:10). Peter assures his people that their suffering is part of God's redemptive plan. Using a rhetorical question in v. 17,
Peter makes a contrast between the present suffering of God's people and that
which will come upon unbelievers. His point is that the pressure on believers,
though intense, is minor compared to what unbelievers will have to endure.

Unbelievers are those who "do not obey the gospel of God." What separates the righteous from unbelievers is not particular actions but one's broad
disposition toward the message and person of Jesus Christ (see 1:12, 25; 4:6).
These unbelievers are the ones Peter described earlier as stumbling and falling
because of their failure to believe in Jesus (2:8).

Peter reinforces the contrasting degree of suffering between believers and
unbelievers with a quotation from Proverbs 11:31 LXX, which translates literally as "if the righteous are saved with difficulty, where will the wicked and
sinner appear?"[8] He does not mean that saving someone is hard for God; the
point is that the journey of salvation is fraught with difficulties even for righteous people due to the pressures they face because of their faith.

Peter concludes this section with an admonition. In essence, he exclaims
to his people, "Don't give up!" Suffering is not a strange idea (v. 12), and it
even comes with God's blessing (v. 13) through the presence of the Holy Spirit
(v. 14). Suffering is the signal that the end is near (4:7, 17) and God will judge
everyone (4:5–6, 17). Consequently, it is best to trust God by continuing to
do what is good.

"According to God's will" does not mean that God wants us to suffer; it
means that Christians suffer because they do God's will (see 4:2). God will

8. See Jobes, *1 Peter*, 297, for more details on 4:18 and its relationship to the Greek and Hebrew
versions of Prov 11:31.

not abandon his followers. Peter's language of "commit themselves" evokes the words of Psalm 31:5, which was quoted in part by the Lord Jesus as he hung upon the cross: "Into your hands I commit my spirit; deliver me, LORD, my faithful God." The word in v. 19 that is translated "commit" (*paratithēmi*) means to entrust something to someone else for safekeeping. As in the case of our Lord on the cross, Christians are to entrust their bodies and souls—their entire beings (*psychē*)—to God, who is faithful. The faithfulness of God is put in the context of God's authority over all creation. Since God is the one possessing the power to make all things—including all people—he is trustworthy.

LIVE the Story

Lessons from the Margins

In my discussion of 1 Peter 3:13–17, I pointed out that Christians in America used to enjoy a degree of religious hegemony. This is to say that there had been times when certain aspects of Christianity served as threads woven into the fabric of social mores, so that Christian holidays and customs were observed openly and without much question. Additionally, practicing any other religion besides Christianity (especially Protestantism) was odd and viewed with suspicion. People who remember those days with fondness may be experiencing a large degree of discomfort while maneuvering about in our current pluralistic climate.

Because of the status Christianity had previously enjoyed in the USA, understanding the original impact of Peter's words in 4:12–19 may be nearly impossible. Suffering has not been part of the American Christian experience for most people. We may have faced ridicule or embarrassment from time to time for refusing to join in particular activities, or for using our Sundays differently than our neighbors, or for holding to certain ethical behaviors, but such humiliation is a far cry from what our forebears faced in some of the earliest days of the Christian movement.

That being said, there are faithful people who have experienced marginalization akin to what Peter describes. Perhaps all of us—even those in the majority culture—can take lessons from those who have been belittled, not enjoying any degree of prominence in society. Two groups serve as examples, although we could surely consider others: (1) African-American slaves and (2) people in other lands who are facing religious persecution.

A Sermon from the Days of Slavery

Slavery in America was an enigma. First of all, it contradicted the founding document, the *Declaration of Independence*; second, many who professed to read the Bible faithfully condoned slavery's practice. Richard Allen, the founder of the African Methodist Episcopal denomination, was born in 1760 to enslaved parents. He managed to purchase his own freedom and became an avid abolitionist. Allen directed his sermons not only to slaves but also to those who approved of slavery; in this example his words resonate with 1 Peter:

> I mention experience [as a slave] to you, that your hearts may not sink at the discouraging prospects you may have, and that you may put your trust in God, who sees your condition; and as a merciful father pitieth his children, so doth God pity them that love him; and as your hearts are inclined to serve God, you will feel an affectionate regard towards your masters and mistresses, so called, and the whole family in which you live. This will be seen by them, and tend to promote your liberty, especially with such as have feeling masters; and if they are otherwise, you will have the favour and love of God dwelling in your hearts, which you will value more than any thing else, which will be a consolation in the worst condition you can be in, and no master can deprive you of it, and as life is short and uncertain, and the chief end of our having a being in this world is to be prepared for a better, I wish you to think of this more than any thing else; then you will have a view of that freedom which the sons of God enjoy; and if the troubles of your condition end with your lives, you will be admitted to the freedom which God hath prepared for those of all colours that love him. Here the power of the roost [sic] cruel master ends, and all sorrow and fears are wiped away.[9]

Rev. Allen's appeals resonate with various portions of Scripture, including 1 Peter. He urges that his readers be patient, refrain from bitterness, and look forward to the end (see 1 Pet 4:7). He also pleads for diligent service so that no one would have cause to dismiss their fight for freedom (see 4:15).

A Letter in Response to Persecuted Christians

In April 2015 the group known as the Islamic State of Iraq and Syria (ISIS) horribly murdered dozens of Ethiopian Christians. A video recording by ISIS depicting those murders served as anti-Christian propaganda. In response, His

---

9. Richard Allen, "The Life, Experiences, and Gospel Labours of the Rt. Rev. Richard Allen," 47–48, Documenting the American South, http://docsouth.unc.edu/neh/allen/allen.html. (Used with permission. "This work is the property of the University of North Carolina at Chapel Hill. It may be used freely by individuals for research, teaching and personal use as long as this statement of availability is included in the text.") Please note that the sermon contains addresses to those "who keep slaves and approve the practice," to "the people of colour," and to "friends of him who hath no helper." I reproduced the section addressed to "the people of colour."

Grace Bishop Angaelos, General Bishop of the Coptic Orthodox Church in the United Kingdom, issued a statement that included the following:

> These horrific murders have not only touched the lives of those in the Middle East and Africa, but have led to a greater sense of solidarity among people and communities around the world. I am thankful, in the midst of this pain, that the ghastly nature of these crimes is bringing a greater rejection of them, and of any ideology that sanctions, justifies or glorifies brutality and murder.... We pray repose for the souls of these innocent men, a change of heart for those who took their lives, but above all we pray comfort and strength for their families and communities, and the many around the world who may not have known them, yet are left to mourn such a tragic and unnecessary loss of precious life.[10]

This is but one voice among many whose Christian community has been terrorized in recent times. In the bishop's words, there is not only a rejection of violence and a support of those who suffer; there is also a tone of love for enemies. This also resonates with the words of Peter.

Sometimes the immediate response in the face of hostility is revenge. Even some Christians will advocate violence as a means of retaliation. I suspect when one is in the majority it may be easier to formulate a plan for retribution. Yet in the above examples, for slaves who had no social status and for persecuted believers under an oppressive regime, there was little hope for a violent reprisal that would change the status quo. While we all can appreciate—even if not understand—such pain, anger, and impatience over such injustice, we must focus on how the Scriptures guide us. Here Peter, who echoes the words of our Lord, pleads for believers to keep doing good work even in the face of suffering (4:19). Perhaps we can learn from those who have suffered on the margins of society how we can handle our own alienation from the mainstream—especially when our suffering has not been as severe as that of our forebears or of our siblings in the faith in many other countries.

10. "Statement by HG Bishop Angaelos following the murder of Ethiopian Christians by Daesh (IS) in Libya," The Coptic Orthodox Church UK, April 20, 2015, http://copticcentre.blogspot.co.uk/2015/04/statement-by-hg-bishop-angaelos.html. Please see the helpful feature, "Persecution," *Christianity Today*, http://www.christianitytoday.com/ct/topics/p/persecution.

CHAPTER 15

1 Peter 5:1-11

 ## LISTEN to the Story

¹To the elders among you, I appeal as a fellow elder and a witness of Christ's sufferings who also will share in the glory to be revealed: ²Be shepherds of God's flock that is under your care, watching over them— not because you must, but because you are willing, as God wants you to be; not pursuing dishonest gain, but eager to serve; ³not lording it over those entrusted to you, but being examples to the flock. ⁴And when the Chief Shepherd appears, you will receive the crown of glory that will never fade away.

⁵In the same way, you who are younger, submit yourselves to your elders. All of you, clothe yourselves with humility toward one another, because,

"God opposes the proud
 but shows favor to the humble."

⁶Humble yourselves, therefore, under God's mighty hand, that he may lift you up in due time. ⁷Cast all your anxiety on him because he cares for you.

⁸Be alert and of sober mind. Your enemy the devil prowls around like a roaring lion looking for someone to devour. ⁹Resist him, standing firm in the faith, because you know that the family of believers throughout the world is undergoing the same kind of sufferings.

¹⁰And the God of all grace, who called you to his eternal glory in Christ, after you have suffered a little while, will himself restore you and make you strong, firm and steadfast. ¹¹To him be the power forever and ever. Amen.

Listening to the Text in the Story: Proverbs 3:34; Mark 10:32–45; John 13:3–11; James 4:6–7.

When I discuss church ministry with fellow pastors, many agree that much of what we learned in seminary did not prepare us well for the role of pastor in contemporary times. Most of my education, for which I am grateful, focused on handling Scripture, understanding theological ideas, appreciating the history of Christianity, and also communicating through preaching and teaching. But churches apparently do not expect their pastors to be resident theologians, counselors, or even teachers. Modern-day pastors are expected to be motivational speakers with managerial skills akin to those of American business professionals. I have attended gatherings on leadership in the church which featured plenty of presentations from the business and political worlds, while studies from Scripture were absent or minimal. Additionally, the current tendency is to laud as successful those who manage with what approaches a dictatorship. Servant-leadership, though often discussed, does not win out among our models of successful ministry. Large numbers of "buildings, bucks, and bodies"—the trinity of ministry—is what determines success.

A young pastor noted that prior to his work with me he'd always been in churches with authoritarian senior pastors. My associate and I agreed that heavy-handed leadership is often more efficient! However, the picture that Peter gives of church leadership is contrary to these contemporary models and offers a rebuke to the autocrats. Leaders must be shepherds who follow the example of Jesus Christ. In this section Peter likely does not have only those we call "pastor" in mind, but all who are mature in the church. For the younger learners as well as the older mentors, humility is key.

EXPLAIN the Story

Peter has said that the church is God's household (4:17), and within that metaphor he now speaks to older and younger family members. Peter has alluded to the virtue of humility earlier in the letter (see 1:14; 3:1, 8). Here humility governs the way the elders lead, the way the younger follow, and also the way the entire community should conduct itself even when ostracized. The ultimate example of humility is Jesus.

Before offering a final doxology, which contains a promise of how God will "restore" the readers, Peter briefly cautions the community about the devil. His readers must be vigilant and stalwart in their faith in Jesus as a strategy against the devil's attacks.

A Final Word for Elder and Younger (5:1–5a)

"Elders" are simultaneously the older people within the congregation as well as its leaders. Peter emphasizes their leadership role as "shepherds" (v. 2) but also makes a distinction between others in the community based upon age

(v. 5). The term *presbyteros* ("elder") may refer to a person advanced in age as well as a leader among a congregation. In both the OT and the NT, Jewish leaders were called "elders" (e.g., Exod 19:7; Ruth 4:2; Luke 7:3). Early Christians also used "elder" as a title (e.g., Acts 11:30; 14:23; 1 Tim 5:17). First Clement, a Christian writing from the early second century, appears to use the term *presbyteros* as Peter does, with the double sense of older people as well as leaders: "For you did everything without partiality, and you lived in accordance with the laws of God, submitting yourselves to your leaders and giving to the older men among you the honor due them" (1 Clem. 1:3, Holmes).

Peter's appeal to leadership is based upon his own position as an elder and also as an eyewitness of the sufferings of Christ. We might expect Peter, as one of the original twelve apostles (see 1:1), to call attention to his high position as an eyewitness of the ministry of Jesus and his resurrection (see Acts 1:21–22; 1 Cor 15:3–8). Yet here Peter more pointedly refers to how he witnessed the sufferings of Christ. We may supply the details from Matthew and Mark, which recount how, upon the betrayal by Judas and Jesus's arrest, the other disciples fled (Matt 26:55; Mark 14:50). Yet all four Gospels also note that Peter followed from a distance to see what would happen to Jesus (Matt 26:58; Mark 14:54; Luke 22:54; and John 18:15, which suggests that John was with Peter). Peter saw at least a portion of Christ's sufferings.

Throughout 1 Peter the sufferings of Christ have served to reinforce the apostle's admonitions (1:11, 19; 2:21–24; 3:18; 4:1, 13). Yet here not only does suffering put the Savior in solidarity with Peter's readers, it also serves as a contrast to the bright future that believers will have at the *parousia*, the return of Christ. Peter, in addition to being an elder and eyewitness, claims status as a partaker in Christ's glory that will one day be manifested (1:13). Peter wants his fellow elders to know what he knows: after suffering there will be glory (see Rom 8:18).

In the meantime, elders must care for the people of God. Peter in 5:2, as do the psalmists, portrays God's people as sheep (cf. Pss 23:1; 78:52; 95:7; 100:3). Leaders, therefore, are shepherds, following the example of Jesus, the Chief Shepherd (2:25; 5:4; Heb 13:20). Paul, in Ephesians 4:11, also refers to some leaders in the church as shepherds, but the word *poimēn* is typically translated there as "pastor," and contemporary readers—especially urbanites such as myself—may miss some of the imagery contained in the word "shepherd." Shepherds are to provide the kind of care that Peter describes as "watching over." That expression, "watching over," is related to the Greek *episkopos*, from which we get the word "episcopal" (see 1 Tim 3:2 and my earlier discussion of 2:25).

Peter describes that task, using three pairs of contrasts:

1. Not out of obligation, but willingly
2. Not greedily, but with eagerness to serve
3. Not heavy handedly, but as examples

There are lists of requirements for leaders elsewhere (e.g., 1 Tim 3:1–7; Titus 1:5–9), but it may be the teaching of Jesus that is uppermost in Peter's mind. On several occasions Jesus taught his followers that discipleship involves suffering, using his impending passion as the example (Mark 8:31–38; 9:31–37; 10:32–45).

Jesus connected his suffering to humble service. In Mark 9 and 10, Jesus uses his disciples' jockeying for prominent positions to give a lesson on authentic leadership. The episode in Mark 9 concludes with Jesus lifting up a child to illustrate that true greatness is found in being last instead of first, and by serving.

> Then they came to Capernaum; and when he was in the house he asked them, "What were you arguing about on the way?" But they were silent, for on the way they had argued with one another who was the greatest. He sat down, called the twelve, and said to them, "Whoever wants to be first must be last of all and servant of all." Then he took a little child and put it among them; and taking it in his arms, he said to them, "Whoever welcomes one such child in my name welcomes me, and whoever welcomes me welcomes not me but the one who sent me." (Mark 9:33–37 NRSV)

A later incident in Mark 10 is even closer to Peter's teaching here in vv. 1–4. After the sons of Zebedee, James and John, request to sit on the right and left side of Jesus "in your glory" (Mark 10:37), Jesus points his disciples to the path of suffering, described metaphorically as drinking from a cup and baptism (Mark 10:38–39). When the other disciples react angrily to the inquiry from James and John, the Lord responds further:

> Jesus called them together and said, "You know that those who are regarded as rulers of the Gentiles lord it over them, and their high officials exercise authority over them. Not so with you. Instead, whoever wants to become great among you must be your servant, and whoever wants to be first must be slave of all. For even the Son of Man did not come to be served, but to serve, and to give his life as a ransom for many." (Mark 10:42–45)

Jesus observes that tyrannical leadership is found among Gentiles, a fact with which Peter's readers would agree. Rather than take their cues from Gentile officials, the leaders of the church are to be like Jesus and lead through service. And as Jesus offered his own style of servant leadership as an example, those elders of the church in turn are to be examples to God's flock (5:3). Although Peter does not use the word "humility" until v. 5, it is fitting to say that vv. 1–3 describe the brand of humble leadership that Jesus taught and demonstrated.

When Jesus the Chief Shepherd returns, those shepherds will be rewarded with an unfading crown of glory. Peter started his address to the elders with an expectation of his own future glory (5:1), and he now ends the section offering the same hope to his readers. Just as Peter points backward to suffering and forward to glorification, the image of a crown may simultaneously point backward as well as forward. A crown recalls the suffering of Jesus, whose royal heritage was mocked when soldiers placed a crown of thorns upon his head (Matt 27:29). At the same time, the depiction of the *parousia* of Jesus in Revelation 19 includes the lord on a white horse wearing a crown (19:12, where the crown is a *diadēma* and not the usual *stephanos*).

In the Greco-Roman world, crowns, typically consisting of woven foliage, served as recognition of high status or distinguished public service. Even though leaders among the Gentiles—who lord it over others—might receive crowns, the leaders of God's flock would receive even better crowns. The "crown of glory" (5:4) is unfading, in contrast to crowns made of foliage, which quickly decay.

The younger people, those who are not leaders, are admonished to "submit." Submission is a godly posture that ultimately recognizes God's authority over everything and everyone (see 3:1–6). Submission is not always easy and it requires humility, which is the very virtue that ties this entire section together and is mentioned explicitly in the following sentence.

The Centrality of Humility (5:5b–7)

As noted above, the words and actions of Jesus seem to lie behind Peter's imperatives throughout this final chapter. That is almost certainly the case in the second part of v. 5. Peter's command to "clothe yourselves with humility" recalls the events of the Last Supper as depicted in John 13:3–11, when Jesus washed his disciples' feet. According to John, Jesus took on the role of a slave as he took off his outer robe and tied a towel around himself, the way a slave would dress to perform the menial task of washing the feet of guests. Behind the command "clothe yourselves" in v. 5b is yet another rare word. *Enkomboomai* is a verb built from the noun *enkombōma*, the word for an apron worn by a slave. In essence, Peter says, "put on an apron of humility, in the way that a slave aprons himself." Jesus dressed himself as a slave to wash the feet of his disciples and Peter wants the church to take a similar posture toward one another.

Humility was not considered a virtue in Greco-Roman society (see my discussion of 3:8). However, God does honor humility. At the end of v. 5 Peter quotes Proverbs 3:34. God's people, even though they suffer at the moment, will be vindicated through their humility. Throughout the letter it has been clear that the broader society is hostile to the people of God. The unbelievers fit into the category of "proud," as they have elevated themselves over God's people and God's word. Consequently, they will face God's judgment since he "opposes the proud." Yet God's people will know God's favor.

Therefore, according to v. 6, the entire community—the older and the younger—should be humble and hopeful; the mighty God will exalt his people at the right time. This pattern of exaltation after humiliation is also the picture Paul paints of Jesus in Philippians 2:5–11.[1]

Exaltation by God's hand will come at some future point, but in the meantime life is stressful and fraught with uncertainties. In v. 7 Peter addresses the concerns Christians have during their time of waiting for God's exaltation and vindication. All worries should be given over to God. Indeed, they should be "thrown" onto God as one flings an item onto a beast of burden (see Luke 19:35, the only other NT appearance of the word for "cast"). Anxiety is not just related to suffering; it can be anything in life that gives us concern. For example, in the parable about seed that falls in various places, Jesus teaches how some seed, representing God's word, falls among thorns, which represent the worries or anxieties of life (Matt 13:22).

God is able to bear the anxieties of his people because he cares for his people. Peter utters the words that hurting people most want to hear: "God cares." God has not abandoned them. Although it is not part of the canon of Protestant Scripture, the LXX's book of Wisdom, a writing that pious Jews would have known, uses the same vocabulary: "For neither is there any god besides you, whose care is for all people" (Wis 12:13 NRSV). That sentiment is of course found throughout the Scriptures, employing a range of vocabulary and images. For example, in the Sermon on the Mount Jesus states that people who know the goodness of God should not worry:

> Therefore I tell you, do not worry about your life, what you will eat or what you will drink, or about your body, what you will wear. Is not life more than food, and the body more than clothing? Look at the birds of the air; they neither sow nor reap nor gather into barns, and yet your heavenly Father feeds them. Are you not of more value than they? And can any of you by worrying add a single hour to your span of life? And why do you worry about clothing? Consider the lilies of the field, how

---

1. Both Peter and Paul use a form of the verb *hypsoō*, "to exalt."

they grow; they neither toil nor spin, yet I tell you, even Solomon in all
his glory was not clothed like one of these. But if God so clothes the grass
of the field, which is alive today and tomorrow is thrown into the oven,
will he not much more clothe you—you of little faith? Therefore do not
worry, saying, "What will we eat?" or "What will we drink?" or "What will
we wear?" For it is the Gentiles who strive for all these things; and indeed
your heavenly Father knows that you need all these things. But strive first
for the kingdom of God and his righteousness, and all these things will be
given to you as well. (Matt 6:25–33 NRSV)

Rather than worrying, people should be focusing on God's rule and righteousness and trust God to provide the basic needs of life. Looking to the ways
of God requires sobriety, which not only includes an understanding of God's
grace but also awareness of the devil's schemes (see 2 Cor 2:11).

Lessons about the Devil (5:8–9)

Verse 8 contains the third and final time that Peter urges vigilance. He has earlier called his people to be alert and sober-minded, for holiness (1:13) and for
prayer (4:7). Presently, Peter's call is for watchfulness and sobriety in light of
the devil's known *modus operandi*. The devil is a prowler. In Psalm 22:13 the
psalmist laments about his human opponents, "Roaring lions that tear their
prey open their mouths wide against me." So too, says Peter, is your adversary,
the devil. The ultimate enemy of God's people is not passive but terrifyingly
active. He does not wait for people to slip into his grasp, nor is he a scavenger
that awaits his prey's death. The devil is a predator, searching for victims.

Yet, contrary to what one might expect, Peter does not advocate a preemp-
tive strike or some aggressive action against the devil. Rather, God's people
must hold their ground against the devil's attacks. Peter urges resistance based
upon solid faith. Here his words remind us of the spiritual warfare found in
Ephesians:

Finally, be strong in the Lord and in his mighty power. Put on the full
armor of God, so that you can take your stand against the devil's schemes.
For our struggle is not against flesh and blood, but against the rulers,
against the authorities, against the powers of this dark world and against
the spiritual forces of evil in the heavenly realms. Therefore put on the
full armor of God, so that when the day of evil comes, you may be able to
stand your ground, and after you have done everything, to stand. Stand
firm then, with the belt of truth buckled around your waist, with the
breastplate of righteousness in place, and with your feet fitted with the
readiness that comes from the gospel of peace. In addition to all this,

take up the shield of faith, with which you can extinguish all the flaming arrows of the evil one. Take the helmet of salvation and the sword of the Spirit, which is the word of God. (Eph 6:10–17)

The list of armor ends with only one offensive weapon, a sword. Paul's main goal is for his readers to stand their ground (Eph 6:13), the same thing (using the same vocabulary, *anthistēmi*) that Peter calls for in v. 9.

The letter of James, similarly addressed to dispersed believers (compare Jas 1:1 and 1 Pet 1:1), echoes Peter's advice: "But he gives us more grace. That is why Scripture says: 'God opposes the proud but shows favor to the humble.' Submit yourselves, then, to God. Resist the devil, and he will flee from you" (Jas 4:6–7). James claims that the devil will flee as a result of the believers' resistance through their submission to God. For both Peter and James, advice for defense against the devil follows a call to humility. Perhaps a lack of pride, the sin presumed to have been the devil's downfall, helps in the work of resistance to the devil.

Further along in v. 9 Peter informs these believers that they are not alone in their suffering. Knowing that God cares can encourage us in the midst of trials and so can an awareness that we do not suffer alone. Others in the world of the first century are familiar with the trials that his people are facing. The shared experience of suffering Christians provides motivation to stand firm in the faith.

Final Words of Praise (5:10–11)

I noted earlier (see 4:12–19) that 4:12–5:11 makes up the ending of Peter's letter proper, prior to the closing greetings. Previous themes are recapitulated in the closing, and both sections end with a doxology. The doxology in 4:11 follows a call for sobriety and vigilance (4:7) just as the doxology here in 5:10–11 does. With these concluding words of praise, Peter celebrates God's favor, offers a promise of future restoration, and affirms the power of God.

The word translated "favor" a few verses earlier (5:5) is the same word rendered "grace" here in v. 10. God does not simply dispense grace; grace is a part of God's character. "The God of all grace" is a way of saying, "God, who is grace." We can compare this Paul's language, "the God of hope," in Rom 15:13. Even more commonly, God is called the "God of peace" (Rom 15:33; 16:20; Phil 4:9; 1 Thess 5:23; Heb 13:20). God gives peace because he possesses peace as a divine attribute. For Peter, God gives grace (1:2, 10, 13; 3:7; 4:10; 5:5) because grace is an essential part of his character. God's gracious nature is evident in his divine election or calling of his people (1:15; 2:9, 21; 3:9).

The famous hymn "Great is Thy Faithfulness" includes the line "strength for today and bright hope for tomorrow." That echoes the sentiment found in vv. 5:1–11. Peter reminds his community of the salvation that awaits them (e.g., "the crown of glory" in v. 2) and also proclaims that God will grant them the ability to remain faithful during the time of trial. Earlier, in 2:5 Peter described the believing community as living stones that are being built into a spiritual house, a strong and stable building. Here in 5:10 Peter reinforces that image of strength and stability with four verbs: *katartizō* ("to restore"), *stērizō* ("to make strong"), *sthenoō* ("to make firm"), and *themelioō* ("to make steadfast"). That third verb is found in Matthew's account of the parable of the wise and the foolish builders, which concludes the Sermon on the Mount (Matt 7:24–27). The wise builder's house was well "established" because of its solid foundation. The Christian community's solidity is made possible through God's eternal might, which Peter celebrated in 4:11.

LIVE the Story

Being a pastor, I cannot help but to reflect on my own calling as I read vv. 1–11. While the verses apply to all Christians on some level, I find them especially relevant for pastors. If you are not a pastor, please read on anyway and take a moment to pray for your pastor and other spiritual leaders regarding these topics of shepherding, the devil's attacks, pride, and humility.

Shepherding God's Flock
I noted in my introduction to this section that contemporary pastors face a pressure to be more like CEOs of corporations and less like shepherds who care for a flock. Clearly we all have different styles of leadership, but we must respect the fact that Peter appeals to the elders principally to "be shepherds of God's flock" (5:2). There are many resources available to assist pastors in defining what their roles are, and I would encourage further reading in that area. For now, I'd like to offer voices from three pastors on the topic. These voices extend from recent times (Joseph Stowell, the president of a Christian university), back to the late nineteenth–early twentieth centuries (Charles Jefferson, a long-term pastor in the heart of New York City), and further back to the seventeenth century (Richard Baxter, the famous Puritan pastor and evangelist).

Joseph Stowell, in his *Redefining Leadership: Character-Driven Habits of Effective Leaders*, teaches on 1 Peter 5:1–7. He observes that "Peter casts leadership in the language of shepherding… It's rare to hear a leader articulate his or her role in the language of shepherding. The metaphor of shepherd and sheep is one that most of us are unfamiliar with."[2] Stowell continues:

---

2. Joseph M. Stowell, *Redefining Leadership: Character-Driven Habits of Effective Leaders* (Grand Rapids: Zondervan, 2014), 87–88.

It's no wonder that leaders today look to the corporate model, borrowing metaphors and images from the world of business leadership. Leadership books and seminars tend to describe and define leadership by encouraging even those of us in ministry to see ourselves as executives, basing our decisions on how a CEO would lead. It's interesting to note that many pastors and ministry leaders actually seem to think of themselves, not as shepherds, but as CEOs. Of course, there are aspects of CEOing that need to be exercised. But even in that, the concept of shepherding advises "how" we carry out our executive responsibilities.[3]

Charles Jefferson was pastor of the Broadway Tabernacle in New York City for nearly four decades. His *The Minister as Shepherd* first appeared more than a hundred years ago, yet much of it sounds remarkably relevant for today. After noting how the culture seemed apathetic toward the role of pastor, Jefferson writes:[4]

> Multitudes care little for worship, less for church polity, still less for creeds, nothing for traditions and ceremonies. Character is everything. Shepherding is the work for which humanity is crying. The twentieth century is the century of the shepherd … the relation of the minister to the parish is now too often that of a platform speaker to an audience, of a reformer to a community, of an engineer to a machine, and not that of a friend to a company of friends. If the minister is simply a Sunday lecturer, he can leave town any day, and no one will be sadder. If he is only a public reformer, he can depart at the end of any week and many persons will be glad. If he is a machinist, expert in managing organizations, his place can easily be filled by another—engineers are abundant. If he is a shepherd, if he knows his sheep by name, and if his sheep know his voice, he cannot pass from one fold to another without a great loneliness and heaviness of spirit, and without deep wounds in the hearts of those he leaves behind him.… If the Church of Christ is to be saved, she must be born again into the glory of the shepherd idea.[5]

Richard Baxter's classic, *The Reformed Pastor*, is replete with counsel that is perpetually applicable. In his chapter, "The Oversight of the Flock," Baxter has many words of advice on what shepherding entails. Apropos to Peter's words about humility, he cautions:

---

3. Ibid., 88.

4. Rather than change the pronouns, I've left them as Jefferson originally wrote them, but his words apply to male and female pastors.

5. Charles Edward Jefferson, *The Minister as Shepherd* (New York: Thomas Y. Crowell, 1912), 104–5.

Our work must be carried on with great humility. We must carry ourselves meekly and condescendingly to all; and so teach others, as to be as ready to learn of any that can teach us, and so both teach and learn at once; not proudly venting our own conceits, and disdaining all that any way contradict them, as if we had attained to the height of knowledge, and were destined for the chair, and other men to sit at our feet... I say of ministers as Augustine to Jerome, even of the aged among them, "Although it is more fitting to teach than to learn, much more is it fitting to learn than to be ignorant."[6]

These are a small sampling over a number of years and within a narrow cultural range (European and American). Yet I chose them because they are voices that celebrate shepherding as a central role of pastors, and I have found them personally helpful and challenging in my own life. I especially take Baxter's advice and continually seek to learn from the people God allows me to know or at least know about.

The Devil, Pride, and Humility

Peter mentions the devil directly after writing about humility; James does the same thing (Jas 4:6–7). Christians have long associated the devil with pride. For many Bible readers, that connection is based largely upon two OT passages that have been understood as references to Satan. One of the passages is the lament against the King of Tyre found in Ezekiel 28:1–19, especially vv. 12–17:

> Son of man, take up a lament concerning the king of Tyre and say to
> him: "This is what the Sovereign LORD says:
> 'You were the seal of perfection,
>   full of wisdom and perfect in beauty.
> You were in Eden,
>   the garden of God;
> every precious stone adorned you:
>   carnelian, chrysolite and emerald,
>   topaz, onyx and jasper,
>   lapis lazuli, turquoise and beryl.
> Your settings and mountings were made of gold;
>   on the day you were created they were prepared.
> You were anointed as a guardian cherub,
>   for so I ordained you.
> You were on the holy mount of God;
>   you walked among the fiery stones.

---

6. Richard Baxter, *The Reformed Pastor*, Puritan Paperbacks (Edinburgh: Banner of Truth, 1974), 116–17.

You were blameless in your ways
　　from the day you were created
　　till wickedness was found in you.
Through your widespread trade
　　you were filled with violence,
　　and you sinned.
So I drove you in disgrace from the mount of God,
　　and I expelled you, guardian cherub,
　　from among the fiery stones.
Your heart became proud
　　on account of your beauty,
and you corrupted your wisdom
　　because of your splendor.
So I threw you to the earth;
　　I made a spectacle of you before kings.'"

The second passage is the taunt against the king of Babylon found in Isaiah 14:4–23, especially vv. 12–15:

How you have fallen from heaven,
　　morning star, son of the dawn!
You have been cast down to the earth,
　　you who once laid low the nations!
You said in your heart,
　　"I will ascend to the heavens;
I will raise my throne
　　above the stars of God;
I will sit enthroned on the mount of assembly,
　　on the utmost heights of Mount Zaphon.
I will ascend above the tops of the clouds;
　　I will make myself like the Most High."
But you are brought down to the realm of the dead,
　　to the depths of the pit.

The "morning star" of Isaiah 14:12 (Heb: *helel*) is translated *Lucifer* in the Latin Vulgate, which also appears as a proper noun in the King James Version. Allusions to Isaiah 14:12 appear in the NT when Jesus refers to Satan falling in Luke 10:18, and in Revelation 9:1, the account of a falling star who has the key to the Abyss. Those two NT verses seem to be intentional allusions to Isaiah 14:12, contributing to the morning star's association with the devil.

It is clear from both prophecies that pride is directly responsible for the ruination of the king of Tyre (Ezek 12) and the king of Babylon (Isa 14), both of whom have been identified with Satan. Consequently, pride is sometimes referred to as the original sin, having been responsible for Satan's downfall, presumably before the sin of humans in the garden of Eden (Gen 3:1–7). St. Augustine of Hippo (AD 354–430) cites Sirach 10:13 when he writes, "'Pride is the commencement of all sin;' because it was this which overthrew the devil, from whom arose the origin of sin; and afterwards, when his malice and envy pursued man, who was yet standing in his uprightness, it subverted him in the same way in which he himself fell. For the serpent, in fact, only sought for the door of pride whereby to enter when he said, 'Ye shall be as gods.'"[7]

Furthermore, in the qualifications of an overseer (*episkopos*) in 1 Timothy 3:6 is the prohibition, "He must not be a recent convert, or he may become conceited and fall under the same judgment as the devil." Conceit, or pride, is directly connected to the devil. Additionally, pride is associated with the devil because pride is consistently seen as contrary to the ways of God. Pride is one of the so-called Seven Deadly Sins (wrath, greed, sloth, pride, lust, envy, and gluttony), associated with Proverbs 6:16–19, which lists seven things the Lord hates: "There are six things the LORD hates, seven that are detestable to him: haughty eyes, a lying tongue, hands that shed innocent blood, a heart that devises wicked schemes, feet that are quick to rush into evil, a false witness who pours out lies and a person who stirs up conflict in the community."

While the biblical connection between Satan and pride is conjectural, the relationship between pride and ruin is not, as Proverbs 16:18 makes clear: "Pride goes before destruction, a haughty spirit before a fall." Many years ago several notable preachers fell victim to scandals. I was a seminary student when Jim Bakker and Jimmy Swaggart, two of the most famous televangelists, were publicly humiliated. Pride was a prominent factor in the downfall of both men. Of course they were not the only preachers to fall—and certainly not the first—but it seems as if their public disgrace provoked hypervigilance on the part of Americans toward all preachers ever since.

While many fear prideful preachers, none of us is immune to that sin; we all need to learn the way of humility. A colleague and friend, Dr. Tom Tarrants, has written on the pervasiveness of pride: "It would be easy to conclude that pride is the special problem of those who are rich, powerful, successful, famous, or self-righteous. But that is wrong. It takes many shapes and forms and affects all of us to some degree. The widespread, chronic preoccupation with self in American culture, for example, is rooted in pride and can give

---

7. "St. Augustine: Anti-Pelagian Writings," in *Nicene and Post-Nicene Fathers I, Volume 5, Christian Classics Ethereal Library*, http://www.ccel.org/ccel/schaff/npnf105.html. Sirach (known to some as Ecclesiasticus) is book found in the Apocrypha, which was part of the Greek OT (Septuagint). Sirach 10:13 NRSV says, "For the beginning of pride is sin, and the one who clings to it pours out abominations. Therefore the Lord brings upon them unheard-of calamities, and destroys them completely."

rise to or intensify our emotional problems."⁸ Tarrants goes on to highlight several passages of Scripture to show how humility is the antidote to pride. He concludes with the practical admonition that "as we refuse to be preoccupied with ourselves and our own importance and seek to love and serve others, it will reorient us from self-centeredness to other-centeredness—to serving and caring for others just as Jesus did for us. In the narcissistic culture of contemporary America, this is a particularly powerful countercultural witness of Christ's presence and lordship in our lives."⁹

In a chapter entitled "Humility and Exaltation," Andrew Murray, the South African mystic of the late-nineteenth and early-twentieth centuries, offers some appropriate thoughts on 1 Peter 5:6 (along with Jas 4:10 and Luke 14:11; 18:14), that we may find helpful today. Murray notes both the command and promise of God:

> Two things are needed. Do what God says is your work—humble yourself. Trust Him to do what He says is His work; He will exalt you.
>
> The command is clear: humble yourself. That does not mean that it is your work to conquer and cast out the pride of your nature and to form within yourself the lowliness of the Holy Jesus. No, this is God's work, the very essence of that exaltation in which He lifts you up into the real likeness of the beloved Son. What the command does mean is this—take every opportunity of humbling yourself before God and man. Humble yourself and stand persistently, not withstanding all failure and falling, under this unchanging command. Do this with faith in the grace that is already working in you and in the assurance that more grace will be available for the victory that is coming. Look to the light that conscience flashes on the pride of the heart and its workings.
>
> Accept with gratitude everything that God allows from within or without, from friend or enemy, in nature or in grace, to remind you of your need of humbling, and to help you to it. Believe humility to indeed be the mother-virtue, your very first duty before God, and the one perpetual safeguard of the soul. Set your heart upon it as the source of all blessing. The promise is divine and sure, "he that humbleth himself shall be exalted." See that you do the one thing God asks: humble yourself. God will see that He does the one thing He has promised. He will give more grace; He will exalt in due time.¹⁰

8. Thomas A. Tarrants III, "Pride and Humility," *Knowing and Doing*, C. S. Lewis Institute, http://www.cslewisinstitute.org/Pride_and_Humility_SinglePage.

9. Ibid.

10. Andrew Murray, *Humility: The Beauty of Holiness* (Apollo, PA: Ichthus, 2014 [orig. 1896]), 53.

1 Peter 5:12-14

 ## LISTEN to the Story

¹²With the help of Silas, whom I regard as a faithful brother, I have written to you briefly, encouraging you and testifying that this is the true grace of God. Stand fast in it. ¹³She who is in Babylon, chosen together with you, sends you her greetings, and so does my son Mark. ¹⁴Greet one another with a kiss of love. Peace to all of you who are in Christ.

Listening to the Text in the Story: Psalm 137:1–9; Jeremiah 28:1–29:14; Daniel 1–6.

In my commentary on 1:1–2, Peter's opening greeting, I offered sentences of a letter to Ireland from an Irish immigrant to the USA as an example of what it can feel like to be an alien and stranger, terms used to describe Peter's audience (see 1:1, 17; 2:11). Now, at the closing of Peter's communication, I offer a letter sent in the opposite direction; i.e., from a mother in Ireland, to her beloved son who immigrated to the USA.

Dear Patt,

I received your letter with the thirty shillings in our greatest of want. I hope God will reward you for it. The day it come, I was without one bite to eat. Dickey's 8 weeks in bed, without a stitch on him, and my petticoat and coat's all pawned. Dear Patt, we've no place to lay our heads. We were lodging under James Street arch, but were put out of it. Then a few nights up in the Sconce, still without a bite. We'd be dead long ago, only for two neighbors that often gives me a bite, for God's sake. Little ever I thought it'd come my turn to beg. No more would I beg, only for your father's death. But thanks bit of God, whatever me or his child here is suffering, your father died and was buried the way he lived: respectable and decent. Dear Patt, I've had not a penny. The blankets, bed and boots of my feet was pawned. You can't know how we're suffering unless you were in starvation and want, without friend or fellow to give you a shilling, then you'd know. But on my two bended knees, Patt, fresh and fasting, I pray to God that you nor none of yours may ever know, nor ever suffer, what we are suffering now. Uncle John said he'd keep little John and Joseph until I write from America for them. I wrote to James and he promised to take them out last June and never wrote us since. Send word if he's in Providence with you. If he be in Providence, tell him that poor little Dickey longs both night and morning to see you and James. The poor child says he'd not be hungry if he was near you. Oh Patt, hurry and take us out of this. It's the poorest prospect of a winter that ever I had, without house or homefire, friend nor fellow nor bit of food to eat. That's my prospects. For the love of God, dear Patt, bring me and little Dickey out of this, as quick as you can. I pray that God's Holy Spirit be with you all. You promised to take us out.

Your loving mother until death.[1]

This gut-wrenching letter demonstrates that life for those left behind could be as difficult or even worse than life for those who emigrated. This is relevant as we examine how the apostle closes his letter, offering greetings from the fellow believers "in Babylon." Babylon likely refers to Rome in 5:13, but it recalls the literal Babylon, where God's people in the OT were taken into exile (e.g., 2 Kgs 20:16–18; 24:10–17; Jer 29:1). By referencing Babylon and calling the Christian community there as co-elect (*suneklektos*), Peter points out that the church in Rome is in exile just like the churches to which he writes. There is solidarity between the churches in Rome and the churches of the diaspora (1:1) in Asia Minor, since all of the believers, because of their faith, are alienated from the dominant culture.

This is true for all Christians. The contours of our suffering may be different depending upon our location, but none of us are fully at home in a world that rejects the "chosen and precious cornerstone" (1 Pet 2:6–7).

EXPLAIN the Story

Peter closes in a fashion typical for Greco-Roman letters. He sends greetings along with a final admonition and echoes his opening wish for peace (see 1:1–2). The conclusion is the only place in the letter where Peter names anyone specifically, and he references these people with familial terms. He also encourages a familial act, a kiss. The church in exile is a family, connected to each other by faith in Jesus Christ, according to the will of the Father (1:2, 14, 17).

---

1. "Letter from Mrs. Nolan, County Kilkenny, Ireland, to her son Patrick, apparently in Providence, R.I., October 8, 1850," *Letters to and from Irish Immigrants to America, 1830s–1880s*, http://risdyeswecan.blogspot.com/2010/02/letters-to-and-from-irish-immigrants-to.html.

Peter's Family (5:12–13)

Silas, a "faithful brother," is likely the man we have met elsewhere in the NT in association with the apostle Paul as a traveling companion (Acts 15:40; 16:19–40; 17:4–15; 18:5; 2 Cor 1:19) and also as coauthor of the Thessalonian letters (1 Thess 1:1; 2 Thess 1:1).[2] Peter's readers may have known Silas by reputation. The commendation of him as "faithful" prepared them to receive Silas in person as the bearer of the letter, in the same way Paul commended Phoebe to the church in Rome (see Rom 16:1–2).

Scholars debate Silas's role in the composition of this epistle, speculating as to whether he was its coauthor, or the amanuensis (i.e., "scribe"), or a courier. Since Silas is not named at the letter's opening, it seems likely that he did not have a hand in writing the letter.[3]

Peter uses "brother" in a spiritual sense, as is frequently the case in the NT. Yet I mention it because the "she" of v. 13 and the reference to Mark as "my son" have drawn attention to questions concerning Peter's biological family.

Because *suneklektos* ("co-elect"; NIV: "chosen together") is feminine in gender, some have taken the term to be a reference to Peter's wife (see Matt 8:14; 1 Cor 9:5). However, that would seem an unnecessarily obscure way to refer to a wife. Besides, feminine terms are elsewhere used of the Christian community (see 2 John 1, 13), particularly because it aligns with the word *ekklēsia* ("church"), a feminine noun. Additionally, Peter has just referred to all Christians using a feminine noun, *adelphotēs* ("family of believers") in v. 9. *Adelphotēs* is the most likely antecedent of *syneklektos*.

Babylon is a reference to the capital city of Rome.[4] Yet Peter's letter is not an apocalyptic writing like the book of Revelation where "Babylon" is a cryptic way to signify Rome's wickedness (e.g., Rev 17:5; 18:2). Peter probably uses Babylon because it symbolizes a place of exile. "Just as the Jews had been driven out of Jerusalem and sent into exile in Babylon by their oppressors, Peter had also been driven out of Jerusalem by persecution and is sojourning in the capital city of his oppressors."[5] Peter and his community in Rome are estranged from the dominant, pagan culture, in solidarity with the readers of the leader, who are part of a diaspora (1:1).

---

2. Verse 12 has *Silvanus*, the Latin form of the Jewish name *Silas*.

3. Also, Peter uses an expression *dia Silouanou* ("through Silas"), which is grammatically similar to Acts 15:23, where a letter carried by Silas and others is sent *dia cheiros autōn* (lit., "through their hand"). The similar grammatical construction may indicate a similar function as a courier, not a writer.

4. See the introduction.

5. Jobes, *1 Peter*, 34–35. Observe that Jobes has a detailed introduction to 1 Peter, including elaboration of a theory of Roman colonization to explain Peter's situation, as well as that of the readers of the letter.

"John, also called Mark" (Acts 12:12) appears at various points in the NT and, just like Silas, is associated with Paul (e.g., Acts 12:25; 15:37–39; Col 4:10; Phlm 24; 2 Tim 4:11). It was common for Paul to refer to spiritual offspring (e.g., 1 Tim 1:2; 2 Tim 1:2; Titus 1:4); therefore, Peter's reference to Mark as "son" probably signifies the same. Church history has long associated Peter with Mark, the presumed author of the second book of the NT. The historian Eusebius (ca. AD 260–340) records an important tradition:

> And so greatly did the splendor of piety illumine the minds of Peter's hearers that they were not satisfied with hearing once only, and were not content with the unwritten teaching of the divine Gospel, but with all sorts of entreaties they besought Mark, a follower of Peter, and the one whose Gospel is extant, that he would leave them a written monument of the doctrine which had been orally communicated to them. Nor did they cease until they had prevailed with the man, and had thus become the occasion of the written Gospel which bears the name of Mark.[6]

True Grace of God (5:12)

Peter's brief letter sought to encourage and bear witness to the true grace of God. The Greek verb *parakaleō*, which is behind the word "encouraging," also carries a sense of exhortation and entreaty (see 2:11; 5:1). That range of meanings characterizes what Peter has been doing throughout his letter. Additionally, Peter has given testimony (*epimartyreō*) of God's grace through his writing.[7] The ambiguous "this" in v. 12 most likely refers to the entire letter, rather than just any one aspect (such as suffering or perseverance). The entire letter substantiates God's favor. "Grace," one of Peter's frequent words, is evident throughout (1:2, 10, 13; 2:19, 20; 3:7; 4:10; 5:5, 10, 12).[8] The God of grace (5:10) offers that which is true (*alēthēs*), genuine, and dependable.[9] Because God's grace is dependable, believers must stand firm, holding on by faith despite opposition. In time, God will restore all things (5:10).

A Kiss with Peace (5:14)

The kiss of love is the same as Paul's familiar wish for a "holy kiss" of greeting (Rom 16:16; 1 Cor 16:20; 2 Cor 13:12; 1 Thess 5:26). Such a kiss may

---

6. Eusebius, *Hist. eccl.* 2.15, Wikisource, Nicene and Post-Nicene Fathers, Series 2, https://en.m .wikisource.org/wiki/Nicene_and_Post-Nicene_Fathers:_Series_II/Volume_I/Church_History_of_ Eusebius/Book_II/Chapter_15.

7. *Epimartyreō* ("to witness fully") is yet another word of Peter's that occurs only once in the NT. However, it is related to the very common *martyreō* ("to bear witness").

8. It is only in 2:19–20 that *charis* (grace) has a sense other than God's favor.

9. Elliott, *1 Peter*, 878, avers that *alēthēs* "describes something that, because truthful and genuine, is therefore 'dependable.'"

have been appropriate whenever the Christians greeted one another, but it may have been especially meaningful in a liturgical context, since 1 Peter, like the other NT letters, would have been read aloud when the community gathered for worship.[10] "The call for a kiss of love turns the attention of the readers from the syntax of the letter to the faces of those around them. The purpose of the letter is not to produce a rich reading experience, even if it does manage to do that. The purpose of the letter is to guide the behavior of these Christians in their relationship with one another and with their non-Christian neighbors."[11] Indeed, the kiss serves to remind the community of the love they are to have for one another (1:22; 2:17; 3:8; 4:8).

Finally, a wish for peace brings us back to the opening of the letter (1:2). The reference to Babylon echoed the diaspora of 1:1, and "peace" is another point of symmetry between the letter's opening and closing, forming an *inclusio*, a literary device used to frame the beginning and the end of a text. Even though the word "peace" appears only three times in 1 Peter (1:2; 3:11; 5:14), "the theme is pervasive, interwoven with the call to mission ... *eirēnē* ["peace"] is viewed as a gift, as something to be received."[12] While in the heart of Peter's letter he calls his readers to seek and pursue peace with those among the dominant culture (3:11), he also knows that these weary believers must experience inner peace for the sake of their own well-being.

LIVE the Story

The closing of Peter's letter reminds us of the interconnectedness that must be part of Christian experience. Christians are connected by faith, even if separated by miles. We are not alone, but work alongside others, doing God's work in the world. Also, when on the margins of society, never fully at home in this world because our faith, we may suffer as a result of being alienated from those who do not know God through Jesus Christ. Such marginal status presents temptation for compromise, trying to dodge ridicule and possibly persecution. However, as believers in exile, we must "stand fast," holding onto God's grace.

My Church-Planting Experiences and the Power of Partnerships

In 1989 my wife, Susan, and I set out to plant a church in Brooklyn, called New Community. We were excited to be part of a church that would reflect the ethnic, racial, and economic diversity of New York, not segregated but

---

10. See Donelson, *I and II Peter and Jude*, 156–57.
11. Ibid., 157.
12. Waltner, "Reign of God," 242–43.

rather a new community of faithful followers of the Lord Jesus. I had attached myself to a denomination that wanted to plant urban churches and looked forward to the prospect of a new church in my home city.

Yet, on one spring day, a month or so before graduation, I was suddenly hit hard with the realization that I had no idea how I would make a living! My name, picture, and other information had been distributed throughout the denomination, but there was no plan as to how I would earn an income. While many seminary colleagues had already lined up assignments with various churches and ministries well before graduation, I had to get out and scramble to find a job. I was open to anything, but I focused my energy on finding a teaching position in mathematics, something I had done prior to seminary. Seminary graduation day came and I had no job.

By the grace of God and the kindness of some Christian friends in New York, Susan and I returned to Brooklyn (with three small children and one on the way), maintaining the hope of starting a new church. Space limitations prevent me from telling the longer version of this story, but Susan and I still look back and wonder how we made it through the first several months in Brooklyn with neither of us having a job. Teaching positions were usually secured before the summer and at this point fall was fast approaching. By September we had made a few contacts and started a Bible study group in our tiny apartment. In October in answer to earnest prayer and as the result of unusual circumstances, God provided a teaching position for me at a high school well after the term had started. Susan and I pressed on.

Looking back, we realize that even though I had a seminary degree, and although we were surrounded by well-wishers and people who prayed for us, we had little focused training or guidance in church planting. In fact, much of what we had received were stories of new and growing churches without all the behind-the-scenes details. I'm sure those who told their stories did not intend to deceive in any way, but my wife and I (as well as others we know) were led to believe that church planters were lone rangers. As entrepreneurs, these church planters went their own way, did their own thing, rejected established patterns, and created something entirely new. While some of that was true, the picture of the lone planter was not always an accurate one. It took me years to realize that many of those planters rarely worked alone. They had partnerships with mature Christians, or with churches, or with denominations, or with community-based ministries. Oftentimes those partnerships produced money, church members, informational leads, and a range of intangible benefits that could help get a new church going.

One key benefit of partnerships is friendship. The value of friendship is unquantifiable. The work of ministry can be lonely, and church planting can intensify that loneliness, as there is little structure at the start, many obstacles, few resources, and even suspicion from onlookers. The planter needs to know that he or she is not alone. Susan and I came to appreciate the value of such partnerships, especially when we saw key people associated with our ministry come and go. Eventually the strain of raising four small children, of being bi-vocational, and also trying to tend to the range of needs in our community took a toll on us. Many of the people we met in Brooklyn were facing life-controlling issues and we wanted to help them all even though there was no way that we could. Facing burnout, we left the work after five-and-a-half years. Sadly, the church folded a few months after we left. While we did make some good friendships—some that last until this day—we did not have enough partnerships to sustain us in the pivotal first years of the work.

After moving to Washington, DC, and serving an established church for over six years, some friends urged me to consider planting a church again, this time in an economically challenged neighborhood of DC, where we had recently purchased a home. We were not sure and took months to pray about it. When we finally agreed, we communicated how important it would be to have partners right from the beginning.

Interestingly, when some leaders within the denomination with whom I had worked while in Brooklyn heard about my new venture, they invited me to several days of training for church planters. These leaders who extended the invitation acknowledged that even though my new church would not be associated with their denomination, they still wanted me to attend the training at their expense! They felt that if such training had been available back in the late 1980s, I would have had a different experience in Brooklyn. They wanted me to get off to a better start this time around. Additionally, these denominational leaders recognized the power of partnerships by not only including my wife in the training but also another couple from DC who would work with us in the new church.

At the time of this writing, the church we helped to start in DC is still going strong. My wife and I left DC after nearly eighteen years. Yes, we had a responsibility to lead others and to make new disciples, but we also realized that we needed coworkers, people who could share in leadership and in friendship.

The Apostle Paul and Partnerships

Not only had I falsely imagined that church planters were lone rangers, I also had that view of the apostle Paul. I may not have been alone in that view. In some educational films as well as popular movies, the apostle is pictured as headstrong and independent. For example, in the 2005 PBS production,

Empires: Peter and Paul and the Christian Revolution, Paul is depicted walking alone except for the heavily laden donkey he is leading. Recently, in a popular television series, *A. D. The Bible Continues*, Saul of Tarsus is virtually alone in his relentless pursuit of new converts. Sometime after his conversion Paul separates from the community of Christians in Jerusalem under Peter's leadership and heads out alone, not to be seen again for the rest of the series.

In actuality, Paul was seldom alone. Regarding Paul, E. Earle Ellis asserts that "the picture that emerges is that of a missionary with a large number of associates. Indeed, Paul is scarcely ever found without companions."[13] The most typical designations Paul uses to describe his companions, in order of descending frequency, are "fellow worker" (e.g., Rom 16:3, 9, 21; 1 Cor 3:9), "brother/sister" (*adelphos/adelphē*) (e.g., Rom 16:1, 23; Phil 2:5), "deacon" (*diakonos*) (1 Cor 3:5; Col 1:7; 4:7), and "apostle" (1 Cor 4:9; Phil 2:25 [NIV "messenger]).[14] Less frequently Paul uses other terms for his companions, such as "fellow slave" (e.g., Phil 1:1), "fellow soldier" (e.g., Phil 2:25; 2 Tim 2:3), and "fellow prisoner" (Rom 16:7; Col 4:10; Phlm 23). Paul, in the same way as Peter, demonstrates that God's work is carried out in community, even when some leader's name figures most prominently.

Dare to be a Daniel

Peter's mention of Babylon triggers recollection of one of the greatest stories of God's people in exile. The book of Daniel details the story of an exceptional young man who was among the exiles taken to Babylon under King Nebuchadnezzar (Dan 1:1–4). Daniel, along with his three companions Hananiah, Mishael, and Azariah, were selected to be trained in the ways of the Babylonians (Dan 1:5–6). As devout Jews, these young men have their faith tested at various points. Right away, after the young men have their names changed, they are confronted with a choice as to how much they will participate in the life of Babylon. They draw a line at partaking in the king's food (Dan 1:8). God rewards the young men for their faithfulness (Dan 1:11–17).

Two other challenges are among the most noteworthy in all the OT: the furnace and the lions' den. In Daniel 3 Hananiah, Mishael, and Azariah, now called Shadrach, Meshach, and Abednego, refuse to bow in worship to an image of King Nebuchadnezzar (Dan 3:1–12). As punishment, the king orders that the three heroes be cast into a furnace and burned alive (v. 15). Facing a literal fiery trial (see 1 Pet 4:12), the young men are not deterred in their desire to worship only the God of Israel. Once again, God rewards their faithfulness by miraculously keeping them untouched by the fire even while

---

13. E. Earle Ellis, "Paul and His Coworkers," *NTS* 17 (1971): 439.
14. I have given a sampling of references, but see the table in Ellis, "Paul and His Coworkers," 438.

in the furnace, and also by having them subsequently honored by the king (Dan 3:24–30).

Daniel is not mentioned in the furnace episode and his friends are not mentioned in the lions' den story.

Daniel, later holding a prominent place in the Medo-Persian government under King Darius, is betrayed by jealous colleagues who force through a law, making prayer to anyone but the king a capital crime (Dan 6:1–9). Daniel openly defies the law and continues to pray three times daily at an open window facing Jerusalem (Dan 6:10). Upon being discovered, Daniel is sentenced to be locked up in a den of hungry lions (Dan 6:16). Once again, God rewards the faithfulness of his servant and spares Daniel's life and also honors him among his naysayers (Dan 6:19–28).

Peter does not draw upon the Daniel stories, but his mention of Babylon is meant to conjure up images of God's people in exile. For us, contemporary readers of both Daniel and 1 Peter, we find encouragement to remain faithful to God despite the pressures we face from those who do not believe as we do, and who may have power to hurt us or at least alienate us. Ajith Fernando, writing from his experiences in Sri Lanka, uses Daniel to encourage Christians not to be isolated from the world nor to accommodate to the world but rather to engage in "obedient involvement."[15] What Fernando means by that is involvement in society but with ultimate obedience to God. Believers with such a perspective "by their life and witness … challenge the wisdom of the world when it opposes God's wisdom, and they demonstrate that God's way is indeed the best way."[16]

Peter's readers, by their conduct in the face of intense pressure, demonstrate that Jesus is dependable, like a reliable cornerstone (1 Pet 2:4–8). Because of this, his followers need not become isolated from society (3:15–16) nor accommodate themselves to the dominant culture (4:3–4) but can engage the world, committed to following Jesus in holiness (e.g., 1:13–21; 4:1–2).

15. Ajith Fernando, *Spiritual Living in a Secular World: Applying the Book of Daniel Today* (Grand Rapids: Zondervan, 1993), 17–18.
16. Ibid., 18.

Scripture Index

Subject Index

abolition, groundwork for, 122
abolitionist, 196
abstain, 101
accusations, respond to, 152
affection, feelings of, 142
African-Americans, example from, 33–34
alcohol, view of, 175–76
alien(s), 102
    to be an, 212
alienation, 34
Angaelos, Bishop, 197
anxiety, 203
apocalypsis, 53, 57
apologetics, Christian, 156–57
apologia, 152
apostasy, 58
Apostle's Creed, the, 161, 166
Aristotle, teaching of, 114
armor, list of, 205
Augustine, conversion of, 81
author, the letter's, 18–20
authorities, subject to, 105
authority, abuse of, 92
    place of, 165

Babylon, for Rome, 20, 29, 213–14
baptism, 41, 164–65
beatitudes, in Judaism, 192.
    See also Sermon on the Mount
beauty, is described as, 131
behavior, 114
    blameless, 151
    his follower's, 52
    toward outsiders, 181
Benedictus, 40
bishop, 120, 126
blessing, insults with a, 143–44
blood, 41

abstain from, 101
    of Christ, 61
    sprinkling of, 32
Bloody Sunday, 110
brother, 214
canon, place in the, 17
Carmen Christi, 142
carousing, 171
character, 207
Christ. *See* Jesus Christ
Christianity
    aspects of, 195
    subculture of American, 96
Christians
    pagans view the, 172
    persecuted, 196–97
    persecuting, 107
    and status, 93–94
    and suffering, 48
    worshiped early, 108
church, the
    absent from, 145
    as community, 122
    comprise the, 107
    in Jerusalem, 28
    vocation of the, 96
    the word, 214
church growth, 93
church-planting, 216–17
Civil Rights Movement, in America, 109, 137
Claudius, 31
cleansing, 41
clothing, in the first century, 131
commands, two main, 100
community
    authentic, 144–45
    God's elect, 87
    love for, 107, 182

renunciation of, 170
slaves to, 106
Sinai Covenant, 91
slander, 78
slavery
born into, 49
dealing with, 120–22
evils of, 33
in America, 195–96
institution of, 116, 122
issue of, 135–36
redemption from, 60–61
in the Roman world, 122
slaves
address to, 113–15
cues from, 133
honored, 118
masters and, 116
reaction of, 116–17
to righteousness, 107
to sin, 106–7
sobriety, 55, 204
society
engagement with, 18
helpful ones in, 111
order in, 105
our role in, 154
solidarity
with Jesus Christ, 28, 170, 191
with the sufferer, 124
soul, six times, 45
spirituals, negro, 48–50
spiritual sacrifices, 89
spiritual warfare, 204
St. Augustine, conversion of, 81
stone, 90
the Lord as a, 88–89
Stowe, Harriet Beecher, 116
stranger(s), 30, 212
black folk as, 34
submission, 103
godly posture, 202
to masters, 115
to secular rulers, 105
way of life, 128

suffering, 103
benefit of unjust, 150
blessed through, 191–93
decides to face, 48
degree of, 194
for our faith, 28
of innocent people, 110
major themes of, 23–24
paradoxical, 47
purpose of, 44
reality of, 39
rejoice even in, 57
relate to our, 124
role of, 168–69
serves a purpose, 118
sign of disapproval, 189
theology of, 174
unjust, 116–17
the word, 40
sympathy, 141

Temperance Movement, 175
temple, 87–89
Jesus is the, 90
Ten Commandments, 91
testimony, 215
thanksgiving, 39
Thomas, the apostle, 45
time, refers to, 194
titles, are given, 91
Torah, the, 52
Trajan, 19, 107
transformation, 41
trials, 40
rejoicing through, 43
Trinity, at work, 31–32
truth, a synonym for, 73

"Uncle Tom," 116
unity, 82–83
attitudes that foster, 140, 143
universalism, 165

vices, and virtues, 77
vindication, of God's people, 104

Author Index